P

Run, Walk, Crawl—A Car  *...ght Between Generations*

"In this book childhood memories combine with family histories to create a moving tapestry of a loving family fiercely dedicated to the well-being of a member, even when things are seemingly at their worst . . .

Readers navigating a similar "onslaught of family responsibility" may feel less alone after reading this book—and have a better understanding of what works and what doesn't. A brave, soul-searching first-hand account of the risks and rewards of caregiving."

— Kirkus Reviews

"In *Run, Walk, Crawl,* Sarahbeth Persiani shares the 24/7 perspective on the days and nights of a daughter, mother, sister, wife and employee. The impact of Sarahbeth's personal caregiving experience on her career is as heart-breaking as her personal losses. Her memoir is a poignant reminder to everyone that our co-workers often show up to work weary from their other job—caring for a family member. You'll feel as if Sarahbeth is a close friend bearing her soul to you as you read her gripping and honest account. Highly recommended."

— Denise M. Brown, founder of CareGiving.com

"A must read for any human resource professional—or any people manager for that matter—who seeks to understand the pressures on and perspective of the millions of working caregivers whose workdays stretch around the clock. Sarahbeth Persiani's personal story eloquently illustrates the non-stop pressures on working caregivers that can lead to collisions between work and life."

— Joyce Maroney, Executive Director,
Workforce Institute at Kronos

"As a professional in secondary traumatic stress and compassion fatigue, I'm grateful to offer *Run, Walk, Crawl* as a resource that could provide solace to clients who are or have been caregivers. Sarahbeth speaks honestly about the true weight of caregiving which will undoubtedly lighten the spirits of caregivers who read it, allowing them to feel seen, understood, and accepted.

Besides being a great resource for caregivers, I suggest human resource professionals, managers, and executives to read this for keen insights as to what their employees are truly grappling with when it comes to caregiving."

— **Taryn Hughes, Founding CEO, Forest Hughes & Associates**

"I loved this book! Sarahbeth writes with a refreshing level of honesty as she shares her story of family caregiving and partnership with professional care teams. Anything less would be a sugar coating of the realities of being a mom, wife, an involved and caring daughter, a sibling and a working professional in a competitive environment. I found myself with equal moments of laughter and tears as I turned the pages of her book. This is an enjoyable, must-read for anyone who knows these challenges, whether you've been through it or if you're in the throes of it now. Through her words and genuine sharing, Sarahbeth is a virtual companion readers can relate to as she captures the positive, life affirming aspects of the challenges involved with the caregiving years."

— **Shelby Marshall, Co-Founder and Senior Vice President, Right at Home, Eastern MA**

RUN

A CAREGIVER CAUGHT

WALK

BETWEEN GENERATIONS

CRAWL

SARAHBETH PERSIANI

For information about this title or to order other books and/or electronic media, contact the publisher:
We Are Sharing the Sun
PO Box 70052
Worcester, MA 01607
www.wearesharingthesun.com
sb@wearesharingthesun.com

ISBN: 978-1-7333990-5-0 (paperback)
978-1-7333990-0-5 (ebook)
978-1-7333990-2-9 (audio book)

Printed in the United States of America

Cover design by Tony Persiani
Interior design by 1106 Design

Dedication
Glory Be to God

Author's Note

This book is a memoir of my own experiences as a woman in business. But it is also a report and commentary on issues that are facing countless men and women who balance work and family duties, including the care of their children and their aging parents. In that sense, this book is my contribution to an ongoing debate in policy and media about matters of enduring public concern.

With the exception of my husband and various public figures, all of the names of and other identifying details about living individuals, businesses, and institutions have been fictionalized in this book. Any similarity between the fictionalized aspects of the narrative and any real people or entities is strictly coincidental.

I have also been careful to omit any trade secrets and other confidential information of my employers, and I intend no harm or disparagement to any of them. Rather, this book addresses the human interactions and relationships that can be found in *every* workplace and is not confined to a particular work environment.

I invite the reader to read the Afterword at the conclusion of this book, where I share additional thoughts and comments on the issues that I've addressed in the text.

Contents

The term "Sandwich Generation" refers to those who are, in effect, sandwiched between generations, simultaneously caring for their own family and for elderly parents. Synonymous with the term "family caregiver," they are typically unpaid family members or friends (usually women) who provide assistance.

Preface

M y story is one of countless cases of family caregiving situations. Mine pales in comparison with some and was harder than others. What we all have in common, though, is that we've been changed. For better or for worse, caregiving responsibilities affect every aspect of your life.

I'm moved by hearing stories of everyday acts of kindness and long-term selfless dedication. I applaud the courage and endurance of caregivers and recipients alike who find themselves in those unwelcome roles. They come from all walks and circumstances, and on occasion we hear about them on the news—young and old struggling with terminal illness, amputee survivors, lives devastated by gun violence, families doing their best with inadequate resources for the mentally ill, elderly veterans who run out of time waiting for help. Not to mention thousands of our men and women in uniform who return home changed forever.

With the knowledge that there are so many others in similar situations, I doubted whether my experience was worth sharing and ran into many stops and stalls along the way. Sometimes all I really wanted to do was let time do its thing and soften the painful memories. That would have been much easier. But I couldn't. I kept meeting other working-family caregivers, and listened to their stories with newfound compassion. I get it now. Conversations and vivid memories replayed, woulda-shoulda thoughts cycled. I also kept bumping into working family caregivers at networking events, attending workshops at WW, even in the grocery check-out line, and I listened to their stories with newfound compassion. We're all one, muddling along in various stages of growth and understanding.

I know the shoes that family caregivers are in and have the utmost compassion for the load you're carrying. For you, I've exposed bare skin—flaws, flab, and all—that, if I were smart, I probably would have kept under wraps. But then my experience wouldn't ring true. One thing we all know from down-on-our-knees moments is the stripping away of pretense. We know that hands-on care is messy, and reveals not only our loved ones' humanity but ours as well. Rather than approach your time in the Sandwich Generation as a marathon, take it in stride. Your desire to be there, step by step, makes all the difference. Your ability to comfort, care, and lend a hand is all that's required.

Introduction

For more than ten years, my mother would ask when I was going to have children. As my biological clock ticked away—turning thirty-three, thirty-four, thirty-five—her approach changed to conversational scare tactics. Drawing on her cigarette (she was a three-pack-a-day gal), she'd say, "You'll have a barren marriage. You know what happens to barren couples?" She never told me the answer, but her words smacked of something biblical—like locust plagues and lions' dens—or sordid, as if it were only a matter of time till we would become swingers.

It wasn't a question of whether we were committed. We just had much to do—careers to build, houses to buy, graduate degrees to pursue, foreign places to explore. We also had two dogs to raise, Ruby (a black Lab-Chow mix) and Buddy (a Sheltie), who had inadvertently become our fur-baby children. We were happy and fulfilled.

Eventually, we did decide to put aside our barren ways and bring a child into our life. Maybe it was the happy chaos that we noticed at the holidays, with our siblings' children running around wild, or the sadness we felt at witnessing our childless neighbor's obsession with their lawn. The husband's nighttime mowing was a familiar sound, and we'd often see the glow and bobbing of his headlamp from our bedroom window. Whatever the case, our concerns about what a baby would mean to our blissful, self-centered lifestyle didn't seem so worrisome anymore. "Don't worry, Sa," my mother would say, "I'll be there to help. That's what families do—they come together around children. You just wait and see."

I *had* seen. My parents played to a T their supporting-cast roles of doting, dutiful Gramma and Grampa for my sisters. And considering that I'm the youngest of five, things were sure to be even better for me. The baby of the family reaps the reward of parental experience and, if you're astute, learns from sibling mistakes. And so we made the leap into parenthood.

Just shy of ten years after our wedding and after one devastating miscarriage, a beautiful girl joined our bliss. I was thirty-seven, and having read *What to Expect When You're Expecting,* I was ready and well-prepared. More than prepared, actually. During the phase when the baby books say your fetus is the size of a cashew, she already had a college fund. Knowing that Baby Cashew would be showered with gifts, I politely (or so I thought at the time) mentioned to friends and family that "contributions should be for the lasting gift of education, over yet another baby blanket or onesie." Practical and a planner to boot!

In November 2005, husband Tony, daughter Summer, and I moved from our quaint honeymoon home (of eleven years) to a raised Cape-style house in a town farther west, in central Massachusetts. My mother's words had rung true, and we realized how important it is to be around family when you have children. We looked forward to the convenience of Sunday dinners with my parents, more time with my sisters, who were living in nearby towns, and the larger home that moving farther from Boston would afford.

Several months after the move, I was laid off from a global corporate tech company and breathed a colossal sigh of relief to be temporarily home with Summer. I viewed it as a gift and opportunity to take time to assess what I wanted to do next. After a year, I accepted a position at a local university as a move toward work/life balance. It was a smaller workplace and I took a pay cut, but I liked that it was a revenue-generating position (a.k.a. sales). It meant that my worth was directly proportional to my contribution. (Again, or so I thought.)

I never self-identified as a "caregiver." Wife, working mother, sister, daughter, chief dishwasher—those were all labels I knew and embraced. But caregiver? Unbeknown to me, I'd just become part of the "Sandwich Generation" demographic.

For me, and I suspect many others, eldercare responsibilities will become the tipping point in an already full, demanding lifestyle. My comfort zone was the halls of corporate America, with its hushed office politics and organized workspaces. In contrast, the world of home health care, where "shrinking the living space" and navigating parental and sibling tensions just come with the territory, was a foreign landscape. I'd first heard the term "Sandwich Generation" in passing, from my sister-in-law, and remember chuckling at the image I had of an actual sandwich, as if we were a generation with a weakness for anything encased in bread. I didn't think much about it or really consider what it meant to be part of that demographic—to have both the generation before yours and the generation after yours making stiff demands on you—until after the dust settled, as they say. And at that point, I felt a failure on so many fronts, realizing that the adage about "you can't be all things to all people" is spot on.

They say it doesn't honor God to remain stuck in your failure. And that's what telling this story is about—getting back up. My failure wasn't that I didn't care enough or do enough. It was that I went head-down, nose-to-the-grindstone with every aspect of my life. I believed that by sheer force of will, with my checklist in hand, I could make everything work out okay. As a self-proclaimed, card-carrying member of the Superwoman Club, it didn't occur to me, even when I was run-down and anemic, that I *couldn't* do it all. I'd love to have a nickel for every time I've asked myself in the aftermath, *Why was I so ill prepared? Why didn't I know better?*

As a form of release, I began to write. I needed the catharsis of venting to make sense of what I had gone through. Waking in the middle of the night, I would replay a cacophony of memories, mainly caregiving- and work-related missteps, and I found solace in jotting down random notes, scenarios, and questions that always ended with me pondering how I could have managed it all differently . . . better. A bird's-eye depiction of my five years in the sandwich would show my dwindling concern for self and my health, namely my struggles with anemia, chronic stress, and fatigue. I just chalked it all up to being weak. Weaker than other working women. Falling prey to the common comparison thing we all do, comparing our insides with others' outsides—how we feel versus how others *appear*. Bottom line, there were too many things to do, places to be, and people who needed me—I couldn't afford excuses.

Even without a magic looking glass or a medical degree, you can probably see where this is going. At the same time as I was stepping into uncharted waters as a new mother, determined to make the most of treasured toddler, preschool, and elementary-school days with my daughter, I was scrambling to find time for checking in at my parents' house, sitting bedside in hospitals, long-term care/hospice centers or nursing homes, or attending funerals. Whichever scenario I was ensconced in, the self-talk was the same: *Be present, be here for the ones you love, cherish them, because this is time you'll never get back.*

It's no surprise, then, that my focus at work was on just that: the work. To me, it was no social soiree. The goal on any given day was simply to get my job done and go home. Compartmentalize and put on a good face. It hadn't always been like that, though. Premotherhood, as a learning-and-development professional in the fast-paced halls of tech companies in my twenties and thirties, I could be Johnny-on-the-spot, even if it meant weeks spent away from home, conducting training for technical professionals and, in my spare time, marveling at the towering neon in Shinjuku, Japan, or walking along the River Thames in the English county of Surrey. Putting in time on the road or late nights in the office was a visible show of commitment. But my fortysomething Sandwich reality meant that the all-important office "face time" suffered. Coming up on a five-year workplace anniversary in a position chosen specifically to help me achieve work/life balance, with a grade-school child at home, a minimal support system, and millennial colleagues who were "leaning in" and had zero awareness of caregiving issues, I crashed head-first into the stigma that comes with falling back on the Family Medical Leave Act to take flex time. Whether it's true or not, taking FMLA days off seems to signal a lack of commitment and, in turn, productivity. It didn't help that the focus of my position and the majority of my interactions were external-facing, as in dealing with clients and partners. As any "how to succeed in business" or leadership primer will attest, building strong colleague relationships and acing workplace savvy are where it's at. But that's not where I was at.

The work environment can be a rough place for someone in a caregiver's state of mind, but for many of us, what's the alternative? What's the employer responsibility, if any, to the caregiver? There's the FMLA, typically for companies with fifty or more employees, and there are paid and unpaid policies, depending on the company and the manager/employee relationship. But what about the more important day-to-day workplace dynamic with colleagues that can either make your life bearable, a buffer from family pressures, or do the complete opposite and compound the isolation factor common in caregiving?

Nobody tells you that mourning begins while your loved one is still alive, that you can miss someone when he's right there in front of you, that you begin to mourn the person he once was. Of course, there's grief and sadness at the time of death, but for me that's not the hard part. I cry at that moment—bawl, actually—but take comfort in knowing our loved one has transitioned back to spirit and heaven above. For me, it's the time between the lines that are exhausting and difficult. Countless trips to hospital rooms or nursing homes, endless chores like fetching soup, doing laundry, paying bills, and still staying awake and animated for bedtime stories with the kids and alone time with hubby—now *that's* the trick.

I began writing this story in the aftermath of my father's passing in September 2012, during an intense period of questioning, soul-searching, and self-reproach. Through musings and memories, it's my best attempt at capturing everyday moments, recollections, and profound experiences from the two years preceding his death; though the reality is that many aspects of my caregiving experience began well in advance, in lockstep with our move closer to family. Except I never considered it caregiving as such—I was simply being a good daughter. If you asked my sisters, I'm sure they'd say the same. Let's just say, we all were doing something to help. In my case, a good daughter who happened to always shop with my parents in mind (buying twice the groceries my family alone needed), and because I lived the closest, cook the lion's share of their meals, regularly clean their house, and accompany them to many doctor's appointments, including chemotherapy. Who knew that constitutes caregiving?

How easy my life was before the move, but I wouldn't change it. Not one ridiculous, painstaking, exhausting, enraging, life-changing, uplifting minute. Cliché, I know, but true.

With deep gratitude I look back at the onslaught of family responsibility, the burdens and joys of caregiving, and appreciate the trials for how they've changed me. The gifted and truly eloquent Jane Gross may have said it best in her book, *A Bittersweet Season: Caring for Our Aging Parents—and Ourselves,* when she described caregiving as "an all-consuming and life-altering experience that wrings you out, uses you up, and sends you back into the world with your heart full and your eyes open, if you let it."

Whether it was failure or divine lessons I was meant to learn about my roles as a wife, mother, daughter, sister, friend, colleague, and, ultimately, servant, what I know now is that trials help to define who we are. They move us closer to God and our own strength. My caregiving experience taught many lessons about what it means to serve. I said goodbye to deeply loved members of my family as well as a career-minded self-image that included an expectation to be successful on all fronts. I agree with the adage that the best way to get around something is to go through it. By the grace of God, my load was lifted and my life changed along the way. Beginning in strength but not always in good cheer, the process of caregiving, of serving, changed my journey from one of annoyance to one of acceptance.

Dr. Charles Stanley, whose radio sermons made a difference in my life, put it aptly: "Whatever you accomplish in life, you accomplish on your knees."

RUN

"Walk with purpose," I hear my father say. It was his caution as we locked up the bank on the corner of Portland and Franklin Streets that we had just finished cleaning. Not that the side streets in downtown Worcester were crime-ridden, but it was after 10:00 p.m. and our car was parked far down the block. It was a school night for my seventh-grade self but no matter, I was used to our schedule and knew his ways.

The memory fades, and moving at a fast clip from the break room, with my fresh brewed single cup of dark roast, I spot them out of the corner of my eye. There are bouquets of daisies on desk upon desk in every office down the hall. They're not professionally wrapped, but laying fresh-cut in wet paper towels, as if from someone's yard.

In step with my stride, a colleague notices, too, and shares, "Mary Anne brought them in for all of us on the team. Pretty, huh?" I nod and make the turn into my office, expectant.

Except there is no cheerful prize. It's my same perfectly kept desk, tidy and organized as the day before.

Cleaning House

Late September 2012

It's a glorious Indian summer in New England and I'm on my knees. Not in prayer, not in sorrow, but to help Bruce the carpet-cleaning dude roll up the huge living-room rug so we can carry it outside and properly wash the floor. In fact, we're washing all the rugs and hardwood floors in my house. I have more energy than I've had in months. I feel stronger. It's not like that superhuman adrenaline surge that people experience when they rescue someone pinned under a car, but I pretend it is as I help to lift the fourteen-by-sixteen-foot rug. My knees are stiff and my arms are shaking, never mind my bad back, but I'm doing it! And the overall physical surge is energizing. *God, it feels good to clean,* I think to myself, laughing and groaning simultaneously as we lift.

Even though Bruce isn't too easy on the eyes, I'm fully enjoying his company and marvel at his floor-maintenance knowledge and dexterity. Though we don't talk much, we're comfortable working together. I don't even feel embarrassed by the numerous random stains in the carpet. The underside holds years' worth of memories. *Ahh, wine spills from parties with friends, and there's that big one from Christmas Eve, a coffee stain, and oh dear, Buddy's pee stains from his final, lame days. He was such a good boy.* (Buddy Barkenstein was our beloved Sheltie.)

I'm still laughing and puffing loudly as we negotiate the rug through the sliders, through the back porch and then down a few steps to the backyard. My huffing and puffing evokes the labored breathing of a weight lifter—or a mom giving birth. Bruce half-smiles, revealing crooked, nicotine-stained teeth, and seems slightly surprised to have such glad-hearted help.

It's been a few weeks since my father passed, and I'm literally cleaning house, *my* house, to get myself back in order. I feel more peace than I've felt in months. I appreciate the ability to stay focused on the task at hand, my mind not cycling through a dozen tasks that need to get done. I'm not hypertuned to the clock, or feeling stressed and conflicted about where I *should* be. It feels good to move my body, to feel my muscles strain, and—pardon the New Age-speak—to be fully in the moment. For the past couple of weeks, I've been in a cleaning frenzy. I can't shake an overwhelming, compulsive need to clean. Deep-clean. To pull the past year's clutter out of closets and sort, pile, and purge. A mix of clothing styles that are normally stored according to season have been sharing space with outgrown children's clothes stuffed haphazardly in bags for donation-box drops that never happened. For most people, this clutter would be a drop in the bucket, a few weekends' worth of inconvenience to clear out, but for me it's been suffocating. There's an urgency to focus on my home again. Spend time in my home again. And breathe again.

Mixed in with my things are some of my father's belongings: extra canes, the tall toilet commode he would use when visiting, bags of clothes, and boxes and boxes of miscellaneous odds and ends that were pulled from his home, my childhood home, in our scramble to clean it out. We called them his "treasures," and try as I might to see the silver lining, to me they represented clutter and unnecessary disorder. Bringing physical items from his house into mine created a psychological burden—I knew I'd have to deal with that added weight at some later time. And that time is here. Time for making all the keep/toss decisions, but mainly toss. I've decided to begin cleaning and focus initially on my own household. For efficiency sake's, I gather up everything I've brought from Dad's house to store downstairs in the basement. The image of floor-to-ceiling clutter in Dad's basement isn't lost on me as I carry bags and boxes down, but I know I'll get to it soon enough.

I go from room to room and appreciate the simplicity of the task at hand—sorting out kitchen cabinets and pitching neglected cookbooks with handwritten recipes and magazine cut-outs stuffed into the pages, for example. Goodbye—unused multiple vases, warped plastic containers with missing lids, broken utensils, and mismatched bowls and mugs. I sit cross-legged on the floor to empty low drawers filled with everything from old phone books to stained tablecloths to sticky, melted votive candles and flashlights with long-dead batteries. From room to room I go, wishing a pleasant goodbye to dated magazines, forgotten toys, and dust bunnies. *You can't hide, because I'm not stopping until everything is clean and organized!* I hum the tune of "I'm Gonna Catch You," recalling the happy tunes of my daughter's toddler years, contagious in their rhythm and with lyrics that were easy to remember. *I'm gonna catch you, here I come. . . .* Yep, without apology, I admit that Laurie Berkner and the Wiggles quite often provide the mental soundtrack to my blissful scrub-a-dub days. I've become a simpleton. But simple and easy is what cleaning is to me and what I need. Straightforward work with satisfying results and instant gratification.

Most days are focused and productive, like this one I'm spending with Bruce. But there are others, when the heavy lifting isn't physical but in my mind. I battle circular thoughts of unfinished conversations with former colleagues and things I wish I'd said, of both rushed and tender moments with my father in his final days, and of petty, angry annoyance with siblings and my immediate family. All of which brings me to frustrated tears. I struggle to hold on to my simpleton cleaning bliss but slip into a sad stillness. To an onlooker, it would probably appear as if I were acting out an old-fashioned soap-opera scene, gazing off screen, deep in thought. Except there's no dramatic background music building before the fade to commercial. It's just me standing in the middle of a perfectly clean room or sitting on the edge of a bed, sorting clothes unhurriedly and remembering.

Actually, I often give in to the circular thinking, my mind cycling memories that revolve around father, family, and work. Scenes come to mind of helping my father—to his great humiliation and mine—to wipe up after bowel movements during his last days in his home. Of breaking down completely while moving him to a nursing home and swallowing the shock of seeing him in the wheelchair lineup in the hall, sometimes hallucinating from prescribed psych meds. Of summertime yard sales and asking pennies for his lifetime's worth of collections in the desperate hope that we'll raise enough money to bring him back home. There are family scenes of putting our dog down on Halloween eve, the wind knocked out of me, while orchestrating the bustle of trick-or-treat. Of undesired insight into sibling motivations and all of our human flaws. And the work scenes depict me feeling isolated and misunderstood to the point of fleeing from a job I loved and undoing a professional persona that took years to build. Father, family, work—I mull these memories, trying to figure out where I went wrong. What could I have done differently? How far back does it go?

In the still of a house on its way to being clean and organized, I contemplate and analyze what it was like to live that rushed lifestyle. A lifestyle where you work so hard for the conveniences of a beautiful, comfortable home and seldom spend time there because the focus is on working, running the race, acquiring, not living. For me, being in the Sandwich Generation, feeling the squeeze of work and family responsibilities on all sides, meant tapping my reserves of selflessness while being completely overwhelmed and pissed off. I was on an almost-military schedule, squeezing every productive second I could out of each day. I was a multitasking savant, seeing five steps ahead as I determined what had to be done and how it could be done at the same time as I was getting *other* things done. I'd wake up in the middle of the night and mentally review my to-do list and steel myself for the next day. Often, not falling back asleep was somehow better than getting a few more hours of sleep, which for some reason was harder to recover from. A low dose of nervous adrenaline was usually there in reserve for whenever I needed it, except on the god-awful days when it wasn't. If I had to choose, I'd take being stressed and anxious over being dazed and exhausted.

My thoughts keep swirling and I retreat further into memory, mentally searching for what used to make me happy. *How do I get back to who I used to be? When I was self-assured, not ashamed for having put Dad in the nursing home—whole.* Kneeling in front of the bookshelf in my daughter's cheerfully painted, fairy-themed bedroom, I sort and swap out age-appropriate books, holding on to some of our earliest favorites. I remember when I started college in 1985, bucking the Madonna-inspired bow-on-head trend while my dormmates' rooms were all blinged out with trendy comforters and posters on the wall that represented their cool selves—a U2 poster here, a Spuds Mackenzie poster there (he was the Bud Light mascot/dog). I had a homemade quilt, a poster of a homely cartoon bird standing among peacocks with the caption "To Thine Own Self Be True," and Calvin Coolidge's quote about nothing being able to take the place of persistence matted in teal and framed. The *Sesame Street* book I'm holding now reminds me of what I realized in that environment: One of these things is not like the others. *True that, Elmo.* Even still, I felt I belonged and I loved everything about university life. I even met my future husband during freshman year. Little did I know how fast those four years of belonging would pass, how close the start of my career was.

I open the doors to my daughter's oversize closet. One of the largest in the upstairs bedrooms, it's where my wedding dress is stored. I kneel again to rummage and sort through a few boxes filled with training guides and miscellaneous items from various jobs. I look through materials and remember how important this all once seemed. My office Achilles' heel was that I tended to be on the more thoughtful side, as in analytical. I went overboard to perfect an instructor or student guide and belabored education-related marketing copy and brochures. In conversation I would always think of the perfect thing to say after the fact, after I'd thought things through. Nonetheless, I did okay, because on the flip side was my secret weapon: persistence. I committed to putting in the effort necessary to do a job well, no matter the time detriment. It felt good to be absorbed in challenging work, to lose myself in it. Premotherhood, I was always at work on time and usually the last to leave. I had time to burn and that's what I did. I never really considered what would become of using my secret weapon when the pull of caregiver responsibilities meant time was no longer on my side.

"End-of-life decision-making wasn't something I had top of mind back then, you know?" I say out loud to Julie, my daughter's American Girl doll, sitting in her perfectly made doll bed on the floor.

I push the box back in place and stand to move the puffy, zippered garment bag holding my wedding dress to the other side of the closet. Now I have a better view of the opaque plastic storage bin at the back of the closet: my daughter's baby keepsake box. The tune of Joan Armatrading's "The Power of Dreams," the lovely song my husband and I chose for our first dance as man and wife, comes to mind and I hum it. It was the autumn of 1995, a full ten years after we'd met in college, when we finally married. We had moved to the song's rhythm, clinging and self-conscious with all eyes on us, awkwardly waltzing the box step we'd learned "in three easy sessions," just like the Fred Astaire Dance Studio advertisement had promised. Together we reveled in the excitement of it all, but really, I was glad to check the wedding hoopla off the list.

At the time, with no need to rush into anything and well aware that life is all about choice, my plan was to make only good ones. "Careful planning and good decisions will get you everywhere," I say to Julie. Her smiling, placid eyes look back at me. *How did those good decisions work out for you?* I tuck Julie into her bed, under her delicate flowered covers, face down.

I kneel to the keepsake box and, through the milky plastic, spot my daughter's tiny Red Sox onesie. Summer was born in October 2004, and my husband is pretty certain she had a lot to do with breaking the curse of the Bambino. I can finally laugh now, years later, at his obsessive preoccupation with the Red Sox's appearance in the World Series during the most important moments of our life. To think, Curt Schilling's bloody sock trumped my baby's delivery.

Such a little peanut she was. My mother preferred to call her a little pork chop, and I smile at remembering how she would say it just before blowing noisy kisses on her chunky baby legs and feet. How we marveled at her thick, dark brown hair and Eskimo resemblance. Making myself comfortable on the floor in the closet, I peel open the lid and pull out the pink baby blanket on top. *Dee-dee* she called it because *blankee* was too much of a mouthful. Breathing it in, I shut my eyes and try to catch even the faintest hint of her baby smell, what I remember as the perfect blend of baby powder and warm buttered toast. But I can't. It's gone. *They're* gone.

As has happened a hundred times, familiar faces spring to mind, faces of family and friends who died in a shockingly short span of time. I see my mother—sitting wide-legged on our beach blanket, calling out "Jonaaathonn" to the occasional seagull flying overhead, winking at me. Lung cancer stole her from us before my daughter turned three, and words she once said to me still echo in my mind: "I'll be there to help. That's what families do—they come together around children." John—my husband's best friend and confidant, grinning so broadly that his eyes squint. Wearing his signature Hawaiian shirt—the tackier the better. His raucous laughter would defuse any tiffs and tension between Tony and me as easily as switching on a light. He died in his sleep from heart-related complications. Jared—my gentle nephew and godson, kneeling in the sparkling snow in a photo taken minutes before the snowboarding/tree-well accident, glorious and beautiful in the sunlight at twenty-two. That Colorado ski trip was his first away from home. Louanne—my sister and childhood best friend, proudly recounting the story behind each gifted Pandora bead with a silly smile. She endured a slow deterioration from pancreatic cancer but managed to bask in the attention of it all. Carmine—my father in-law, the Brooklyn-born Italian patriarch who, from the head of the holiday dinner table, kept the joy of family traditions alive. He quietly battled congestive heart failure without complaint. Yes, I've had a front-row seat to the indignities of terminal illness, the complications of old age, and the shock of unexpected deaths.

Our time here is so short. I see that now. I have no more cleansing tears to cry. I just have these vivid, nagging thoughts that haunt me, call me.

I replay the memory of driving away from our joy-filled starter home, down Magnolia Street, ours the only yard on the street that boasted one of the namesake trees, now visible in the rearview mirror. I look from the beautiful tree to our daughter, just turned one, smiling contentedly in her car seat. With a bittersweet mix of tears and excitement, we were heeding my mother's call and moving to the area where my own childhood had played out. "Family looks after each other," she had said, and we agreed. With chemo and radiation treatments for her breast cancer wrapping up and her energy returning, it was to be a win-win for us both. She'd get to spend more time with her granddaughter, and I'd be able to go to work relaxed and secure in the knowledge that actual family was watching my precious girl. No longer would I have to swallow hard on the doorsteps of the drop-off for the megasize daycare chain, keeping maternal instincts in check, before speeding to work in tears. Or fool myself, like so many others, that it was better when hubby made the drop-off.

I'd lived that scenario for Summer's first year and still wince remembering the endless colds for both of us. Worse, the who's-who rotation of daycare attendants and the trendy long fingernails of a young woman in the infant room. Fighting the urge to scream,

I had asked one of the several managers in charge, using a measured professional voice, if it would be possible for the infant attendees to have a more appropriate nail length. Moving to stand up in the closet, I can still picture the creased, delicate skin of those beautiful baby legs being held by blood-red daggers.

Always so damn polite, reserved, and professional when I should have railed. But I'm no longer thinking of my dealings with daycare. *What would have happened if I showed my vulnerable, terrified self?* I consider my good decisions in the still painfully raw turn of events. *Which do I regret more, leaving, how I left, or the things I didn't say?*

As I hurriedly repack the cherished keepsakes into the bin, I remember exactly when I realized that the move back, to be closer to family, was much different from what I'd expected. I push the bin back into the closet corner and lie on my daughter's fairy-themed comforter. Sinking into its softness, I allow myself permission to be still, to not do—to just be and let the memory come.

On an early-morning conference call in the late summer of 2006, it dawned on me, with gut-level certainty, that the arrangement wasn't going to work. *My mother is not well.* The call had been scheduled before our East Coast workday began to accommodate some members of the education department of the tech company where I worked at the time who were located in various international time zones. I was sitting in the still of our parked car, at home in the garage. It wasn't running, but it served as a buffer zone to block the sounds of my crying toddler in the great room above. My mother had gotten there in the nick of time to watch her so I could be on the call. Rather than feeling relief that she'd arrived, though, there was an unease in the pit of my stomach. A morning blend of coffee and anxiety. I had passed Mom on the landing, on my way down the stairs, as she slowly scaled the four stairs up from the entryway. "There's only a few more stairs to go and you're home free, Mom. She's all fed and changed."

"Oh, baby, stop fussin' and fussin'. Grandma's comin'," my mother said, breathing heavily but focused on her prize at the end of the trek.

"She would love it if you rock her a little. Just don't you fall asleep, too." Undeterred, I hurried down, noticing her grimace and the familiar smell of cigarette smoke thinly veiled by Estée Lauder perfume, and slammed shut the door to the garage. As I punched in the participant code for the call, I pictured the rest of her stair climb, her arthritic steps as she struggled with spinal bone spurs, knowing I'd just put more strain on her pained body and quite possibly placed my daughter in harm's way. Rubbing the back of my neck, I tried to loosen the knot that was forming there. *I'm a horrible mother and an even worse daughter.*

Those guilty conflicted feelings were new to me then. Before the move, I used to think I was a pretty good daughter, for years showering my parents with as many conveniences and financial help that my well-paying job afforded. My husband and I hosted dozens of gatherings for my siblings and their young children—cookouts, birthday parties, and major holiday get-togethers to give my parents a break. Nothing gave us more pleasure, and we gave whatever we could out of heartfelt appreciation and love. A few bucks toward their house taxes? No problemo. An all-expense-paid trip for Mom to Arizona to visit her new online friend. You bet! A new (used) car and a modest kitchen renovation? Got it! All without a second thought.

Rather than discuss my situation with my manager (whose mom picks up her kids before she leaves for work, fresh from her morning workout at Curves)—rather than tell her that I had once come home from work to find my daughter standing in her crib red-faced, damp with sweat and hoarse from wailing while Mom slept soundly in my bedroom down the hall, heavily sedated by painkillers—I began to leave work like a shot out of a cannon to get home every evening. I drove with precision race-car maneuvers on the westbound Massachusetts Turnpike but far too fast. And I spent more time making calls and checking in at home than I should have to make sure everything was okay. Panicked, I eventually visited daycare centers during lunch to scope out an alternative, sometimes adding my name to month-long waiting lists, sometimes driving away knowing I would never be back.

The crib incident had been a one-time thing and I was made to feel the hovering, overreacting newbie parent who had nothing on the expertise acquired in raising five children, but I knew that having my mother watch Summer was too much to ask. She wasn't up to the task. I wanted my daughter to be in a safer environment. And I didn't blame Mom for her dependence on painkillers. The cancer was back. This time she had masses categorized as squamous cells on both lungs. She had described them to me as salt- and pepper-sized tumors, as impossible to eradicate as sand on a beach. My dad, retired, went almost everywhere with her and insisted everything was fine.

Whereas my thoughts used to be occupied by work-related projects, deadlines, and who would be selected for visible team assignments, I now obsessed about my mother's health, worried neurotically about my daughter, and deliberated over daycare options. Having had the big-chain daycare experience, I wanted the personal touch of a small, in-home setting. Ultimately, I located one, the closest thing to Maria von Trapp that I could find, an in-home daycare that was up to my standards. But, of course, Marias are in high demand, and the initial arrangement was for only a few days a week until a full-time spot opened up. It wasn't ideal, but it was something, and it meant that soon enough I'd have things back under control. The damage had been done, though. Even with the flexibility that I had been granted at work, it was evident to more than just me that I wasn't the same person anymore. I was distracted, nervous, not as focused.

My stomach growls. *I should get up and fix something to eat.* But I don't want to move. I want to figure it out, put my finger on the exact point where I went wrong, so it will all make sense. I used to wonder how other women seemed to manage and cope so easily. I assumed they were stronger than me. Every day at the office, thirty minutes away from home, I felt tethered to my daughter at all times. The sound of her little voice, her cry, stirred a deep response in the center of my being. Motherhood changed me at a cellular level.

I reasoned plenty with myself. *That's your heart talking. Your head knows it takes the earning potential of both of our college educations to achieve the same comfort of living that once was met by a single high school education.* I'd thought it would be easier. I wished I could be stronger. Try as I might, I wore my heart on my sleeve to work and would overshare with a band of close-knit colleagues at lunch about how nice it would be to get the severance package that was awarded to lucky ducks who were laid off.

Ultimately, magically, I got my wish. With my box-o-desk-stuff and walking papers in hand, I breathed a colossal sigh of relief at having my "position eliminated," as they deem it in the corporate world. It felt like permission to be a full-time mom, and now I could also be a help to my mother. I was filled with gratitude that management had made the decision that I could not and had pushed me from the nest.

During my time between jobs, I helped with cleaning and made meals regularly for my parents and my ailing sister who lived with them, and I felt I'd done the right thing by saying goodbye to my career-minded self. Something nagged at me, though, a comment that the quiet, all-knowing finance operations manager had shared when I returned from maternity leave. She said the muckety-mucks in the higher ranks (my descriptive, not hers) were surprised to find it took a contracted headcount of two and a half to cover my workload while I was out. I remember being simultaneously flattered and confounded. *I always assumed everyone knew I was a hard worker,* I thought. *Doesn't it show? I won't make that mistake again.*

With time off to think about things, I came to deeply regret not having been braver and more upfront with the tech company management team back then, not having shown my vulnerability with the simple admission that I was needed at home. And that disappointment with myself wasn't something I could just sweep under the rug. I needed to find another job. Even a pay cut would be fine if the job came with a shorter commute and less intense work environment. Like Goldilocks, searching for just the right bed, I made up my mind to find just the right position to achieve just the right balance of work and personal life.

I did find that perfect job, at a local university, and began my new position in the fall of 2007, but not even a week in, my mother passed, and so began a period of loss and crushing responsibility that has lasted five years. I remember so much of it so vividly; I don't know why. Perhaps there's some truth to the notion that the events we remember best are the ones that occur when we're truly in the moment. It may even be a form of posttraumatic stress. I honestly don't know, and I'm hesitant to use the term out of respect for the servicemen and -women who have full-on PTSD after sacrificing so much for our country. Whatever the reason, for the past five years I have had vivid recollections of events that distract me until I write them down. It's my only release. Then I'm freed and

I can function, at least until some other doubt or fleeting image sneaks up again.

I get up from the warm bed and head into my bedroom at the end of the hall to grab a sweater and my notebook from the bedside table. I decide to sit out on the screened porch overlooking our wooded backyard. Not bothering to read the last entry, I scribble quickly: "blood-red dagger nails, rearview mirror, persistence, so weak, same mistakes? stand up, what have I done?"

I turn the notebook sideways, landscape orientation, and draw a horizontal line to use as a timeline to earmark caregiving and jot names of friends and family now gone: "Fall 2007: Mom, then John. 2008: Jared. 2010: Louanne. 2011: Carmine. Fall 2012: Dad." The writing just flows and I include hash marks and summary notes to label key events. It's messy but it feels good to get it down. I home in on the years 2010 to 2012 and draw a wide, repeating circle around that stretch of the timeline. I recall the summer before my father passed as the pinnacle of change. When I was able to let go of spending days and nights in hell, albeit self-imposed, and began catching glimpses of heaven. I realize that although the summer before my father passed was one of the most intense, in some ways it was no more hectic than any other summer. Although the days flowed together like they always do, heartfelt moments, important decisions, and turning points are easy to recall. . . .

> *The night is far spent, the day is at hand. Therefore let us cast off the works of darkness, and let us put on the armor of light.*
> Romans 13:12

Summer Breeze

2

Summer 2010

Our backyard sounds like a bird sanctuary and the morning cacophony of activity drifts in on the gentle breeze. Inside the house, our own morning scramble is on. My husband, Tony, has already left for work, but the steam from his shower still lingers in the bathroom and it smells soap-and-water clean. Now it's my turn. Not that I spend much time on myself. Truth be told, my personal grooming has dropped off to a bare minimum. Deliberations I used to have over what to wear, hair styling, and makeup now seem trivial. As long as I'm clean and presentable for work, that's good enough for me.

I dress quickly, mechanically, always for comfort, and rarely use the mirror for a last check. These days my primary focus is my father, living alone, battling congestive heart failure, and my precious little girl, Summer, age seven. Even though I have an eye on the clock, I never mind helping her to get ready for her day at summer camp. In the kitchen, slapping peanut butter onto the bread, I hear the thumps in the bedroom above and know she's dancing around as always.

"Summer, you sound like a herd of elephants," I yell up the stairs. "Are you getting ready? Do you want—"

"No jelly, and an extra juice box today, 'kay?" she bellows back. I smile to myself, appreciating that she's just as in tune with what I'm doing as I am with what she's doing. "Can you come up when you're done? I want to put on my sunscreen before we leave so we don't have to do it there."

A few minutes later, sitting on the edge of her bed, I slather sunscreen on her child-soft skin. Then we're on to the big decisions of what to wear, T-shirt or tank, shorts or capris. And which of her numerous bathing-suit options will be chosen to go into the swim bag? I don't know why, but I have a soft spot for—and possibly an addiction to—bathing suits. Both of us have far too many, but like a flower to a butterfly, the bathing-suit rack has a colorful, irresistible pull on me. Summer has so many that we've made a game of the selection process, addressing the bathing suits and cover-ups in the drawer as if they weren't inanimate objects. "Whoooo's goin' swimmin' today?" Summer yells as she swirls her hand inside the drawer and pulls out a sporty tankini with a color-block pattern of Day-Glo yellow and green. "The winnah!" She laughs and holds it up. She knows her exaggerated mocking of my Worcester accent always gets a laugh out of me, and this time is no exception. We head downstairs to the kitchen, where she dances and dawdles while I speed-pack the purple polka-dot, insulated lunch bag with the PB-and-no-J sandwich, snacks, and drinks for the day, and then we're off.

The morning drive to the YMCA summer day camp in Sutton is always my favorite part of the day—windows down, fresh summer air, woodsy smells, back roads that wind through picturesque, central Massachusetts lake towns. These same roads lead to the campground my siblings and I used to stay at when I was Summer's age. Catching the faint hint of campfires or fresh-cut wood, I'm heady, seeped in pine-infused memories of carefree days. I glance in the rearview mirror and it's obvious that Summer is as sensitive to the seasonal fragrance, with her eyes sometimes closed and her serene expression angled to catch just the right gentle breeze through the window.

Driving along, I cherish the innocence of the talks with my little peanut butter cup and the songs we sing together even as I'm silently bolstering myself to say goodbye. I'll encourage her to enjoy the day, look forward to new friends and activities, while knowing that she really wants to be with me. And the same goes for me, but spending the day with her isn't possible for the working mom, the "sandwich mom," the "get-it-all-done-in-a-day mom." This lifestyle is all about compartmentalizing each persona with an eye on the big picture.

Thinking back on my childhood, I'm amazed at the time we had to laze the day away in the seventies. For the entire summer, our family camped with trailer and tent on Lake Manchaug, in Douglas, just a few towns over from Worcester. To my younger self, it felt like hours and many miles from home. I spent the days with my sister closest in age, Louanne, three years older than me, and summertime friends. We mostly swam and played board games while listening to Carole King, Jackson Browne, the Beatles, and the Guess Who on eight-track cassette. "American woman, get away from meee-hee, American woman, Mama set me free-hee," I would belt out at the top of my lungs while Louanne and I played Monopoly, Trouble, or Life in our sun-dappled campsite, never mind that it was on a rotting picnic table. With great command

and confidence, I would move my plastic piece around the game board while taking giant slugs from an oversize Pixy Stix tube. Sugar-dust-induced bliss! (Slim Jims and Funyuns were our other dietary staples.) Louanne hummed along, but her focus was on the game. Naturally more competitive than me, she won nine times out of ten, so she knew that to keep me in the game, she had to suffer my boisterous antics. Most of our games ended with her laughing maniacally and proclaiming herself "the champion once again!" and me running away bawling. Ahh, good times.

Sometimes I share things that come to mind with Summer and laugh to hear her questions. "Do they still sell Pixy Stix? What's a Slim Jim?" But more often the memories are my own to mull. Those days were such a contrast to the highly structured times we live in now. Free-range childhoods are a thing of the past. In my family, adult supervision was optional, which suited me just fine. I know that many changes are for the better, though, and I shudder to think of how many near-death experiences I had while swimming alone. I especially loved to explore under the docks, shallow-breathing and staring up at dozens of rusty nails jutting through the wood. In retrospect, my childhood freedom bordered on neglect, but I harbor no ill will toward my parents. It was a time filled with acceptance and love, just none of the traditional trappings of childcare. As the youngest of five, I was raised by my siblings as much as by my parents, so our home was a little like the Wild West. You did well to fend for yourself. Though it was never expressly said, we knew the house rules—You want clean clothes? Wash 'em. You want something to eat? Make it. You're tired of being dirty? Take a bath.

My mother earned her nursing degree and went to work as soon as I was school age. Perhaps for her own sanity, she chose second shift, three to eleven, which meant she was gone when we got home from school, she came home when we were in bed, and she was asleep when we got ready for school. And being an avid reader, she was distracted even when she was present. By today's standards, her hands-off ways, albeit unintentional, might be heralded as an innovative technique in modeling educational excellence. Like her, all of us kids always had our noses in a book. Never mind that I was the youngest student at school learning life lessons by reading *Love Story, The Thorn Birds,* and other cast-off titles lying around the house. I'm fairly certain I was the only girl who was naming Barbie and Ken dolls "Meggie" and "Father Ralph."

It was all okay though, from the rusty-nail escapades to my sporadic, personal-hygiene schedule. I loved the freedom that my parents gave me and that most of my friends didn't seem to have.

So different from my parenting style, but who's to say mine is any better? I certainly learned to be self-sufficient, and I often wish Summer would do more for herself. Ironically, that thought usually occurs as I'm doing a task myself, such as pouring lemonade, in the name of efficiency, to get it done without a mess.

As I pull up at the Y, there's no more escaping into the past. It's time to face another goodbye. These goodbyes are silent torture. They are unspoken words and a forced smile of resolve from us both. I'm silently willing my kindhearted daughter to have a good day, and she will, even though we both could use more time together. Holding hands, we walk down the dirt trail toward the check-in spot, and I rattle off a superfluous list of questions as a means to fill a space, an inevitable void where we begin to miss each other in the last minutes that we're still together.

"Got your money for the snack shack and extra sunscreen if you need it?"

"Yup," Summer replies, looking down as we walk.

"Do you think your friend Abby will be here today?"

"Not sure."

Some days she's quiet and I don't push for a reply. She knows as well as I do that the checklist and the small talk doesn't really matter. I feel like she can see right through my lame attempt at a happy face.

The conflicted feeling and the hint of panic in the pit of your stomach as you hand off your most precious prize are simply the price of entry to the Working Mothers Club. And I especially resent it in the summer. Summers are supposed to be carefree, lazy, exploratory—*fun.*

God, I hate this part. Goodbye, my dearest girl. I take a deep breath. *I can do this.* "I'll see you soon, my little love bug," I whisper as we share a quick hug. She squeezes tight, but then she looks away and runs off to join a group without looking back. I do, though. I stand and watch to make sure she's with someone and not alone. When I head back up the trail to the car, I pass by a well-dressed mom and a boy who looks younger than Summer. They're having a similar exchange, and I smile and nod to a fellow member of the club. Not surprisingly, she doesn't even notice. I glance at my watch and see it's eight thirty. *Ugh, I've gotta hustle.*

Back in the car, I retrace the ride back, but this time with no regard for the fresh summer breeze and woodsy smells. Bound for work at lightning speed, I'm heading away from my heart and mentally shifting gears. Those same picturesque winding roads are now a pain in the butt because it's nearly impossible to read email on my iPhone and dial return calls.

I make good time until I spot a black car backing out of a driveway and I'm suddenly forced to drive the speed limit, something I usually regard as an option rather than a requirement. "Great, perfect!" I say out loud. I glare at the insipid sticker on the back window depicting a stick-figure family of four: Mom, Dad, soccer boy, and ballerina girl. There's also a bumper sticker that says, *"The scientific name for an animal that doesn't either run from or fight its enemies is—LUNCH."* "That's great, soccer mom, take your time," I say. "Heading to yoga?" I edge closer, right on her tail at a mere thirty-five miles an hour. "Yeah, that's right, let's slow down to read the menu sign in front of the golf club. . . . How nice—the National Grill features fresh local vegetables." Finally, the driver of the Acura pulls to the side of the road, allowing me to pass. Impatience being one of my virtues, I wave sarcastically as I veer around, wondering why the hell everyone moves so slow. In the blur of passing, I notice that Soccer Mom is actually an older man in a gray Stetson driving cap, similar to the one my father-in-law used to wear. I dismiss the elderly image of my father-in-law, dozing in front of CNBC's *Mad Money* in the recliner at his Long Island home. Having softened in his old age, he was no longer outspoken and full of bravado, and I much preferred him that way—quiet. It was easier to get closer to him.

No time for that. I feel about five seconds of guilt before I gun it and fix my eyes on the road ahead, mindful not to wear out the brakes. When I reach the ramp to the wide-open expanse of Route 146 heading north toward the city, I feel relief and finally remember to breathe.

I arrive at work a few minutes before nine, which is something of a feat. Like today, most days are a race to get there, a race to get butt-in-seat by nine, so that the colleagues most inclined to notice won't have any dirt on me that day. And today I've done it. *That's right, watchful eyes, I'm here. Sound the trumpets.* Although the nonexempt workday officially starts at eight, "that's not me", success for me is arriving any time between eight-thirty and nine.

After all, I took this university position as a move away from the fast-paced, well-paying tech environment and toward greater balance between work and my personal life. My colleagues have no idea I used to be the last person to leave the office for the day. As a condition of my hiring this time, I required the option to shorten my workday as long as I was able to get the job done. I shared the example of a former colleague who'd told me she wished her kids could drop and roll from her moving car so she wouldn't have to take time for chitchat at daycare. "I'll never be one to shake my daughter from my leg at daycare drop-off so I can get to work on time," I said to the dean, who was the hiring manager at the time. He had nodded approvingly. *Plus, I'm in a sales role—isn't the true measure supposed to be revenue, not punching in?*

So plays my internal dialogue every time I feel the slightest twinge of guilt. But the fact is, internal team relationships are paramount, and so is being in lockstep with office culture. It's all about how it looks. And how do I look to my officemates and my young rising star of a manager? Tired, frumpy, overweight, and middle-aged. With bad hair. I admit, no amount of smoothing gel products seems to work against my coarse, graying roots. Thanks, forties! So, I've given up trying. *Perhaps it looks deliberate,* I like to think. *Windblown and casual, like one of the women in a Sundance or J. Jill catalog.* But in reality, I'm more aptly a run-of-the-mill, disheveled working mother stuck in a perpetual "before" photo, as in "before the makeover." There's probably a certain justice to it, though, call it what you will—payback, karma, the circle of life. Early in my career, I used to look with disdain at working moms. I viewed them as train wrecks coming and going, completely absentminded. Back in the early nineties, sporting my latest *tres* chic Dress Barn fashion, I would think judgmentally, *How nice it must be to leave the office earlier than everyone and at the same time every day. Hmmf.*

Now I know better, having lived the irony of "What goes around comes around." *I'm* the train wreck with hair from hell.

This I know because of the day that an older, well-dressed colleague who works only on Fridays brought in a flat iron that she "just happened to pick up at a yard sale."

"Here, honey," she said with a twinkle in her eye as she handed over the brand-new hair tool, still in the package. "You're still a young woman. This might help." I know she acted out of genuine concern for me, but I felt the blush rise in my cheeks. I swallowed my embarrassment and forced a smile of thanks.

But despite my unruly hair and not being in the best of shape, I consider myself quite adept at doing my job—selling on-site graduate programs. True to all sales jobs, practices such as diligent follow-up, making the right connections, and sometimes just being in the right place at the right time contribute to success. Early in my career, I held positions that supported the sales function (delivering training and creating sales enablement tools) so it seemed a logical and easy enough transition to try. I'm glad I did, as I love the cachet and the energy associated with being part of a university environment. And the fact that there were twenty-five colleges and universities within a twenty-five-mile radius of the city from which to choose certainly helped.

Representing the university to area companies is like wearing a badge of honor. Since I never aspired to drop anchor in a sales role indefinitely, I made peace using the mind-set that if I had to be in sales, what more altruistic function is there than helping working professionals to pursue their dreams for advanced education? My noble goal was to convince senior-level managers of technical employees—information technologists, software or systems engineers, or people who worked on a range of defense weaponry, (from manned/unmanned ground vehicles, to helicopters, to nuclear submarines)—that their employees would be happier and more productive if professors from the university came to their place of work to teach graduate courses rather than making the employees schlep to campus after working all day. Whether for a business or a technology degree, it is a win-win for all involved. And it matters not that I know close to nothing about such complex and sophisticated job functions. If I can say "master of science degree in electrical engineering" (or mechanical or computer engineering), I can sell it. Well, actually, position it. Really, my primary goal is to "open doors"—I guess it's really about *knocking* on doors and, if they crack open, finagling my way in. The prestige of the university name helps with that.

It's been a few years in this role, and I enjoy it. Whether visiting with companies at their sites or in the office doing outreach or prepping for functions, there's seldom a dull day. In a nicely refurbished brownstone separated from the main campus, my sunny office is where I can slip away from the pain of whatever illness or tragedy is happening in my personal life and be a capable professional. My buffer zone against the complexities of family dynamics, against the calls from testy siblings, the school nurse, or my father's doctors. I make no secret that work is my haven and often the best part of my day. As I rinse out my coffee mug in the sink of the small kitchenette, it's hard not to read the neatly typed reminder taped to the wall above the faucet: "Wash Your Own Dishes." Every day I read this and the dozen other labels that have been carefully positioned by the über-efficient facility manager, who's clearly very deft with a label-maker. My favorite is "Watch Your Own Toast," smack-dab on the front of the toaster. Despite its conspicuous presence, burned toast can sometimes be smelled wafting down the hall and word of the transgression quickly gets around.

It's all good, though, a welcome change from the impersonal environment of the large corporations where I'd always worked.

From the first days on the job, I was told, "We're a family," and it's probably been repeated by this person or that one more than a hundred times since. During my first year in the position, it was music to my ears. I felt like Dorothy stepping out of the shadow of the twister into the colorized world of merry Munchkins full of glad tidings. But as with most things, once your eyes adjust, you see that some Munchkins carouse and whisper and might be inclined to villainize people whom they don't understand. In time, the "family" line seemed more like a strong reminder, and it became clear that it pertained only to certain people. *Well, okay, I guess so,* I often thought, although with my actual family I never have to be circumspect about how much I share about my work "family." And I don't feel as if my comings and goings are fodder for lunchtime kibitzing. With them, my real family, I'm not guarded.

But still, I know there *is* a closeness to this group, something that comes from the bonding over a shared goal, a revenue goal to help the university top line. The conveniences and perks and personal touches in the kitchenette are tangible reminders that this department stands out from others in the university. It's more than the requisite automated coffee brewer stocked with a variety of gourmet options and a range of flavored creamers to match, there's the friendly banter and group photo hanging on the bulletin board along with cute cartoons, an oversize table that's always crammed at lunch and two oversize refrigerators to house the medley of leftover treats from department-hosted, graduate-student functions and employee lunches.

And, of course, there are labels on the refrigerators. Both say the same thing: "Eat Your Own Lunch."

> *A man's heart plans his way, but the Lord directs his steps.*
> Proverbs 16:9

Early Signs

3

Fall 2010

I t was my father's doctor who made the decision to take away his driver's license. There hadn't been a precipitating event, but she was wary, and I suppose part of being a geriatric doctor is knowing when the time is right. What she didn't know was that it would have been better to talk with him and allow him to be part of the decision. Or maybe she did and he forgot. I don't know because, at this stage, I wasn't with him for doctors' appointments. I was still very much wrapped up in my own life, thank you very much. Bottom line, he received notice by way of an official letter in the mail telling him his license had been suspended.

"Sa, can you believe this?" he'd said, handing me the letter, his hand shaking and tears welling. My mind raced. Not knowing what to say, I looked down to read the letter, taking a little longer than necessary, and pulled out a seat at the kitchen island counter. He followed me and stood beside me, looking down at it as well. I knew the impact of this. To men of his generation, this is a huge blow. Far more than a means of getting from Point A to Point B, driving is proof of adulthood and autonomy and all things that say you're a capable, contributing member of society.

And it hit my father especially hard. The eldest of six siblings from the Green Island neighborhood of Worcester, he'd always been scrappy and resourceful, doing his part as a boy to provide for his family during the Depression and, when he was old enough to drive, learning every side street and shortcut in the city. When most people were holed up during big storms—say, the New England blizzard of '78—he'd be off helping someone in need or running yet another errand through the deserted streets in a rundown jalopy just because he could. He wasn't reckless—it was just that mobility was an extension of himself, vital to feeling alive and independent. I knew that this "hand it over" decree caused him shame, feeling like a public indictment of both his judgment and his capability.

"Dr. Vahini did this," he said. "She can't do this, can she?"

My mind kept racing. I know the doctor—she'd always been good to both him and my mother. I really wanted to say the right thing to him, provide an explanation or some comfort like he had for me in so many situations. I'd rarely seen him upset, and I'd never seen him afflicted with shame or self-doubt.

"I know, it doesn't seem right, Dad," I said. "It *is* an injustice. But I suppose it's all about safety." Back of mind, I thought about stories my mother used to share, about how he would run to the store and come back without half the things he was supposed to buy or even forget how to get there altogether. I'd never thought much about it—it seemed natural enough, like something that could happen to anyone, especially as you get older.

He considered my response, still standing and studying the letter. Just as I was about to offer more lame solace in the form of logical explanation, he folded it up and put it in his shirt pocket.

"Safety? Whose safety? Screw safety—I'm going to get it back. What do you have for tea?"

Over the next month, he took driver's ed classes to try to sharpen his skills, but what he came away with was the realization that he didn't have the dexterity of his youth. Without much discussion or explanation, he stopped pursuing the road test. And something more than just driving privileges has been lost. The indignity has taken a chip out of his self-confidence. For the first time, he seemed to accept his status as elderly.

So now my siblings and I pitch in to drive him where he needs to go, and on this crisp Sunday afternoon in October I'm picking up my eighty-three-year-old dad to take him to Walmart for his four-to-eleven shift as a greeter. I arrive in plenty of time to give him any help he might need in getting ready. Lately, he's been a little less coifed, his grooming habits falling short. My sisters and I can't help but notice when he's wearing a stained shirt or when he's missed an obvious patch of scruff while shaving. Nothing earth-shattering, just a little off.

Anyone who knew my father in earlier times knew he had a unique sense of style. He had a signature look, born of practicality and his time in the navy. His appearance seemed to be part of his work ethic; clothes were like a uniform. He had multiple shirts that were identical and multiple pairs of the same pants, and to the casual observer, it may have appeared that he wore the same clothes every day: a button-down shirt over a white crew neck T-shirt with flat-front khakis. In reality, although his outfits were all monochrome, they did come in different colors, albeit only a few: navy blue pants with a lighter blue button-down shirt, dark gray pants with a lighter gray shirt and—his favorite—dark brown pants with a tan shirt. The same outfits for years on end (though he did change it up by rolling up his sleeves on a hot day). Never mind all our attempts to force a patterned short-sleeve shirt or a Perry Como-style sweater on him as a birthday or Christmas gift. You could almost hear him thinking, *No way, José—ain't gonna happen,* as he faked a smile and said, "Why, thank you very much!"

So it's come as a major upheaval that Walmart's dress code requires him to wear tan pants with a navy shirt, but he's taken it in stride. On occasion, he's even agreed to wear a dark blue fleece vest! It seems ridiculous, I know, but it's quite a sight to his kids after decades of seeing him a certain way.

As we stand in his kitchen, sort of sizing each other up, his is the softer of our gazes. He's glad to see me. And while I'm glad to see him, too, I look at him more critically. I want to make sure he's clean and presentable. As I take in his five-nine frame, his receding gray hairline, his brown eyes, and his olive skin, I realize that I'd taken for granted that one of his distinctive traits was that he never seemed to age. Until recently, he was one of the lucky ones, perpetually fit and trim and always clean-shaven. Being healthy mattered to him, and he took a natural, common-sense approach to eating. He taught his five growing children (four daughters, one son), "Eat what you like, just not a lot of it." Judging by my zaftig figure, I guess I took the "eat what you like" part more to heart.

I assure him he looks good, and he does, with his name badge securely attached to the breast pocket of his nicely pressed navy shirt. He's had the Walmart job for only a few weeks, but he always seems like a kid on the first day of school when he's getting ready. He's excited in a nervous kind of way, wanting to look the part and fit in. I give a quick swipe with the lint brush on his chest, arms, and back to catch any stray dog hairs. Then I perform the not-so-subtle sniff test to see if he smells like pee. Hugging him tight and breathing in, I sniff loud enough that he knows my motive.

He shakes his head and laughs, annoyed. "Cut it the hell out, Sa. You girls are all crazy."

"Yup, I know, but I still want to make sure you don't smell," I say and give him a quick peck on the cheek.

Since taking the job, he's begun to regularly wear adult incontinence products, mainly Depends. To my sisters and me, it's a relief. It means fewer pee stains on the front of his pants from his constant trips to the bathroom, themselves a result of the Lasix he's taking for water retention caused by his congestive heart failure. For months we'd noticed these telltale signs of body betrayal, and he would downplay and try to ignore them. When we suggested he start wearing Depends, he initially balked at the idea, but he ultimately agreed to wear them at work as a precaution.

The final touch before we're good to go is a recent gift from eldest daughter Pat, an armed-forces baseball cap recognizing his time spent in the navy, aboard the USS *Joseph P. Kennedy Jr.* just after World War II. It's a symbol of pride worn by the men of his generation, and he doesn't go anywhere without it. To us girls, it's another win—a gift actually worn!

Together we lock up the house, leaving the porch and kitchen lights on. "You watch the house," he tells the dogs as we close the side entry door and start down the familiar walkway to my car. In one spot, a pine tree root has created a bulge in the concrete that we've casually stepped over for our whole lives, but now it seems a minimountain that he has to navigate. I'm glad to be an arm to lean on, his ride to work, but at the same time it's unsettling, this new role of being in the driver's seat.

Some of the final drives that Dad took before losing his license were to visit Louanne at the St. Francis House nursing home/ rehab/hospice center where she was living out her final days, wasting away from pancreatic cancer. He'd make the trip to see her every day, bringing goodies and treats, until she finally passed after battling the cancer for a full year longer than doctors had predicted.

"Hi, Lou-lou," he'd say cheerfully, ambling into her bedroom door and always with some sort of snack in hand. "I didn't know if you would want cereal or a Table Talk pie, so I brought you both!"

No food was off-limits. Privately, he would tell me, "Eating is a good sign, and once her appetite goes, it won't be long."

And it wasn't just food that she was inundated with. By the time she passed, cleaning out her room was like emptying a fully stocked kitchen *and* a gift store. Over the course of the year, visitors had given her quite a selection of stuffed animals, decorative doodads, and general miscellanea. And family members took to adding Pandora charms to her growing collection of bracelet pageantry. In the end, she had an extra two pounds of weight on her wrists alone. Who knows who had more joy, us in giving or her in receiving? Whatever the case, the offerings became a ritual.

Through it all, Dad would sit by her bed, sometimes without saying a word. Growing quieter every day, I suspect, because there were no words left.

Louanne had chosen the same fate as her second husband, Alex. She put the needle to her arm to see why the love of her life had fallen under the sway of heroin. "I wanted to see what was the big deal, was all," she said so matter-of-factly when I asked her why she would *ever* make that decision. "Plus, it was another way to be with Alex, you know?" Whether it was based on true love or just a thoughtless choice, her subsequent addiction wreaked havoc on our family, bringing lies, sadness, and pain. And the ordeal aged her exponentially. She was forty-six years old when she died but looked like she was well into her sixties.

I've imagined the Hollywood movie version of her character, played by, let's say, Anne Hathaway, who can gracefully depict facets of the human condition in decline. Early scenes would depict my sister's self-conscious weight struggles, having bought into what her sixth-grade cheering squad considered to be acceptable beauty. I know because I was there beside her on the living room couch, under the handmade afghan, eating Beefaroni and watching the ever-mesmerizing drama of Luke and Laura while her tear-stained cheeks dried. She was never quite comfortable in her own skin until she met Alex, when she became blissfully happy—or blissed out, depending on how you want to look at it. Later scenes, set after Alex's death, would depict her moving back home with my parents, her life becoming entwined with theirs. She continued to march to the beat of her own drum, though, even if that drum said to stay in bed all day and chain-smoke. Granted, she was probably bipolar and severely depressed, but without an actual doctor's diagnosis, she was just our sister who lived a hop, skip, and jump outside societal norms. She was quirky, but she was also as smart and crafty as a fox.

But that's another story entirely, and Louanne's part in this one is the role she played in keeping my dad active and engaged on her behalf. Or maybe it was the other way around. Whatever the reality, it seemed to work both ways. As a means to stave off her depression, Dad found a way to keep her interested in a passion from her former life with Alex: finding and restoring antiques. They'd once owned an antiques store called "Oldies but Goodies," and it was a happy time for them during which they managed to stay clean. To help her find that happiness again, father and daughter went out in all types of weather to flea markets and auctions, and both seemed to thrive on their time together.

Dad paid a price, though. By thoughtlessly spending down his reverse mortgage-account balance, he forfeited the nest egg that could have afforded him years of home health care. By the time Louanne went into hospice, Mom had died and Dad was left in a house full of impassable rooms, stuffed with artifacts and antiques. Some would say he'd served as an enabler, but being there for his family was what kept him going. Mom used to say, "Your father is the consummate provider."

With Louanne's passing in early September, we all slipped back into normal life. And during fall in New England, normal life comes with a melancholy that sometimes catches you off guard. As the deciduous trees drop their golden leaves, it's a reminder that a piece of our lives is falling away, too. My close friends and I serve as an informal 1-800 hot line for each other, talking each other off the ledge when the melancholy hits. Sometimes it's just a quick message: "*Beep* . . . Hi, Sa, it's Fran. There's that frickin' smell in the air today. Gotta love it, right? I bawled on the sidewalk watching Sam get on the bus for school. Granted that was fifteen years ago, but that damn leafy smell brought it all home, you know? I know Summer is going to school . . . Hope you're doing okay. Call me . . . *Click*." And I *was* okay, just really busy, but isn't everyone?

The hubbub of back-to-school activity helped to distract from the gloom and allow me to jump back into the hectic pace of life as usual. For me and my sisters—Patricia, the eldest, and Colette, the third-born—the routine now included calling to check on my father, talking loudly into the phone. Often, it would ring for ages before he would answer in his usual way.

"Who goes there?"

"Hi, Dad. Everything all right? Do you need anything?"

The reply was usually either dead silence or "I can't figure out this goddamn phone. Is this on? Is anyone there?!"

It was rare, but on occasion we would have the satisfaction of a regular reply: "Yup, all set. Bye now."

The three of us would call each other to learn who had talked with him on that day and how he was doing. An informal network was thus formed, with my father as the central topic.

When I visited, I'd usually find him either at the kitchen table reading the *Worcester Telegram & Gazette* or watching TV in the living room, sitting on the couch. That ridiculous couch. We all called it "the red couch," and it took on its own place in the family. The red couch was Louanne's and it moved in when she did. Best described as kitsch, it was better-suited to a 1920s Hollywood movie set than my parents' living room. The fabric was a heavy blend of suede or velvet, and the design was very sleek, with a narrow seat and a low back. In its brash newness, it stood out from the rest of their worn-out living room furniture like the one colorized item in an old sepia-toned photo. It didn't belong among the dark paneled walls, the upright jet-black piano and classic marble-top accent table with maple claw-foot legs. Not that this was a living room of refinement, but there were nice pieces among the clutter.

The animals who lived there—the dogs, Max and Elsa, a mix of Chihuahua and Pomeranian, and the cat, Simon—loved to sit on the red couch alongside my dad. At first, there was a comical element about seeing them there all together, connected and overlapping like kids cozied up during a sleepover. But ultimately, there was something heart-wrenching about seeing him sleep there, preferring the couch to a room steeped in memories of my mother's sick days.

During Mom's battles with breast cancer and then lung cancer, we'd painted the bedroom radiant orchid in an effort to cheer up the space. After her passing, the effort came off as gaudy and a stark contrast with the neutral palette in the rest of the house. There was a distinctly false energy to it, like the creepiness of a clown. Codependent and sharing pills, my mother and Louanne—also terminally ill—had spent so much time in the poorly lit room, chain-smoking in the queen-size bed, that a smoke cloud was usually visible, the thin cirrostratus type that cover the sky like a veil. In my mother's final days, I dreaded going over there even for brief visits. I would inevitably leave enraged because of their lounging condition and the stench of stale cigarette smoke clinging to my daughter's hair and clothes. I tried to look past the dysfunction and secondhand smoke, but I found it intolerable on my toddling girl's behalf. In time, I stopped going over altogether.

It was a sick room personified, with drawers full of personal items no longer used and a dust-covered jewelry box to rival Miss Havisham's, frozen in time. Dad obviously felt it, too. "I don't like the draft in there" was his simple explanation, and like a chapter in a sad story, the bedroom door on the first floor of his Cape-style home closed and remained so. So, in place of a proper bed in a proper bedroom, Dad would fall asleep sitting upright on the red couch. It was such a lonely and sad sight to find him and the animals all crammed together. It was his nature to inconvenience himself so the animals would be comfortable. It seemed as if the red couch lost its fresh form in tandem with Dad's weakening health.

He also spent large portions of his days on the red couch, sleeping. His body clock was off, and when he wouldn't answer the phone (which was happening more and more often as winter approached), I'd often find him asleep on the couch with Fox News blaring on the TV, the cordless phone right by his side and the house smelling of dog pee and poop. I'm ashamed to admit how, at this stage, I would usually breeze in and out, annoyed at him for not answering the phone and causing me worry and the inconvenience of dragging myself over there after working all day.

"Dad, *Dad*, wake up," I'd shout. "It's after dinnertime. Have you had dinner? Have you taken your pills today?"

"Christ, you scared me, Sa. What the hell time is it?"

"It's around six and I can't stay long, so what do you need while I'm here?"

I wouldn't wait for the reply, and while he roused himself, I'd clamor around the house like a white tornado, humorless and bothered, either collecting dirty dishes or rolling up the soiled newspapers on the floor, where the dogs had learned to relieve themselves, just in front of the sliders to the backyard. I'd force myself to sit at the kitchen table for a proper visit, even if it was only for fifteen minutes, and try to be conversational. He loved to hear news about the family, about Summer (usually right there beside me) or about what project Tony was working on at Hasbro. "How's the toy maker?" he'd ask, smirking with pride about his witty allusion to my husband as Kris Kringle. Or he'd ask about what companies I was meeting with in my position, genuinely interested in the various industries and which companies were investing in their talent by bringing graduate education on-site. But truthfully, the conversation often deteriorated to my grossed-out commentary about the condition of the house.

I'd watch while he puttered quietly around the kitchen. Unless I brought an already-cooked meal to drop off, he preferred to cook in his own kitchen despite my offers to whip something up. And such concoctions he would create—odd meal combinations that he truly loved. For example, he'd spoon canned salmon or tuna onto crackers and have a can of B&M baked beans on the side, or he'd heat up SpaghettiOs on the stove and stir in some soy sauce or milk. It looked gross, but he really enjoyed it. A common practice was to add milk to whatever was left in the pot on the stove from the previous day—"to loosen it up—it's still good, Sa," he'd say.

"Compared to what?" I'd reply.

I usually hosted him for dinners on the weekend, and a few times during the week either Tony or one of my sisters' husbands would drop something off for him to eat. This isn't meant to sound saintly—quite the opposite. It's amazing how little I anticipated and thought about what was likely to unfold. So consumed in my own family, career, and life, I guess I thought it would just work itself out. Like scenes from *Groundhog Day*, repeated over and over, my rushed, after-work visits almost always ended with me leaving in a huff. Wanting his space and tiring of criticism and the intrusion on his privacy, he didn't like my visits any more than I liked stopping over. "I can't stand these dogs, Dad. Why are they constantly digging at my leg to be picked up? They're overweight, they smell, and they eat so badly. Can't you just feed them their food instead of always tossing them greasy leftovers? And why is the birdseed all over the floor? Can't we just organize it in the bin *outside*?"

"Hey, look, I don't need to be told how to feed the dogs, and I have a system for how I feed the birds," he'd fire back. "If you don't like it, just stay the hell home!"

"You've got it! I still have plenty to do, you know."

I'd leave brusquely, but always with a quick kiss on the cheek. By the time I got home, I was usually drying my eyes and feeling guilty about my behavior. Calling him to apologize wasn't much of an option because he didn't hear the phone, and I'd tell myself I'd do it the next time I saw him, but more often than not, a similar scene repeated.

My sisters had their own unique run-ins and stories too. One weekend afternoon, Pat stopped over for a visit and to rummage in one of the upstairs bedrooms for a vintage picture frame. She has an eye for recycling odds and ends that I would just as soon toss. They're knickknack dust collectors to me, but to her they're family heirlooms with history and memories attached. Halfway up the stairs that afternoon, she excitedly asked, "Is it okay if I explore to find me a treasure?"

He shrugged. "Depends what it is."

Opening the door to her childhood bedroom, she found more than she'd expected: beautiful Simon, collapsed and nearly dead on the floor. He'd been locked in the room for over a week and was surrounded by dried-up excrement. We'd all known he was missing and suspected that Dad had inadvertently let him out with the dogs. He was an indoor cat, declawed by a previous owner, so we feared for him and assumed the worse. Everyone in the family, my husband included, had walked the perimeter of the overgrown backyard, calling his name during the course of the week searching for him. Even if you're not a cat lover, it would be hard not to appreciate Simon's gorgeous coat. He was such a beauty, with his black, long-haired angora blend. His most distinctive attribute was his verbal nature. Through the years, he had no problem making his needs known. His meow was deafening—loud and proud—and for the average person, it would have been impossible not to hear Simon crying in the bedroom.

Holding his hand to his mouth, Dad was devastated to see Pat carry Simon downstairs in that condition.

"Didn't you hear him crying, Dad?" she asked.

"Well, no, of course not," he stammered and scrambled to fill a bowl of water, not taking his eyes off the limp cat. "Can he drink?"

"We're lucky he's still breathing." Pat gently placed him down, and miraculously, he was able to drink.

During an emergency vet appointment, he was diagnosed as malnourished and dehydrated but okay. Though he was down one of his allotted nine lives, for the next one Simon led the life of a pampered prince. As had been the case with Lou-lou, who had brought him home with the red couch and other unique finds, no food was off-limits. Ultimately, though, Pat intervened and took Simon home to live with her, and Dad was glad for it, agreeing that it was for the best.

Now, a few months after he started the job at Walmart, we're all in a groove, with us girls and our husbands taking turns dropping him off. As far as I'm concerned, it's the obvious remedy to his idle days on the couch. It seems we've found the perfect solution to keeping him more engaged with people and given him a newfound sense of purpose. Something he can look forward to, not to mention make him more appreciative of rest on his days off! Together, we had filled in the online application at the kiosk in the back of the store. Together, we went to the interview and he aced it. I remember he had commented on the way out, "Jeez, that was more like a conversation with a pretty young lady than an interview."

"Dad, she was easily in her mid to late fifties," I said, laughing.

"Yeah, like I said, just a spring chicken. When do you think I'll start?"

He got the call, the next day, and here we are, with me dropping him off for a job he's an old pro at after just a few weeks.

"See you at eleven," I say after walking him to the entrance.

"You bet," he answers and gives a quick wave without looking back.

Two months later, on a night in mid-December, I arrive to pick him up and he looks weary. Actually, he's grimacing as we begin the trek to the back of the supersize store so he can punch out. He'd been off to a good start, but over time the shifts have become hard on him. Even though he has a note from Dr. Vahini requesting that he be able to take breaks and to sit while greeting, he pushes himself more than he should. He insists on standing for the duration, and I know his feet are sore and swollen.

"Hey, Dad, why don't you just wait here and I'll walk ahead and punch out for you?"

"Nope, against the rules, Sa. I'm fine."

As luck would have it, one of the store's electric scooters is parked in a nearby aisle, and I start it up. "Hop in, Dad. Let's take advantage of a free ride." I wonder why I haven't thought of this sooner and congratulate myself for thinking of it now. *Another problem solved. Cross that one off the list—check!*

I'm not totally without concern, though, and on the ride home I ask him if he thinks the job is worth the cold, late nights for us both.

"You bet, Sa. I don't mind as long as you think it's the right thing and don't mind getting me."

This is impossible to answer. How can I sum up my appreciation for a lifetime of love? So I take the easy route and use a comparison. "How could I mind when I think about how many times you used to drop me off before I could drive? Remember when I couldn't wait to have my work permit to begin my illustrious grocery-cashier job at Goretti's on Grafton Street? How else was I going to pay for all of those acne treatments?"

We chuckle, and yet I can't help thinking about everything I have to get done the next day, mostly work-related to-do's. *How many people I work with are out in the frigid cold of winter after 11:00 p.m. picking up their elderly father from work?*

"Why do you suppose the ladies like to kiss me?" he says, bringing me back to the warmth of the car. "I had several today and hugs too."

"Ah-hah!" I say, playing Sherlock Holmes and holding my pointer finger straight up in the air. "The *real* reason why the job is not so bad!"

We laugh again as I pull up at 19 Cliff Street. Then a fit of giggles takes over, perhaps because we're both tired and a little slap-happy. Like sharing an infectious yawn, we laugh about it all the way down the walkway. I hug him good night once he's inside and smile about it on the ride home.

The next day is a blur and pretty much goes downhill from the moment I leave the house at 5:30 a.m. for an important meeting with high-level systems engineers at a nearby army base. Even with the free pass to sail off to the eight o'clock meeting, obstacles seem to be strategically placed at every turn. The commute a few towns east to Natick that usually takes forty-five minutes takes a little over two hours because of what turns out to be a fender bender on the highway. Listening to the radio banter of paid professionals who, I suppose, are trying to take our minds off this mess, I take consolation in knowing that my colleague attending the meeting will probably be there on time. She's been in the department for much longer than I have and actually secured this account, so it's actually preferable from the account's perspective for her to be there instead of me. Regardless, on paper the account is mine and my being late looks bad no matter how you slice it.

Leaving her a voice mail, my aim is to apologize in a professional manner, but instead I end up rambling. "Hi, Lilith, it's Sarahbeth. I'm sorry but it looks like I'm running late to the meeting. I'm on the Pike staring at an endless line of red taillights. Who knows why? Accident maybe or road work, I don't know. I can't believe it, actually. I was sure I was leaving with enough time to spare, but here I sit, ready to scream. So sorry to do this. I know it looks bad. I'm sorry. Uh, I'm sorry for how many times I'm saying sorry! Maybe things will start to move and I'll be there soon. Okay, sor—I mean bye."

The checkpoint procedure for clearing civilian admittance on-site, which normally moves along with military precision, is backed up as well. After my turn waiting behind a handful of others checking in, I walk into the meeting a full thirty minutes late. The good manners of everyone in the room preclude any hint of judgment, and by nine o'clock the meeting wraps. Afterward, my colleague's cool demeanor is another matter. She says nothing, which says it all. For the rest of the day, I replay the image of my apologetic stammering reflected in Lilith's blank expression. I try to shake it off in the busyness of the workday but can't.

I'm no slacker. The thought pops into my head, and to prove it to myself, I squirrel myself away in my office for the rest of the day, avoiding chitchat in favor of productivity.

By the time I leave for the day, I'm in my usual rush. But it's not to pick up Summer on time from our neighbor, Joy, who watches her after school. It's to take Dad to dinner before his shift begins at six. We made plans last night to stop for chicken jo-jos at his favorite place in the Village. I'd been expecting that Summer would be with us, but she stayed home from school today with a cold. It felt like hitting the lottery when Tony agreed to work from home to be with her. Granted, the Bizarro World lottery, where the prize is the luxury of going to work.

When we get to the greasy spoon restaurant, I'm already thinking about tomorrow's workday schedule and lineup of scheduled calls as I stand with my dad in the cramped foyer, rubbing the knot at the back of my neck. I'm not so preoccupied that I don't notice that something isn't right, though. He's wheezing! I've never heard this before and it's strange to hear the whistling, raspy breaths. *What is it?*

"Are you okay, Dad? You look so tired and sound awful." I see now that his color is off.

"Well, I am tired. I don't have my energy today. Maybe I'm slowing down." He seems to look to me for confirmation, and I'm suddenly conscious of my own breathing and feel my heart beating faster as panic sets in.

"You're not slowing down—you're sick! I think you should skip work today," I say more intensely than I intend.

"But what about my shift?"

I borrow his way of speaking, "Screw your shift. Let's go home and call the doctor."

We get our dinners to go, and as I help him into the car, I can feel his body relax with the knowledge that he isn't going to work, like the relief a sick child feels when granted permission to stay home from school. Which reminds me—Summer! I need to call Tony and find out how she made out today and let him know that this won't be the quick drop-off I'd expected. Suddenly I'm faced with conflicting pulls and I begin to cycle options for how the rest of the evening can play out. *Who needs me the most right now?* The smell of our greasy takeout is wafting through the car and my stomach constricts. *I had planned to spend the night with my little one, but I need to get Dad settled and wait for the return call from the doctor with instructions. There might be a trip to the ER and a long night before I can go home.* I dread the conversation with Tony, but I know he'll understand another request for him to pinch-hit for me with Summer. *I'll wait to call him once the doctor returns my call, but what if Summer is still sick tomorrow and I need to be home with her and Dad? I suppose I could use a sick day from work.*

"So, I guess I'll miss the fringe benefits of the job tonight, huh, Sa?" Dad says with shallow breaths and the sickening wheezing sound.

I just smile and cringe inside, thinking of strangers hugging and kissing him last night, exposing him to germs while he stood in the frigid draft of the Walmart entryway. *What was I thinking?!*

I'm seeing the situation clearly for the first time, and I'm in shock from the weight of it. Dad is sitting beside me trying to put on a good face but clearly very sick. *Can this really be happening?* Has he really deteriorated this quickly since the slow but surefooted steps to visit Louanne? Even worse than my realization about his failing health is that I suspect he's known for a while and has been pushing himself for my benefit. *What have I done?*

After we pull up to the house, I turn off the car, and as we sit briefly in the quiet, the sound of his labored breathing is exaggerated. Like the calm reserve that automatically kicks in when I need to bandage Summer's occasional cuts and scrapes, the necessity to be in control takes over and I help him from the car. "Let's call Dr. V and get you comfortable, Dad. How about we have a nice hot cup of tea?" He nods, and without talking we make our way along the walkway.

As the weight of the realization sets in, I become determined to make everything all right. I'm as determined as someone poised at the starting line, ready to give it everything she's got. But rather than the crack of a gunshot to start the race, his frightening whistle-breathing rings out and rattles me to the core. A bell toll of sorts, that we've both heard, and there's no ignoring.

> *To everything there is a season, A time to*
> *every purpose under the heaven.*
> Ecclesiastes 3:1

Push and Pull

4

Christmas 2010

"I can't tell what it is yet," Summer says, having a hard time using her inside voice today. Her pitch rises as she tears and crumples Christmas wrapping in frustration. "It's some type of curtain, I think. Maybe a bedspread?"

"You don't have to video every second, Tone," I say flatly, trying to wake up. "Try not to get me, okay?" Still a little unnerved by the shrieks and sheer joy that Christmas morning ushers in, I'm sitting beside Summer in front of the tree with a cup of coffee in one hand and trying to discreetly wave Tony off with the other.

"It's a *puppet show*. I knew it." She's jumping now. "I knew he would bring it. Didn't I say Santa would bring it? And look, there are furry forest animals that go with it! I knew it, I knew it, I can't believe it! Dad, when we play, you can be the bear—no, the moose! Mom, you're the rabbit." For the second time this morning she does her giddy jig, sort of an in-place, one-person conga line, with hops, kicks, and chanting. "I love Christmas day, hey! I'm gonna puppet play, hey!" The earlier rendition of this chant was "I'm gonna Barbie play, hey!" Depending on the gift, I have a feeling this holiday carol will be repeated all day.

Like your wedding day and the first time you hold your newborn baby, Christmas morning is one of those times when you want to be in the moment, to enjoy and soak in every detail. I try to commit these special times to memory so that I have a store of happy, keepsake treasures I can call to mind during times of sorrow or during my golden years when I need some clarity to clear away the gossamer of time. No pressure here. Even as I'm telling myself to enjoy the moment—and I am—I'm also reviewing the schedule for the rest of the day. I've planned it all with Rolex precision. Smiling along and going through the motions, I know I have exactly thirty minutes to open gifts, one hour to straighten the house, thirty minutes to get dressed and two hours to visit with Dad at the hospital before company arrives for Christmas dinner. He was admitted to the hospital, weak, breathless, and wheezing—all related to his congestive heart failure—and with blood in his stools.

After fixing up the house, I try to cut corners with my own fixing up. *Maybe I can save some time if I just brush powder through my hair instead of washing to restyle. It still looks good from the Christmas Eve service. Well, maybe not good, but good enough. . . .* I rush downstairs to wriggle into my bulky winter coat.

"Bye, guys. I'll tell Grampa you said merry, merry!" I shout over the sound of their racing My Little Pony remote-control cars. In the hallway leading to the garage, I grab Dad's present that I'd put aside earlier in the week: a package of plain white, crew-neck T-shirts, a "Dog Days" calendar with oversize printing, a gift basket with a few of his favorite foods—pickled herring, dark chocolate-covered orange peels and Bigelow organic green tea—and a handmade Christmas card from Summer. I'm moving quickly to stay focused and distracted from the pull of staying home, cozied up with my family.

"Bye, Mom. I'm better at this than Dad. Hug Grampa from me."

"Yeah, she is," Tony yells back. "Tell your dad we love him, Sa."

I think of my father sitting alone in a hospital room and I'm pulled just as hard in that direction. *Oh yeah, holiday cheer.* I quickly rip a few of Summer's candy-cane construction paper decorations off the back door as I leave, to brighten up his hospital room.

Adjusting to the frigid cold as the car heats up, my mind cycles. *The table is set, the vegetables have been peeled and the turkey is in the oven, so everything should go fine as long as there are no hiccups in the day.* Unlike my daughter gleefully unwrapping gift upon gift, I wish for *no* surprises. No surprises like the scene I witnessed the day after Dad was admitted to the hospital. I was shocked to see how confused and disoriented he was, to the point of not recognizing his doctor or knowing what day it was. As he sat quiet in the hospital bed, with fear and panic in his eyes, the attending nurse casually informed me that elders can experience a "mental status change" during hospital stays.

That change also raised the question of whether he has dementia, so a room at a rehab facility was being arranged to assess and allow more time for rest and recovery before he returns home. But that was a few days ago and he's improved every day since they regulated his Lasix prescription for water retention.

"Well, hello!" he says as I enter his hospital room.

Relieved to see that he's himself, I feel myself relax for the first time today. It's nice to see him sitting comfortably in the guest chair reading the paper rather than in bed. He's clean-shaven and wearing the hospital gown under his unzipped blue fleece sweater. "Hello, yourself, and Merry Christmas, Dad." I give him a hug that lasts a few seconds longer than the usual quick squeeze. He smells soap-and-water fresh. "At first I thought it was nice that you had the room to yourself, but now I wonder if it would have been better to have a roommate for company, especially today. Too bad you couldn't have timed getting sick a little better." I smile as I peel off my heavy coat to hang in the narrow closet alongside the clothes he wore on the day he was admitted. "You know, most people prefer home-cooked turkey over hospital food."

"Naw, to tell you the truth, I don't really even notice. I'm fine with the quiet and I've never had a problem with hospital food. You kids fuss over everything." He notices the wrapped presents. "Whatcha got there? Did the big man find his way to your house?"

"Of course, but these are from Summer and the cat!" I say and we laugh together over my lame joke.

While he opens his gifts, I hang the candy canes on the cork bulletin board on his side of the room and share news of our morning, embellishing a little in the hope that it makes him feel part of our day. At one point, a nurse's aide comes in to take his blood pressure and tell us that some holiday activities have been scheduled. With the exception of the culinary delights, not much of it holds interest for him, but we make polite comments about how nice it is for the hospital to have planned Christmas carolers and gingerbread-house making.

Compared with the frenetic energy of the morning, our visit is relaxed and comfortable. Even so, it passes quickly. While the Disney Parks Christmas Day Parade plays on TV, we talk mostly about his health. Both interested in the marching bands and floats, we sometimes pause to take in the commentator's details. And during Mariah Carey's big finish, conversation stops altogether. He can't take his eyes off her.

"Wow, what a set of pipes on that one," he says when she's done. He winks and laughs quietly, and I laugh, too, having grown up around his brand of humor.

When it's time to go, I find that it's just as hard to leave him as it had been to leave my husband and daughter this morning, if not more so. I use logic to remind myself that he needs the monitoring of this hospital stay, but still I feel my throat tighten and the familiar heavy heart. Being pulled between my immediate family and Dad is becoming a way of life. Since Lou-lou's gone and he lives alone, I stop in as regularly as possible after work, with Summer always by my side. But the challenge for me is more on an emotional level, or maybe it's psychological. When I go back to the bustle of my family life, I'm always thinking of him alone there with his dogs. It's a constant worry. And it seems an even greater injustice to leave him alone on Christmas Day.

Tensing, telling myself, *don't cry, don't cry,* I say goodbye and hug him quickly this time so I won't break my resolve to keep a good face, a face of forced good cheer in the spirit of the day. He sees right through me, though.

"It's okay, Sa," he says just as I'm at the door. "It's just another day."

I keep walking and wave without looking back, letting the tears flow while I wait for the elevator to come.

By the time I get home, my tears have dried, and it turns out that my Christmas wish is granted: The rest of the day goes without a hitch. Well, sort of. Hosting dinner for the extended family is deeply rewarding but a lot of work. The day is a blur of chaotic commotion accompanied by my husband's handpicked soundtrack of snappy Christmas carols blaring in the background. He calls it his "ChrisMix" and makes one every year for colleagues, friends, and family. He always gets rave reviews.

Over dinner, much of the conversation with my siblings is about Dad. We're so used to his being independent, and it's our first real conversation about what may lie ahead. There are more questions than answers about when we might need to step in, with opinions about his situation varying greatly. Again, in the spirit of the day I try my best to keep the strained topic light, but somewhere between the pecan pie and the shrill sound of cousins trying out Summer's new toy violin and recorder, I end the conversation entirely.

"*What are you talking about?*" I burst out at Colette and Pat. "Admission to a nursing home already? Are you *kidding*?!"

Even the budding musicians in the next room pause until oxygen is breathed back into the air and atmospheric pressure restabilizes.

A few tense minutes later, over the clinking of table cleanup, my sisters debate the best strategy for squeezing in their visits with Dad. "It's so late in the afternoon," Pat says, yawning. "He's probably beat. We should stagger our visits so we don't tire him out."

"That's exactly why we should just go up together!" Colette says and blows out the candles, which have melted down almost to the bottom.

I stay out of this one and keep my head down, packing Dad's plate of leftovers from dinner, although I suspect it matters more to me than to him. It's a comfort knowing I'm sending up his favorite fixin's: Mom's cherished recipe for meat stuffing, drenched in Bell's seasoning.

I make it to the end-of-day finish line, numb from the waist down, back aching and legs feeling like lead. I say goodbye to our guests, relieved to check this holiday off the list. Emotionally, I'm wound as tight as one of the characters in Summer's brand-new collection of Littlest Pet Shop figurines, worried about my father's health, our sibling differences of opinion, about a game plan, and about the days ahead.

My father made no plans for his senior years. Strike that—from his standpoint, I guess there was nothing to plan. He would stay in his home until the day he died, and he would rely on his children to be there just as he had been there for us, and that was that. Age sort of sneaked up on him. With so much of his attention focused on caring for my mom when she was ill and then for my sister, his own health was never the priority even when it should have been. He regularly took blood-pressure pills, enjoyed his regimen of vitamins, and had his own cultivated way of eating, but that didn't head off the intestinal bleeding that had set in a couple of years ago, possibly the result of duodenal ulcers that had plagued him in middle age or his aspirin regimen for staving off heart attacks. Now it's his time to receive care and support from his family, and I fear we're failing him.

During his stay in the hospital and then at a rehabilitation center for the first few weeks of the new year, my sisters and I argue about the long-term outlook, and I feel like I'm the only one fighting for his life. He isn't ready to be admitted to a nursing home long-term, but for some bizarre reason, they're considering it. It's surreal to have these conversations. For the first time in my life, I feel utter and complete panic. Not like the butterflies caused by, say, walking down the aisle or taking a standardized test, but gut-wrenching, chest-constricting, mind-racing *panic*. It's a sickening feeling accompanied by the realization that, just like my dad, I don't have a plan.

I call my older brother, Will, in Florida to update him on our trusting dad who's diligently doing his physical-therapy routine at the rehab center while nurses, therapists, and caseworkers are evaluating him for dementia and administering a battery of tests to determine whether he's fit enough to go home. Like something out of a Shakespeare classic, there's plotting behind the scenes and dire need of a hero to save a frail old man who doesn't know half of what's being whispered about.

"Will?" I say in a high-pitched squeal as I sob through the phone. I'm crying so hard that I can't say another word. As far as he knows, this is a random call from a dolphin or the Tin Man.

"Sa, is that you? Who's there?"

Squeak.

Thank God he doesn't hang up and just waits.

When I finally speak, it's a fire hose of incoherent information.

"You wouldn't believe everything that's going on. Dad can't remember much of his stay in the hospital and they said he experienced a mental status change because of how fast they took off the water in his system. He was lethargic and confused and now they're saying he has dementia. I'm not exactly sure what that means, but I know he's not crazy. Anyway, Colette missed the meeting with the hospital discharge administrator, and as result he's been admitted to the armpit of all rehab facilities in the area. She said it would only be for the weekend until they could find him a bed at another location but, come Monday she decided to leave well enough alone and brought him up a TV for his room. Can you believe that? She said one thing and did another." I finally inhale.

Such is the beginning of a series of frantic calls in which I wail and tattle, reminiscent of my earliest role as the baby of the family. Whether he likes it or not, I keep him in the loop with a play-by-play every few days.

"Hi, Will. This rehab center is worse than I thought. It smells to high heaven, and there are rows of elderly people sitting in wheelchairs in the halls. Daddy really doesn't belong there. He's improved tremendously and is doing much better, but they won't allow him to get up and walk until the team evaluates him. That still hasn't happened! He and I take strolls around the entire floor because they only allow him to walk when supervised. Oh, and they won't listen to his plea to stop giving him Milk of Magnesia. Colette keeps saying she'll get around to calling the doctor for a change order but hasn't. I don't understand why there's no sense of urgency, why no one is listening to him."

The majority of my calls to him are in the evening, after I've visited with Dad or during dinner prep, with my neck craned sideways to hold the phone in place. An exception is during a mid-afternoon drive back to work. "Hi, it's me. I answered a call from Colette at work this morning and the panic in her voice sent a chill down my back. She said, 'Are you sitting down? I have the worst possible news about Dad.' All I could think was that Daddy had a heart attack or stroke or fell and broke something. Nope—that wasn't it at all. She said the rehab facility wants to send him home. Since when is *that* the worst possible news? But then she clued me in, it's all about money.

So I raced out at lunch to attend an emergency meeting that she arranged. I ended up writing a check for five hundred dollars for someone to complete a Mass Health application that I could probably do if I had the time to actually look at it. Anyway, she told me it was necessary or we would have to pay the daily rehab rate or—even worse—they would send him home. Again I ask, since when is that the worst-case scenario?"

I'm always sure to include updates on Pat as well, not playing favorites in my panicked attempt to provide the entire picture. "This entire situation is awful," I tell Will during another call. "I've been so stupid and naïve thinking we all feel the same responsibility and gratitude toward Daddy. Pat's pretty much indifferent about what facility he's in, but she had an idea for me to research the facility and program where her in-laws are enrolled. She keeps warning me about what could happen if I get too involved. She says the IRS will come after me for his back taxes and that I'll lose my house! She seems to think a nursing home is inevitable. This is *Daddy* we're talking about. I can't believe any of this!"

As always, he's quiet, listening and waiting for his turn to talk. When it *is* his turn, his reply is delivered calmly. "You know we all love Dad. It may be different from your way, but we all have a unique relationship with him."

"So how can they be so quick to decide his fate? Why are they talking about admittance to a nursing home? We can't do this to him. It's all moving too fast, Will."

"Unfortunately, we're all a little clueless in knowing what to do just now. Daddy's always been so healthy. You know there's a lot that goes into eldercare, Sa."

"Oh, and they know what goes into eldercare? They don't even seem willing to try! You should hear the fights and power struggles. We can't even agree on whose house to meet at to—"

"Now, don't you go jumping into crazy-town mode. Don't jump to any conclusions yet. You should see the services they have here in Florida. Too bad we can't bring him here."

"I just want to do what he wants, and he wants to go to his own home. Daddy really needs us now."

By the time of my final update, I'm no longer hysterical. I'm closer to being in shock. My embarrassment pours out with my tears. "Hi, Will. I ended up moving Dad to a facility closer to my house today. Tony and I decided to just pay their daily rate out of pocket until we have a game plan and this new team can evaluate him. It was so odd, though—when I went to pick him up, no one at the rehab place provided any instruction or help. I got him ready myself and we waited for almost two hours in the lobby. There was a question as to whether we needed a van and which facility was paying for it. I just sat there like a dummy waiting. I finally called the new place to ask what to do and the administrator assured me that it was all right to leave, so we walked out to my car and left. It's so strange to feel like you need permission. They have this way of making everything so official, so scary.

"On the way to the new place, he asked to stop at Arby's for his favorite sandwich, and, of course, I was glad to take him. We were making jokes about him being sprung from jail and he was so thrilled to be out and about again. It never occurred to me how his system would react, especially with all of that Milk of Mag they'd been giving him. Oh gosh, it was awful, Will! I had to help him get cleaned up after going in his pants. It was the most embarrassing, humiliating thing for both of us. Poop went everywhere, on his back, down his legs, in his socks and shoes. I was shaking trying to help him. Honestly, I've been sick about it all day.

"He wasn't himself, Will. It's like sometimes he gets stuck midprocess and seems lost. I think it was too much excitement for him in one day. Maybe it was that thing that they say happens when you move elderly from their environment. What am I going to do when it's time to bring him home?"

Deflated and exhausted, I no longer have the energy to talk. So I just cut to my white-knuckle plea. "Can you come home, Will? I think you need to come back to Massachusetts."

Now I'm the one who is silent, listening.

"I'll give it some thought," he says finally.

And now it's my turn to wait.

In the space between my frantic calls to Will, there's been constant speculation from my sisters about what's to come, on every front, but my father's finances usually take center stage. A month before Louanne died, I'd taken over paying his bills and learned—no surprise—that most everything was overdue. She'd been in charge of paying bills while she lived there, or more aptly, she'd been in charge of borrowing from Peter to pay Paul. Actually, she didn't pay Paul at all. I can still hear her hoarse monotone as she told me her tips and tricks, with eyes closed and lying under the crisp, white sheets. "Only pay the minimum on the electric 'cause they can't turn the lights off on him anyway. Keep Sears in good shape, he likes Sears. Don't worry about the phone. Most of the time, he can't find his cell phone, and then can't figure it out anyway."

I listened quietly and held my tongue. To me, the organized Virgo princess striving for perfection, whose bills are paid on time and in full, it was a nightmare looming. I'm not sure if it was because this was my big sister and earliest friend or because this was a deathbed conversation, but in that moment, the mass of overdue bills seemed a minor detail to be addressed at a later date.

"Okay, Lou-lou, I got this. Nothing will be paid and everything will be fine," I said, and we both chuckled.

And now that later date has come. As I'm mired in phone calls to and from bill collectors and my own household takes a back burner, anger and resentment start to set in.

"For I know the thoughts that I think toward you, says the Lord, thoughts of peace and not of evil, to give you a future and a hope."
Jeremiah 29:11

One Man's Treasure

5

It's stating the obvious (and the crux of the matter) to say that if I didn't have a family of my own and a pressure-filled, full-time job, I could more easily organize my father's affairs and arrange a well-thought-out plan. Instead, most activities are done hurriedly, in broken intervals and with half my attention given to Summer. While Dad is in rehab, I stop at his house after work to sort and organize bills. You name it, every utility and credit card that can accumulate a large balance has done just that. It's a confusing mess.

And the house is a mess, too. Beneath the bills, paperwork, magazine subscriptions, and junk mail, his kitchen table is no longer visible. The counters are overflowing with everything from cans and boxes of food to gadgets and half-dead plants. My father saves *everything* and has carried up, from the depths of the cellar, boxes of bills and paperwork from several previous years for reasons that are unclear. Perhaps he wanted something to do. Whatever the case, the dining room table is also covered, and boxes line all four walls. My goal is to try to find the current bills and get things under control.

I consider Summer and myself lucky on days when we have arrangements for her to play at a friend's house after school. This is not a child-friendly home, with little to no seating available, clutter everywhere, no games, and the dogs digging at our legs to be picked up. I give her small tasks to do to help out, but she's not easily distracted and incessant in her requests to leave.

Without sitting down, I work as fast as possible and try not to take out my annoyance on her. *How can she understand why we're here doing this? I don't even know why this task has fallen to me.* I rip open envelopes, sort the relevant from the outdated into piles. Like a crazed robot, I scan bunches of documents, bills and envelopes, and efficiently stack papers into minipiles, deciding when I open envelopes to either rip and toss, or stack for later review. Open, scan, toss or stack, repeat—I'm my own one-person assembly line. Try as I might, I can't achieve the mindlessness of a robot and an inner dialogue begins.

Jeez, are these actually bank statements from the old South Works Credit Union on Greenwood Street?

Open, scan, toss, or stack.

The miracle vitamin clips I understand, but why would he save a clipped article from the Weekly World News *that "Hillary Clinton Adopts Alien Baby"?*

But I *do* know why: because it might come in handy one day. My father could bring up from the depths of his cellar *anything* one might need. For all our various school reports and projects, we had the best show-and-tell accompanying artifacts. Fossils for science class from the Paleolithic era? No problem. Actual soldiers' gear from World War II to make history reports come to life? You got it. A little somethin' brought back from lunar missions? You just hold on to your hat! So I smile knowingly to see Hillary's alien baby announcement neatly folded into the mix. Quite simply, one of us might need adoption know-how someday.

"Summer, honey, toss the squeeze toy for Max and give Elsa a treat," I suggest while maintaining my sorting rhythm.

"I don't want to touch it. I think it rolled in the poopy papers before you picked 'em up."

"No, it didn't. Just play with the dogs, okay? Find another toy. There's a ton around here. Can you imagine how much they miss Grampa?"

"When are we leaving?" she asks as she kicks a toy cautiously. It rolls two inches and stops. Max stares at it, then at her, and puts one ear back. I suspect he and I are having similar thoughts. He gives up and lies down while keeping an eye on us. Since they're all alone at night, we must be high entertainment for the dogs. I've hired a pet sitter, and between her stopping in and my own visits, it's the best I can do.

I keep up with the small talk as I slip into a sorting trance. *Goodbye, giant stack of car-insurance coverage notices.* "Summer, what did you learn in school today?" I know from learning theory that the ability to restate and share the experience helps to solidify the learning.

"Well," she jumps right in, "did you know that we're all more than just one thing?"

"Mmm-hmm." Open, scan, toss, or stack. Every scheme and sweepstakes that's targeted to the elderly is here in the pile, with promises to pay out prizes and cash galore.

"Well, did you?" she asks again.

"What do you mean, honey?"

"And we get bigger every time!"

I look up when I notice it's quiet. She takes that as her cue to continue and begins again.

"I'm a member of my family, a member of my class, plus the school, I'm a member of our neighborhood, then the town, and a member of the United States. Or does the country come before the state?"

I notice that some entry forms are half filled in with shaky penmanship and cringe to think of how much money has been spent on these gimmicks. Open, scan, toss, or stack.

"You're not listening anyway. I'm going to see if he gets the Disney Channel." She makes her way to the red couch, the dogs following along.

Glad for the chance to really focus, I see in the margins his growing confusion and his attempt to stay organized. I well up to see his handwriting in the margins of bills, notes to himself about when to pay and reminders of this or that. "Pay Peterson Oil, #1." The loneliness of the situation hits me and I feel the stirrings of loss. A mourning of sorts, but I don't fully recognize it for what it is. Mired in stacks of paper, I'm holding at bay memories of growing up in a household of clutter and disarray. I try to keep the focus on him and remind myself that he's just down the road a few miles, at the town Elder Rehab and Health Center, but I miss the dad I knew. The dad who would hop into the car on a moment's notice to run an errand, the dad who knew every shortcut and back road in the city. Even as he grew older, he would always be up for something to do.

In fact, just a few months ago he had said, "Hey, Sa, let's go down to the ol' ice house to cash my check early," something he always used to say when his Social Security check arrived at the end of every month. The ice house is long gone, though, and in its place is an unattractive Check Depot in the bustle of Kelley Square. On the way home from cashing his check, we stopped, as we always used to, at Coney Island, on Southbridge Street, for two hot dogs apiece. "Load it up with everything," he said when he ordered his, and he remembered how I liked mine too. "Just a touch of relish and mustard for the little one," he said, referencing my younger self. This was clearly confusing for the counter help, who kept a straight face while sizing me up.

"*Mom*, for the third time, when are we *going*?!" Summer shouts from the other room above the ever-annoying Disney *Hey, Jesse* theme song, which I now notice is deafeningly loud. Quick as a snap, my musing dissipates and I'm back to robotic scanning. Open, scan, toss, or stack.

"In a minute, honey. I'm just wrapping up," I say even though I've barely made a dent in the pile. I make a mental note to arrange for the modern-day convenience of direct deposit for his Social Security check and consider how to be added as a contact to get on top of these bills. Like it or not, I'm in the mix. *This mess is mine to fix.* I sit down for the first time since being here and take stock of the situation. Looking around, almost from a bird's-eye view, I know it's not good for me or my daughter to be in this depressing chaos. I'd been hesitant to bring any of his paperwork mess into my home, but the sadness and sheer magnitude of the task at hand is taking too much out of me and away from my family. *I'm depressed being here.*

"Mom, are you mad?" Summer asks as she enters the dining room, the dogs still at her heels. "Why are you crying?"

"Ah, I'm just tired, Sum. It's been a long day and this is too much to tackle at once."

She's quiet and looks around, taking it in. She gives the squeeze toy a good hard kick for the dogs, and they scramble across the kitchen floor, grunting from the effort of carrying their excess weight around. "Well," she says with a hand on her hip, "like Gramma used to say, Rome wasn't—"

"Built in a day," I chime in. This, by the way, is the philosophy my mother had adopted to stay sane living here.

Together we scoop reams and bundles of bills and envelopes into large shopping bags to bring home to sort. We get the dogs settled with fresh food and papers on the floor, and I leave with a heavy heart. Besides feeling guilt-ridden for leaving the dogs alone, I'm flat out overwhelmed. *How could he leave this mess to us?* Having grown up in a hoarding home, I feel an unfounded shame similar to what the child of an alcoholic must feel. This house is my childhood secret. I always wanted to have friends over after school but seldom did. The upshot is that while some of my siblings inherited what I call the "clutter gene," a genetic passion for collecting and a tendency to have an emotional attachment to inanimate objects, I went in the opposite direction. While I'm not a neat freak on the OCD extreme of the spectrum, I certainly appreciate a house that's in good order and rarely shy away from an opportunity to clean. Nonetheless, every time I've brought something from 19 Cliff Street into my home, it's been with dread and considerable psychological impact.

> *When my spirit was overwhelmed within me,*
> *Then You knew my path.*
> Psalm 142:3

The High Ground

6

Somehow, amid the chaos, Tony and I find ourselves talking about something other than Dad or Summer one evening. Granted, the topic is work-related—not exactly the stuff of a fun night out—but it does my sanity good nonetheless.

"Thank goodness for info sessions that bomb," Tony mumbles through a mouthful of chicken tenders and reaches for yet another cold spinach triangle.

"It was actually a success, just no one ate much," I say, trying to wrestle the Styrofoam container, overflowing with appetizers, away from him and into the refrigerator so I can take it to work tomorrow. "What time did you put Summer to bed?" I hand him one final mushroom miniquiche.

"She was easy. We went up around eight-thirty, and after a speed round of rose, bud, thorn, she was out."

The rose game is our family tradition of sharing the best part of the day (rose), the interesting/learning moment (bud), and the worst part (thorn). We usually play over dinner and sometimes at bedtime before saying prayers.

"And. . . ." I'm waiting for any little nugget of information about her day.

"Let me think, her classroom seating arrangement was changed up and she learned that her new neighbor picks his nose. That was the thorn too."

I follow him out of the kitchen to the living room, where we take our favorite spots, the couch for his full-body spread and the leather recliner for me. The TV is on but muted.

"That's it? Did she have anything *good?* I usually start with the rose."

"Oh, yeah, the teacher noticed."

"Really? Are you making this up? That's it, really?"

"And she winked at her when she brought the little picker a tissue. Anyway, why didn't anyone eat?"

"My sales helper set up the food table at the front of the room, just aside the podium and projection screen. It's the rare attendee who wants to drift to the front of the room to refill their plate. It's too bad, 'cause I chose the Holiday Inn because of their gorgeous atrium with all the lush plants and Muzak piped in. I pictured the food table set up just outside the meeting-room door and hoped for a relaxed presession mixer. Instead we had pin-drop quiet and wasted food."

"Where were you during the setup?" he says, plumping up the couch pillow behind his head.

"Getting the lay of the land. I took a drive through the office park to scope out some of the other companies in the area. The whole point of doing the info session at this location is to add to an existing program that is running at a defense company close by. Their tuition reimbursement policy was scaled back, so we expect some students will drop out of the program. We're trying to add a few more, for margin's sake. This spot is in a huge pharmaceutical company's backyard, and it would be great if someday they wanted their own on-site program. The associate dean from the MBA program was nice enough to come as the guest speaker."

Tony nods in my direction, but his eyes are fixed on *Dancing with the Stars*. I'm pretty sure I'll lose him altogether as soon as Peta comes on.

"Anyway, it went pretty good."

"Did you say anything to the helper lady? Are you going to say anything to her manager?"

"I couldn't help being annoyed when I saw the setup but ended up thanking her up and down in the parking lot afterward. I'm not going to say anything—what's the point? It's not a big deal."

"Didn't something like this happen before when you got to the place and something was set up wrong?"

"Hmm, are you thinking of the time I got to the company and the setup kit was completely empty of the table skirt, sign-in sheets, handouts, and whatever else I can't remember? Although I think I had the giveaway pens. That was another helper person."

"Don't you check before you go?"

"Nah, I used to, but I don't want to look like I'm nitpicky. Plus, the upside is that it teaches you to handle anything that comes along."

"Yeah, right. That's not how you felt that time you were stressing about that super important new IT or software development something-or-other program. Remember that one, where the helper said she wasn't available to help because of a meeting with the exact same faculty guy that you needed as the guest speaker? It wasn't so funny then, when she didn't know it was her role to cue it up with him."

"Oh, yeah, you're thinking of Cisco. Wow—good memory. I'm impressed. That's not a sales helper but a faculty liaison. That's right, instead of saying they both could join, she said they both weren't available."

"And if I recall, you never said anything about that one either."

"Yeah, I know. It seemed like tattling, and I knew it would play out. They both ended up coming and it went fine."

Tony releases the "mute" button and we hear the familiar "dah, dah, dah da duh da dah" *Dancing with the Stars* theme song and the MC with the British accent announce, "Donald Driver and partner Peta Murgatroyd!" Tony's eyes glaze over.

As Peta whirls away half-dressed, I think about my conversations with a former vice president at General Dynamics and how he'd been a mentor of sorts. He shared one of his favorite quotes, a nugget from Truman, or maybe it was Reagan: "You can accomplish much if you don't care who gets the credit." I've mulled it more times than I can count and wonder why I've never seen it in the context of career or leadership tips for women. It seems the antithesis of most "how to succeed" and "see and be seen" messages in corporate America, but for some reason, I like it. In the day-to-day, though, it doesn't help me out much. Neither does my work philosophy that being a good employee is about how much you contribute in an intelligent, meaningful way as opposed to looking the part, being über-friendly and, most of all, being in your seat. I've buckled under the same scrutiny that all working mothers face, often from other women on the same path, ironically, or even worse, those who have gone before. With their hard-earned battle stripes, they carry an air of toughness that hints, "If you can't take the heat, get out of the kitchen. I survived it—why can't you?" I suppose I'm inadvertently doing the same to women younger than me. I just don't have the time to be the mentor type—I view myself as a hired gun who opens doors and gets out of the way.

I especially love the classic Madeleine Albright quote, "There's a special place in hell for women who don't help other women," and wish I had the nerve to hang it somewhere in my office. That would be too obvious, though, maybe even aggressive, which isn't me. Given a choice between fight and flight, I'm flight every time. "I don't care what score she gets—she is by far the best dancer on the show," Tony says and looks at me, smiling a devilish grin in a Peta-induced afterglow. "I have one more for you and then we can let it go."

"Jeez Louise, what is this? A *This Is Your Life* recap of info sessions?"

"I'm just showing my interest. For every time you've said I don't listen, looks like I am, right? Plus, I'm seeing a trend. Anyway, is this the same lady who rolls her eyes when you go into her office and who you defended at some new account you were trying to get into?"

I pause, a little surprised that he's mentioning it, and nod. This particular woman can be brusque when she has her game face on. I recognize that focus and, sometimes in her manners, catch little glimpses of my younger self. I don't mind it, though. The duplicitous culture of nice has trumped all, and I respect any inkling of genuine personality. But not everyone shares that appreciation, especially not hotshot executives. Once, she decided to use a newly learned, sales-training questioning tack during an account call, clarifying and repeating the problem statement to an almost-comical degree. Mr. Exec, with subtle ease and sleight of hand, changed the dynamic in the room by making eye contact mostly with me and the men in the room. The next day, in my follow-up call to thank him once again and recap next steps, I conversationally worked in supportive words to the effect that my colleague was competent, albeit a tad eager. He understood—people rarely rise to his level without being able to read between the lines—and said he appreciates colleagues who stand up for each other. The conversation actually seemed to strengthen our relationship, and the groundwork for a new account was in place. Afterward, there was no need to fill in either my brusque colleague or my manager about the call—"it had just been the right thing to do," I say as Tony flips through the channels, having grown bored with *DWTS* as he always does. I can tell I've lost his attention and reiterate more loudly, "I said, I always try to do the right thing."

Still nothing. He nods but keeps clicking. I'm not deterred and continue, "Plus, it's not like it would ever come up casually in conversation. How exactly would *you* share something like that?"

"Dunno. How about, 'I'm on your side. Stop blowing me off and shooing me out of your office'?"

"Ha! Yeah, right, that'll work. I'm sure that will break right through the established perception of me. She's bought into the word on the street, that I'm above it all, from when I first started and had a little too much swagger from years of mainly male role models and working at technology companies. As you know, all of the previous corporate cultures either operated under a startup mentality of act first, ask permission second, and beg forgiveness if necessary, or exclusive top-down decision making. In every case, being a good corporate citizen meant you just needed to implement and execute. I didn't read the landscape and understand that I had entered into the land of alliances and consensus building. Honestly, I just want to get in and out without any drama."

"Well, that's a bummer," he says and settles on a wife-carrying championship on a sports station and mutes it again. Women with bums to the sky and legs wrapped around their running husbands provide a comic backdrop to our conversation. I love my husband's sense of humor, and that he's taken the time to have this talk.

"It just seems that everything is so melodramatic in the office and it's so not necessary. There's something about the hours of juggling time with Summer and my dad that separate the day into things that really matter. You know?"

I continue, "These various home health aides that I'm meeting, some who barely speak English, make more difference in the day-to-day. The majority of people signing up in our graduate programs do it because it's a free benefit their company pays for and it's a résumé builder. Good for them, but let's not kid ourselves that we're conducting open-heart surgery. You would think it would be less intense. We have elaborate process flow charts and timelines for when materials need to be collated into the attendee handout. We call it 'the packet.' Like, we start weeks ahead of time to orchestrate 'the packet.' Which no one reads anyway. I'm talking high-tension, high-stakes stress over where's the darn presentation printout for the packet?!"

I pause, thinking of the personalities at play, and wonder where the undertone of pervasive competitiveness stems from. Like scrolling through a Rolodex of faces, I think of my colleagues and soften, knowing some people's personal struggles. "I know the lead time is necessary because there's so much going on that it has to be organized, but it's just a small example of how little details get blown up into overanalyzed issues. I shared once that I would be glad to do my own packets and that Summer could help me in a pinch."

"Ahh, nice," he says, laughing. "Now, that must have been a feel-good moment. My seven-year-old can do your job. That must be very reassuring, not slighting at all."

"Okay, thanks, Mr. Flip-Side-of-the-Coin! Maybe it does, but I don't mean it that way. I'm just trying not to be a bother and stay out of the fray. *And* it's the least of my worries right now. The good news is that I actually believe this latest manager, the new sheriff in town, has her finger on the pulse. There are major trust and role-definition issues, and they aren't mine to fix," I say, moving to get out of the recliner, not easily, or gracefully by any stretch, a definite turtle on its back moment, before I muster enough leg strength to get the footrest down. I stand, folding up the fleece blanket I've been under, trying to suppress growing annoyance.

"Are you ever planning to speak up and share your two cents?"

"You know I would if I was asked, but I'm never asked! I feel like I'm carrying too much baggage anyway, like if I began, a torrent would flow, and that can't be good for one's career, can it? So, instead I opt to be really low-maintenance. I'm good at that, right? Just like my upbringing has taught." The mention of which conjures ingrained teachings that begin with "Do unto others" and "If you don't have something good to say" and shifts my mood. "There are closed-door cliques, though, who talk about it in secret. Actually, they instant message each other, too."

"Now, how do you know that?" he says, his villainous eyebrow twitch a sign that he's trying to lighten my mood.

"Because of random outbursts and snickering that sporadically come from offices and cubes. Anyway, almost every other day someone is making reference to how we're 'a family,' so it's best to put on a happy face."

"Now, I believe the low-maintenance part, but you have a happy face?"

It doesn't make me laugh, but I like that he's trying. "There must be a secret handshake to get in 'the family' that I haven't figured out."

He forces a quiet laugh, which catches my attention. He looks me in the eye and pauses. "So, you're doing the right thing by never talking to anyone about anything that really matters to you during the workday?"

I'm confused. "I talk to a close friend, but mostly to prospective clients."

"What's that saying that you shared that one of the exec's always uses . . . 'how's that working for you?'" With that he half-smiles politely and turns his attention back to TV, having made his point and not really expecting an answer. Which is fine, I don't have one.

I lean in and give a quick hug before heading up to bed, glad for our time together. I'm still mulling his question on the way up the stairs and know in my heart of hearts that I'm so low-maintenance I'm invisible.

> *I will instruct you and teach you in the way you should go;*
> *I will counsel you and watch over you.*
> Psalm 32:8

Getting to Know You

Winter 2011

With the holidays behind us and the decision of whether Dad should be admitted to a nursing home or return home hanging over us, I schedule a meeting for my sisters and me with an attorney in the center of town. Right now there are two votes for the nursing-home option and one (mine) for bringing him home, and my intent is for us to collectively hear and better understand basic matters about all things eldercare.

Leading up to the meeting, with prompting from my sisters, I'd called two attorneys specializing in eldercare to inquire about the implications of being on my father's checking account and whether I would become responsible (that is, personally liable) for his bills, his debt, or any other scary obligations that might come out of the woodwork. I was reassured both times by a definitive "no." This was no consolation for my sisters. Whenever I chatted with Pat on the phone, mostly to complain about my lot in life and the endless mess of paperwork I was sorting, she would reprise the same line again and again: "They'll come after you! All of them will. If you add your name as a contact or forward his bills to your home address, they'll never stop hounding you. The IRS too. You'll be sorry!" She might as well have been channeling the Wicked Witch in *The Wizard of Oz,* because what I heard was, "They'll get you, my pretty." After our chats, even with legal assurances fresh in mind, I would doubt myself and question whether I'd heard them correctly.

"Sa, your sister's concern is warranted," Tony would reason. "It is legitimate to wonder if you can become intertwined in someone else's affairs, all in the name of trying to help."

"Someone else? You mean Dad? Since when do you use words like *warranted*? What is it about legalese that makes everyone talk so official?" Though I was snapping at him, I knew it was possible that I was hearing only what I wanted to hear.

Because my siblings and I are operating in fear mode, the tone of most of our conversations is strained. Everything is more intense than usual, emotions are high and criticism of each other is off the charts. I'm told quite often to "calm down." Colette constantly calls attention to my pitch and asks me to lower it so as not to sound so hysterical. "What do you mean 'calm down'? You calm down. Don't tell me to calm down—I *am* calmed down!" At which point I shut down, becoming quiet and deferential.

So it's in that light that we sit around a ten-foot, oval mahogany table, with pin-drop quiet among us, to be schooled in eldercare legalese. On one side of the table are Colette, Tony, and me; on the other side Pat and her husband, Sam, and the attorney sits at the head. The enormity of the table widens the divide between us and makes me feel small, like Lily Tomlin's *Laugh-In* character Edith Ann, but a less wise, endearing version. As if on autopilot, the attorney explains in an even, emotionless tone the differences among health-care proxies, power of attorney, conservatorship, guardianship, executors. Dispassionately spouting just the facts, he might as well be reading from a dictionary.

"At some point, a family member or other concerned individual may need to assume responsibility for decision-making and will need legal authority to do so," he drones. "Have the elder designate a person to manage his or her financial affairs. . . ."

Just-the-Facts-Jack makes no recommendations on how to get started. He offers no reassurance that others have been in our shoes and we'll come together. Granted, that's not necessarily his role, but it's what we need. He drones on about Medicare-related topics and I begin pinching myself under the table to remain focused.

"Medicare discharge planning services require that. . . ."

I've been so looking forward to this meeting and now I feel as if I've been drugged. Like Dorothy in that field of poppies. *I hope one of us is able to make better sense of this than me.*

Jack provides no handouts, brochures, or pointers regarding website resources that will help us make sense of the phase we're in. I was hoping for a roadmap to help get us started on our way. Even Dorothy had the jovial Munchkins and Glinda to put her on the right path. We have Jack, who answers questions flatly as they're posed.

We each take turns asking questions like "How exactly do we apply and request Mass Health benefits?" and "Will they do a 'look-back' at previous income to determine his monthly rate?" Our concern is his reverse mortgage, which was paid out in a lump sum and blown through in just a few years. Almost every answer we get begins with "It depends." I'm glad to have other pairs of ears around the table so that later we can recap what's being said. Among us all, I hope, we'll remember everything.

I wonder how we appear to Jack. *Is this how all families come to the table? Do we seem uncaring to be concerned about associations with our father's debt when he needs us the most? Can he see the same posturing between us that I can?* One of us visibly prickles when the other speaks. Colette raises an eyebrow when I become overly polite, trying to facilitate the meeting, for example. Pat shifts when Colette uses her authoritative, professional medical language. She counterbalances both my and Colette's demeanors by becoming something of a townie: "Ah, just to get this straight, are we gonna be responsible for his bills and stuff?"

Wondering at the pronounced differences among us, I study my sisters. It's obvious that we're all related, with somewhat similar features and the same sandy-brown hair color, although Pat's short, layered look is enhanced with deeper shades of auburn to contrast with her fair skin and blue eyes. Colette's going au naturel with a straight, shoulder-length cut that's the longest among us and bucking the cultural hair-color conspiracy, allowing her grays to have their way. And she's pulling it off. The salt-and-pepper streaks are in keeping with a self-accepting euro vibe, whereas Pat and I fall prey to the conventions of Nice 'n Easy. To employ Hollywood comparisons, picture Pat as a polite and less comedic Vicki Lawrence and Colette as a larger-than-life, straight-talking Kathy Bates.

The meeting lasts less than an hour, as Jack doesn't belabor any points with examples or small talk. We thank him stiffly and shuffle out in the same awkward silence in which we'd entered, but I'm relieved. Glad to check this one off the list. *At least now we all know the deal and there's no need to be so wary. We can all help and do what's right!*

Colette and I collect our waiting daughters in the lobby, and then we all gather in the parking lot. In my firehose manner, I start rattling off the to-dos that are top of mind. "See, all of my sorting and organizing will help us get his bills under control. I still have to fax proof of residency that he's living at home to Wells Fargo and Aurora, his life insurance company, so they'll continue to mail his measly check. I'll take care of that at work next week. I'll have important things redirected to my house to save time sorting things out over there. I'll make those calls next week, too."

There are blank stares and no comments from anyone, which I don't interpret as good or bad, just as a sign that they're listening and that I have their attention. Rather than wait for the group decision on whether Dad will be admitted to a long-term-care home, I simply presume he's going home and have already put the wheels in motion.

"I have an interview with a home health agency lined up tomorrow," I add. "Who wants to join me?"

"It doesn't really matter," Pat says enthusiastically. "I trust you. You go ahead and do it, Sa!"

Is that mocking?

"Tomorrow doesn't work for me," Colette says, her tone very controlled.

Is she angry?

"Okay, I'll let you know how it goes. Most important"—now I'm brimming with excitement—"I've called to get rates on dumpsters so we can clear pathways in the house so he can maneuver with his walker. As we all know, the nursing home needs that as part of his care plan before he can go home. In terms of a timeline, we need to have it all ready and done by the end of next week. And then there's the dumpster issue. The best drop-off rate I could find was for one week, so we need to maximize our time and commit to a plan."

As if we had been under water, holding our breath, the tension that had been building since the meeting with Jack began is released. But instead of the exhalation of a cleansing deep breath, frustration comes pouring out. Coming up with days that everyone's schedule can accommodate proves impossible. As we listen to each other's existing plans, it's obvious that each commitment is more important than the last. Never mind that, aside from the legitimate need to tend to our kids, we're talking about kitchens that "need" to be cleaned, dirty clothes that "need" washing, and dirt bikes that "need" to be ridden.

This is ridiculous. The Big Dig was probably organized more easily than this.

I suggest that the dates be based on our husbands' preferences and convenience, since they'll be doing the bull work and heavy lifting. "It makes perfect sense," I say. "Let's just roll up our sleeves and get going, right?"

A moment later, I'm left standing alone in the parking lot. Tony helps Summer into the backseat of our car, doing that little nervous laugh that he does. He's acting like it's perfectly normal that Colette scrubbed away in her Jeep leaving the burnt smell of rubber in the air, and that Pat and Sam would say something to the effect of "We'll get back to you, but don't make plans to discharge him too soon."

On the ride home, Tony tries to lighten the mood by humming the tune to "Getting to Know You." It doesn't work. I sit seething, trying to figure out why this is such a battle. *Is this just the petty notion of "Who put you in charge?" or that the respite that we've had since Louanne's vigil is now slipping away?* Or maybe it's that the weeks I've spent going to Cliff Street, to tend to the dogs and sort paperwork have given me a head start on internalizing that we're now our father's keepers. I've had that moment of realization that my life is no longer my own and is about to become much more complicated. I've had time for it to sink in. It hadn't occurred to me that the others haven't.

Perhaps it's all of the above and then some.

The first scream of the day comes from the side porch.

"What the *#*?!"

It turns out that a family of mice has been uprooted and left homeless by the removal of three large, air-conditioner window units from the porch, where Tony and Sam are working.

Two weeks after the meeting with Just-the-Facts Jack, we're cleaning out Dad's house, making it presentable and livable for his return home from rehab. The cleanup crew consists of me and Pat and our dutiful, albeit somewhat grumpy husbands. Even though we're smack-dab in the middle of winter, it's an unseasonably warm and drizzly weekend. I'm not allowing the wet weather to dampen my mood, though. In fact, I have to keep myself in check in order not to annoy the others with my giddy enthusiasm.

While the guys tackle the floor-to-ceiling clutter at the side entry to the kitchen, Pat and I start with the dining room closet, where we find evidence of another mouse dwelling. And much more. Anyone who's seen the hoarding shows on TV can guess at the variety of items that are packed into this space and lots of others. The difference about my dad's clutter, though, is that there's a semblance of order about most of it. Things are packed within groups and categories. For example, air conditioners are stacked together in neat precision, never mind that none of them work.

There are plenty of remnants of Dad's janitorial service days, when he ran a part-time moonlight business. Buckets, mops, cleaning equipment, and commercial-style, stand-up, floor buffing machines line the porch like inactive soldiers, perhaps old companions he didn't have the heart to sell or kick to the curb.

Colette had brought his sense of order to my attention many years ago. For one of her college courses, she'd made a photo journal depicting what on the surface looked like backyard junk and chaos but was actually more organized than not. I remember thinking she was a genius for seeing beauty and divinity in my father's ways.

As the weekend marches on, we do, too, like an orderly platoon of ants, making trip after trip to the thirty-yard dumpster in the driveway. In the divine clutter, we find things we've stepped over and around for years. Stacks of newspapers, computer monitors and TVs that no longer work, and, on the back deck, broken patio furniture, random swimming pool components, and a few models of well-used gas grills. From time to time, we also stumble onto memory lane, here and there finding keepsakes and tokens from our childhood. For Mom, we molded numerous handmade ashtrays in pottery sessions after school at the Girls Club on Providence Street, and there are also souvenir magnets and mugs from trips and vacations. We uncover boxes of warped albums and moth-eaten clothes from the fifties, sixties, and seventies. *Is that the shirt I wore when I was a hobo one Halloween?* We make only a dent in the variety of household items that span a lifetime. We place aside treasures that we know are near to Dad's heart in the hope that he'll be able to enjoy some of his hobbies again.

At some point, I look up from my work to see Tony and Sam carrying the flea-infested red couch through the now-passable side porch and down to the dumpster. I clap and hoot. *Good riddance, sad red couch. We're making room for better days ahead!*

Like a starving runway model at an all-you-can-eat buffet, I'm awed and sickened at the same time. With extreme efficiency, I grab at long-expired canned goods and boxes of dry goods, all tightly packed together. In a way, the kitchen cupboard is a time capsule, with brands from yesteryear now considered retro.

"Aw, remember Hills Bros. coffee in the red can?" I say.

"Of course," Pat answers from her position on the floor in front of the Lazy Susan, and pulls out the perfect companion piece from the rotating cabinet. "I also remember that 'Chock full o'Nuts is that heavenly coffee,'" she sings to the tune of the jingle. "'Better coffee a millionaire's money can't buy!'"

One minute I'm marveling at relics from my childhood, the next I'm feeling my stomach turn at the sight of little bugs and mites in some of the boxes. Below the counter, I open the cabinet doors to expose multiples of everything. There are enough pots and pans to cook for an army, including three crock-pots, the avocado-colored, electric fry pan that was used specifically for Swedish meatballs, and dish towels (both clean and dirty) and potholders adorned for every season.

I have a strong urge to toss everything, but Pat talks me down.

"Sa, let's not throw out the baby with the bathwater," she says, inspecting my work and gingerly picking out handfuls of Beanie Babies, still in their plastic wrappers, from one of the oversize trash bags I've stuffed full. "Let's make a yard-sale pile, 'kay?!" she says in her patronizing singsong. "Don't throw out perfectly good pots and pans. Maybe one of my boys can use them, 'kay? Calm the hell down, 'kay?"

So, with dreams of sugarplums and yard sales dancing in our heads, we push on into the first-floor bedroom and store every item that's in good enough condition. You name it, we organize 'em: random musical instruments (dozens of violins, several accordions, even percussion spoons), hundreds of videocassettes, hundreds of DVDs, hundreds of Beanie Babies, dozens of cameras, stacks of books new and old, bags of clothes, pet things, bedspreads and curtains from throughout the ages, and knickknacks that span various trends (macramé!) and ethnicities, from Asian elephant collectibles to Swedish Dala Horses to pieces that appealed to Mom's passing interest in Southwest décor and Native American crafts. There's endless costume jewelry, bags of rolled coins, dozens of coffee cans chock full o' fossils, gems and coins, and miscellaneous medical equipment—stethoscopes, blood-pressure cuffs, unused diabetic needles (well, mostly unused), plastic urinals, and boxes of gauze.

There are sentimental treasures among the mess as well. By either happenstance or divine intervention, Pat happens on a love letter that had been inserted into an old book. What are the chances that, among the hundreds of books, the one hiding this letter would present itself? I have goose bumps reading it. Written to my father in my mother's delicate cursive, dated midnight February 23, 1959, it begins:

Dearest Sweetest Love,

> *I am sitting here thinking of you my love, regretting that I sent you home so early. I was a little stinker tonight, I'm sorry for acting that way. . . . I resent anyone who comes along because I want you to myself. . . . my Benny, if you ever, at any time, doubt what is in my heart, my love, my faithfulness, please open this letter and you will see. I love you now until forever.*

> *Love, Cam*

Gold amid the rubble! Using expressions and language of the time, it's a five-sheet double-sided apology and love letter to rival anything from Abigail to John Adams, or at least from Nancy to Ronald. Finding the letter softens the weekend for me, and suddenly it's no longer about a cleaning frenzy or annoying aches and pains from physical labor. As I bend, lift, and clean, I'm reminded that we were raised in a house founded on love. We had the gift of parents who cared deeply for each other and for us, their children. Although they weren't conventional by any means, they nurtured us with emotional support and unconditional love. In a sense, this clutter represents evidence of a full life well-lived.

Quiet in thought, I reflect on our different approaches to this "Dad situation" as I continue sorting. Tensions are high, and our behavior has been disappointing. *How did we so quickly morph into bickering adults?* Maybe it's not so much an attitude as a coping mechanism. One sister incessantly recites her mantra "He should have planned better for his golden years! Why the hell did this fall to us? He's lucky we're doing this much!" That's the same sister who's knee-deep beside me right now, executing tasks small and large on his behalf. My other sister is ambivalent much of the time. She spent countless hours by Louanne's bedside as health proxy and primary caretaker, and the time away from her own family took a toll. She prefers distance (mostly from Pat and me), and while less interested in rolling up her sleeves, she provides priceless emotional support to our dad. As for myself, my growing obsession with the clock rivals Captain Hook's. No one else seems to hear the constant ticking. My sense of urgency stems from an innate pressure that there's always the next place to run to, the next thing to do, always someone depending on me. Not to mention someone I often miss—my daughter. This "clean-out" weekend to grant my father a safe living space means that a friend or neighbor is watching my little one.

I'm not unique or new to having multiple responsibilities, but I can feel that this is the beginning of a pressure-filled mind-set, with one too many things always on my plate. It's the beginning of having to hone my multitasking and list-making abilities, my ability to be fully invested in one task while thinking of what I'll do when I get home or to work or to the grocery store. My emotional pendulum begins to swing from contentment—*I'm here for him, helping Dad during the time when he needs me most*—to guilt—*I'm not there for my family. I miss them.* Tick-tock, tick-tock.

Soon after our own version of the Big Dig, Dad is home. Amazingly, he doesn't mind or seem to notice the drastic changes to his living space. He understands that as part of being home, there will be a constant flow of home health aides and visiting nurses checking on him. Quietly, he watches the installation of the personal-safety alarm system and practices using the wrist monitor. When I ask him if he's going to use it, he raises an eyebrow and nods and smiles, as if once again saying we're all crazy. But he's resigned to going along with the new normal.

A requirement for being accepted to the Pinnacle Elder Care PACE program[1]* that provides this extra help is that he attend

---

[1] *The Pinnacle ElderCare PACE (Program of All-inclusive Care for the Elderly) program is a Medicare and Medicaid program that helps people meet their health-care needs in the community rather than at a nursing home or other care facility. Medical, insurance, and social support programs are offered for people ages fifty-five and over.

their adult day program two or three days a week. So he and I tour the program facility a few days later after he's settled in and sort of ready, and it turns out to be even more than I'd hoped for. The staff is kind, the rooms are sunny and décor is cheery, and the schedule of activities looks genuinely interesting. But I can also see it all through his eyes, and it looks different. It looks like adult daycare. I have the same feeling I did when Summer and I toured preschools, although I'm not oohing and ahhing and up-selling like I did with Sum. I owe him that respect. Instead, I remain quiet during the tour, and he does, too, taking it all in. We pause the longest in front of the window looking into the physical therapy room. "That seems like a good idea, Sa, to stay fit," he says, and I breathe a sigh of relief.

Our next stop is the great room used for dining purposes. "Well, this is where I leave you," the friendly social worker giving the tour says, "but we hope you'll stay for lunch. I'm sure there are plenty of people who would be interested to meet you and enjoy your company just as I have!" It's impossible not to notice the appetizing smells wafting out of the kitchen area, but I can't tell exactly what they are. We notice the obvious pun on the sign outside of the lunch area: "We Have Good Taste," and beneath it the menu for "Today's Lunch" printed in large letters:

Salisbury steak ~ OR ~ Meatloaf

Choice of: Mixed Vegetables, Wild Rice,
or Mashed Potatoes

Dessert: Peach Cobbler

Selection of: Rolls, toast or cornbread
and coffee/tea

"What do you say, should we stay for lunch, Dad? I want to see how it all works and who else is part of the program."

"You bet. I kinda want to see what they consider good taste. What's your poison?"

"I'm going for it, Salisbury and rice."

"Then I'll go for the meatloaf and mashed," he says, already walking ahead to find a table.

When a few senior ladies, all dolled up and smelling good, make a bee-line in their wheelchairs for the table he's settled on, he doesn't seem to notice the attention he's drawn. They take in this potential new dance card and make small talk with me because he's focused on cleaning his plate, head down. Midway through the meal, though, he sets his gaze on one special lady: Mrs. Dash. With his salt intake now monitored and very limited, Mrs. Dash's salt-free seasoning blends are the answer to his prayers. All eyes are on him as he unscrews the bottle cap and pours a heaping pile of deliciousness directly onto the spoon, which he then puts directly into his mouth. I can see the other ladies' disappointment after lunch as they wheel away from the odd newcomer with the bad table manners. On the drive home, I clue him in to the impression he made, and we have a good laugh.

A few weeks later, Dad seems to be adjusting well and enjoying his new schedule and the attention from nurses and home health aides, and it occurs to me on a quiet afternoon to share the recovered love letter with him. I take a break from doing dishes in the kitchen and dig it out of my pocketbook.

"I have something to show you," I say, standing in front of the new recliner where he's sitting (we got such a deal at Bob's Discount Furniture in Lincoln Plaza that we got one for the home health aides, too). "Pat found it when we were cleaning. It fell out of one of your books." I hold out the letter as if it's a Fabergé egg, a delicate treasure to behold.

He seems less enthralled with this gift from the past than I am. "I know she loves me, Sa." But he plays along when he sees my face fall. "But sure, I'll take a look." As I head back to the dishpan, he throws in, "Still love her, too."

I'd like to say that it's a special, poignant moment, but the truth is, it's a long letter and when I peek back into the living room, I see he's not even two pages in and fast asleep. I laugh and find I can't stop. It's obvious that he doesn't share my reverence for the precious artifact Pat unearthed. As always, he's living secure in the knowledge of the reciprocal love that exists between him and his family. To him, the letter is no big revelation, and while Mom may be gone from sight, they're just as much in love. Just as I'm sure the ladies at lunch concluded, he's doing his own thing and not necessarily on the lookout for new love. He doesn't see himself through my eyes, as a frail and aging man. He's just his normal everyday self who, with his example of simple contentment, unknowingly continues to teach his children. As I was during clean-out weekend, I'm reminded again that this home is founded on love. The strife between my sisters and me over the lack of a plan and shame I feel about our clutter-filled childhood are lessened when, like him, we stay grounded in the present.

Later, I remind him that he fell asleep before finishing the letter and ask if he'll try again.

"You bet," he says, laughing. "Probably just before bedtime."

For the next few days, I notice that he carries the letter in his shirt pocket, never far from his heart. Just like Mom.

And be kind one to another, tenderhearted, forgiving
one another, just as God in Christ, forgave you.
Ephesians 4:32

WALK

Gleeful conversations drift down the hall. From my office I hear the squeals of delight—"What a nice surprise, they're beautiful, thank you!" I can't help but smile to myself, even though it has nothing to do with me.

Their gifted peonies are lovely. They're the same blush pink hue as the ones my mother planted along our walkway at home. The small bushes were the only pretty plantings in our unlandscaped yard. My father would maneuver around them with the lawn mower. Passersby would be more apt to notice the junk cars in the yard, just sitting there, rusting. But I saw the flowers.

Where There's a Will

8

June 2011

"… baby, I was born this way, haaay.…"

Lady Gaga is playing on the TV's pop music channel and together we're belting it out on this summer day. The tempo of the song is perfect for treadmill-walking, something I haven't done in ages but think about often. Instead, my replacement form of exercise is basically bobbing to the beat while cleaning counters and doing dishes. Besides Lady Gaga, my bobbing is inspired by the good news that Will has agreed to come home to help. In addition to clean counters, I've conveniently swept workplace woes under the rug as well. That's something to be resolved another day.

As soon as I'm finished with Saturday morning straightening at home, Tony and I are heading over to Dad's to finish painting the upstairs bedrooms. We're still getting ready for Will's grand return, which is expected to happen in a few weeks.

"Let's git 'er done, Sa," Tony says in his best redneck imitation as he heads for the downstairs entryway. "Grab your dishwashing gloves and I'll meet you out in the car."

He knows that my yellow rubber gloves are my lifesaver. There's no job too messy when my gloves are on. We've spent the past several weekends at Dad's, emptying rooms and renovating to create a fresh new living space for Will. Summer usually stays at a friend's house or with Colette to play with her cousins. And during these weeks, we've had the blessing of extra help with Dad's hands-on care from the home health aides. A requirement for his release from rehab at the nursing home was that he have coverage in place for round-the-clock care. Seemingly overnight, his hearing, eyesight, and memory aren't what they used to be, and when I sought out the extra help, my eyes were opened to a network of people I never knew existed. For a family in need, they're angels in disguise.

As I kneel on the floor, taping off the baseboards, I think about my first encounter with one of them, a brazen, middle-aged blonde whom I'll call Rhonda. She actually owns the health agency and came on the first day to scope out the scene. Perhaps from years of working with the elderly, when Rhonda speaks, she invades personal space, not by much but enough to make you notice. Let's just say, in general, she stands just a little closer, raises her voice just a little louder, and enunciates just a little slower than necessary. That said, she has a natural enthusiasm and seems ready to jump into any situation and lend a hand. For some reason, I find myself humming the Beach Boys' *Help Me Rhonda* tune before and after encounters with her.

Within five minutes of her arrival at my Dad's house a few weeks ago, just after the formalities of greeting my father and surveying the cluttery scene, she homed in on the most important thing to him: his dogs. Because he loves to overfeed them with table scraps, they are overweight and often constipated, and when Rhonda noticed the dried excrement matted into the fur on Max's behind, she nonchalantly snapped on a pair of latex gloves that she had handy in her pocketbook.

"Hello, little man. Let me see how handsome you are," she cooed to Max, kneeling down and immediately winning his affection.

"I have an appointment set with the groomer, but they can't see him until next weekend," I rushed to explain. "Most of the time, I can get it off with a paper towel, but this is the worst it's ever been."

"No time like the present," she said. "Mind if we use your double sink to soak, wash, and rinse?" Without waiting for an answer, she cleared off counter space and searched the drawers for a kitchen towel. She set up a little prep area on the counter and handed me a pair of gloves. As natural as could be, but not without my notice, she started running the show. "Grab a pair of scissors," she said, "just in case we need to trim the area, too."

Thus Max's day at the spa commenced, and as we chatted, my father got up from his recliner and began puttering around, straightening the stack of newspapers to be used for the dogs' ever-revolting indoor bathroom area.

"Hey, Benny, why are you feeding your dogs your dinner?" Help Me Rhonda asks, loudly, over the sound of the running water, holding the quivering dog in her steady hands. "Don't you like your own cooking? Or are you tired of your daughter's?" She laughs and winks in my direction. "What should we make you for the next few nights so I can be sure we have the right groceries?" Just like that, with a new energy infused into the house, she began chatting him up, getting a sense for his ways and winning him over. And winning *me* over. Miracle of miracles, I was able to hand off an errand and the shopping list.

I'm fairly certain that washing a dog's bum isn't a part of a home health aide's job description, but there she was, doing what needed to be done. And she was just one of several HHAs who had their own unique ways of confidently stepping in to help out. They offered not only helping hands but also a piece of their heart in the form of simple kindnesses. Depending on the day, it could be anything from ironing his shirts to rubbing lotion on his feet to making meals that sometimes introduced him to their particular ethnicities. And he ate it up, whether it was Portuguese or Ghanaian, Hispanic or white-bread American, just like he ate up the attention. The HHAs showered Dad with care that I know touched his heart, doting and kidding around and creating a lightness that made it feel perfectly normal for a rotation of complete strangers to come and go at all hours of the day and night.

I created a makeshift schedule to hang on the refrigerator to track the HHAs' shifts as well as mine and Tony's. Colette and Pat were conspicuously absent from the schedule because they'd made it clear on multiple occasions, using straight and direct language, so as to leave no room for misinterpretation of any kind, that they were *not* signing up or available for overnight duty at any time or under any situation, so just don't ask. So I added another layer to the mental and emotional weight I was carrying and blindly accepted the physical toll exacted by a lack of proper rest and sleep.

With Tony's name and mine as part of the health-care team roster, we use a simple, wirebound notebook as a "care plan" and a way to record details about his day and health. We write notes to each other about his overall condition, "mental status" (mood), and ways to help him "better ambulate" (move around) by shrinking the living space. In this way I've begun learning health-related terms, and I feel on top of the situation to some degree.

The notebook is also a nice way to stay in touch with comical moments from any given day. One entry reads: "A Buddy Holly impersonator was here today. I came in to find Benny reading the paper at the table, sporting jet black wayfarer rims! Does anyone know where his regular prescription glasses are?" My father has stashes of eyeglasses that he can conjure from the cellar, or from midair for all we know. Not only his own but also pairs we'd grown out of as kids and pairs he must have collected from his relatives or at yard sales. Literally dozens and dozens. Besides the circa-1950s Buddy Hollys, there are suave, round, tortoiseshell frames, classic ovals with silver frames, even my red, oversize Sally Jesse Raphaels. Obviously, he's spent years preparing for the day when he'd need a stockpile of prescription-strength glasses in styles from yesteryear.

Amid all the choices, though, nothing works well, and we began a series of eye appointments to find something that does—which proves easier said than done. Anyone who has to make trombone motions to find just the right reading distance understands the link between eyesight and aging, but for most it's just an inconvenience. For Dad, it's not something that can be definitively rectified with new glasses. Add to my steep learning curve the discovery that a common symptom of congestive heart failure is changing eye pressure that can affect vision. Dad is now facing the loss of his most treasured pastime, reading. But he's not letting it go without a fight. As testament to his spirit of resourcefulness, as we've begun to gather up the random pairs of glasses to minimize his frustration and everyone else's confusion, we've noticed that hand-held magnifying lenses have begun popping up to take their place.

And then there was this entry in the notebook: "Max running through the house wearing (a.k.a.—chewing) Dad's dentures." We all laughed picturing feisty little Max scampering around wearing a broad false smile. But, in reality, it was a blow to Dad's long-term health and emotional well-being. His well-worn, well-fitting dentures have been replaced by a new set that's ill-fitting and painful, causing him discomfort on a daily basis. Another addition to the learning curve, this one a lesson learned the hard way. Our new rule is for whomever is on the night shift to remember to safely store his dentures so they won't slip out and fall prey to his ever loyal but mischievous dogs.

The clamor of barking dogs is notice that the man from Eddy's Carpets has arrived to take measurements for the entire upstairs—the final touch and, I'm hoping, the final big expense. I try not to mentally tally the expense of helping Dad in all these ways. Until we have arrangements in place for Medicare, this month of assistance from HHAs has been one of many out-of-pocket expenditures. Thankfully, Tony and I are on the same page when it comes to money. We contribute financially in numerous ways, not only directly toward my father's care but also toward the greater supporting network, from the upstairs renovation to dumpster fees to caregiver thank-you gift baskets to pet-related expenses (long-overdue vet care and pet food) to grocery staples and takeout meals to new clothes, undergarments, toiletries, and even monthly heating fuel. My kindhearted father in-law would occasionally send us a check, knowing what we were juggling. Somehow, he knew what was involved even without an accounting. It always seemed miraculous timing and generous to the point of embarrassing, and we would accept the help with humility and gratitude. *I'm just grateful we have help and the means. If we didn't, how would we handle this?*

The irony is that Carmine has been living with the same congestive heart failure diagnosis as Dad. My sister-in-law Angeline and I are living a similar Sandwich Generation lifestyle, as she works full-time, has an only child, a busy husband, and demanding career. I feel such ease talking with her, even though we don't talk as often as I would like. The only difference, the big difference, is that her father lives with her family. She has even more to manage than I do to split her attention between her daughter and father, both competing for her time. She often wakes in the night to the sound of Carmine, *her* childhood hero, calling her name over and over. Not because there is anything actually wrong; it's just become habit and, I suppose, a need for a sense of security. Needless to say, her sleep is also dramatically affected, along with every aspect of her life. *I don't know how she does it, how do any of us do this?*

"Sa, can you finish taping off the baseboards while I help the carpet guy take measurements?" Tony says, putting aside the roller used for the first coat of "Dove White" ceiling paint.

"Sure, do you still think we'll have time to get started priming the walls today, or are you planning a second coat on the ceiling?"

"I don't see why not. Wet paint dries a little bit darker, so the ceiling might be fine with just one coat. The thing is, I ended up buying the thundercloud shade of gray for the walls, and I want you to trust me that it's going to look great."

In the background, I can hear the dogs settling down as the carpet guy makes his way upstairs. There's a familiar creak and groan from the worn section of the stairs. "It looks more like battleship gray to me but fine, you win. Bring on the thundercloud. Will probably won't care either way."

"Let's play it by ear, and more important, good progress is made when no one is hungry."

I take that as my cue to begin thinking about whether to order out or cook in Dad's kitchen. Although I know Dad would appreciate the scents of something cooking in the kitchen, I'm leaning toward the easy path. Plus, if I run out to get something, I can pick up Summer, who's been playing at a friend's house. It's the same friend who joins us for the occasional minor-league baseball game in Pawtucket, and we're planning to go again in a few days, since Tony's birthday and Father's Day are around the same time this year. *That reminds me, Father's Day is bound to be packed, and I should order the tickets for the game online.* Taping the blue edging tape as straight as possible, I'm only vaguely interested in the pricing that Tony and the guy from Eddy's Carpet are talking about in another bedroom down the hall as they consider varying weights for the pad that goes under the carpet. *I also need to get a card out in the mail for Carmine.* I smile thinking about him in healthier, more headstrong days. Not to mention his love for the hip, swanky songs of Ol' Blue Eyes and the Rat Pack. And he loved to cook. He introduced me to the simple deliciousness of pasta fagioli.

With the measurements taken care of, Tony joins me to finish taping off the final section of baseboards. The Lady Gaga-inspired bounce that had been in my step earlier in the day has been replaced with stiff knees from all the kneeling.

"I noticed your cell phone rang a couple of times while you were with the guy," I say picking up the phone, "it looks like it was Angeline. Do you want me to call her back now or wait until you're done rolling?"

"Could you? I want to get started again. I can see a few areas that need touching up. Otherwise, I think the ceiling looks fine. Just put it on speaker."

While he spot-rolls and I hold out the phone while picking up bits of the border tape, she answers right away,

"Hi, Anth," Tony's sister says softly, and there's no mistaking her tone of voice as anything other than dead serious. We look at each. "It's Dad. You need to come home."

He grabs the phone and switches it off "speaker." The tiny hairs on my arms and the back of my neck tingle when he closes his eyes. Standing motionless and cradling the phone tightly to his ear, he doesn't ask any questions, just listens. I take the roller from his other hand and lay it in the tray.

"Yes, I love you, too," he says, his voice breaking. "I'll book a ferry home as soon as possible, see you soon."

Your word is a lamp to my feet
And a light unto my path.
Psalm 119:105

So Many Goodbyes

9

October 2011

Nowadays, I pick up groceries on the fly. It's yet another indication of how scattered I've become. But every once in a while, I take the time for a major shopping trip. I love getting stocked up on pretty much everything. It's a great feeling when the shelves in our makeshift laundry/pantry area in the basement teem with backup dry goods and canned foods. For any emergency situation or postapocalyptic scenario, we'll be all set with petite diced tomatoes, peas, corn, kidney and cannelloni beans, and an assortment of ten-for-ten-dollars boxes of pasta, Ditalini being Summer's favorite. As I neatly stack the cans on this Sunday afternoon in October, I hear the ruckus of Tony and Summer horsing around in the great room above. I allow myself a moment to stand

and listen to their laughter and bask in the beauty of the cornucopia of cans I've arranged. But only a moment.

"Hey, Tone," I yell up the stairs, "can you come down and help me carry up the rest of the groceries?" Lugging the heavily packed bags up from the garage is my least favorite thing in the world, and I always marvel at how many he manages to carry up at once.

"How were the roads, Sa?" he asks, pulling five of the colorful, reusable shopping sacks from the back of the car. "They're saying this storm will be fast-moving, high winds, not much accumulation, but it will pack a punch."

"Not too bad yet, but the grocery store was mobbed." I lower my voice as we trudge up the stairs. "I'm going to try and hide all of the Halloween candy for tomorrow night, so could you please not dive into it in front of Summer?"

"Who, me? It depends on two things: the kind of candy and whether Halloween is even happening because of this storm."

Summer catches the end of our conversation as we near the top of the stairs. "The weather people are saying it's an early wintry mix," she says. "Are they going to cancel Halloween?"

Tony laughs. "It's hard to know, Sum. We could always do some activities at the mall, or trick-or-treat a day later because of the weather."

"It's too soon to know for sure," I tell her, "but have no fear—your long blond wig will not go wasted. Have you decided who you'll be yet?"

"Of course," she answers, as if I'm nuts for asking. "A mermaid who likes snow."

Considering how many times she's changed her mind about her costume—first it was Barbie and then Little Red Riding Hood and then a good witch, a repeat of last year—there's no telling what plans are brewing in her head as she factors in the wintry mix.

The TV in the great room depicts the weather pattern of white swirl over the New England map, and Storm Team Five is already on location in towns in the western part of the state.

"Visibility will become extremely poor as wind gusts increase," one of the reporters says. "Side roads are beginning to get slippery. Police report no accidents at this time but are advising residents to stay home."

As I put my grocery-stuffed bag on the kitchen counter, I see Buddy, our sheltie, doing exactly what he was doing before I left for the store: walking in circles on the living room carpet with his head tipped to the side. Two days ago he was suddenly struck with labyrinthitis, an infection of the inner ear that affects older dogs and causes abnormal posture. The antibiotic ear drops from the vet don't seem to be doing a thing—his coordination is still off, and occasionally he vomits and loses his balance. When he's had this before, it's usually cleared up quickly, and I'm praying for the same now. This dog has been my boy since our eyes met when he was a puppy. So smart and loyal, we have a fourteen-year bond that's as strong as my bond with anyone in the family. I don't spend half as much time as I used to with him, but he's been such a little helper to me through the years. While Ruby, our late Lab-chow mix, would turn a deaf ear, together Buddy and I would make the walk to the nursery down the hall to settle our crying baby in the wee hours of the night. His protective ways and herding nature kept us all together and accounted for during walks in the woods and safe from strangers who might dare walk too close to our parked car during an errand run.

Sitting on the floor, I gather him in my arms and rest his head under my chin. "It's going to be okay, little Bud. It's a Sunday-dinner day and we'll be together here for the storm, okay?" I can feel him trying to relax but know from the rapid movement of his eyes that he can't control what's happening to him any more than we can control the looming storm. I'd feel better if the vet's office were open on Sundays, but then again, because of the weather, there's little chance I could take him in anyway.

An hour later, with the groceries all put away and my home-made lasagna in the oven, the good smells of sautéed garlic and Italian sausage permeate the house. Buddy seems to be slowing, and I'm hoping he'll soon tire out and be able to lie down to sleep. I'm trying my best to create the usual cozy Sunday afternoon, but something's off. There's an uncomfortable energy in the air. The combination of poor Buddy's pacing and the nor'easter squalls visible outside the kitchen window make it hard to feel settled. Not to mention the noise factor. Summer is playing "Monster Mash" over and over in the playroom while on-location newscasters shout about the storm's progress on the TV in the great room.

"National Grid is reporting many power outages across the state, mainly in central and western Massachusetts. . . ."

I strain to hear Will on the phone above the din.

"We're all set, Sa, I told the aides not to come, 'cause I'm here all day. We're definitely not coming over for dinner, though. It's not just the weather. It's a little like crazy town over here. Dad's not himself and he won't take his medication."

The newscaster is insistent. "Keep the station tuned here for the latest updates on the pre-Halloween snowstorm. . . ."

"Which ones?" I ask, and then the power goes out.

In an instant, all is quiet. After all the noise, the silence seems exaggerated.

"Momm, Daaaad?" Summer calls out and runs to me in the kitchen.

It's not quite dark yet, but it will be soon. Tony comes down from the bedroom, where he'd been watching football. "Do you know what is the most important thing to do in a situation like this?" he says playfully. He takes Summer's hand and walks to the stove and slowly pulls open the oven door. "Check to see if dinner is done!"

"Tone, don't you think we should wait a few minutes to see if the power will come back on?" I ask.

"Naw," he says, already slipping on the oven mitt and pulling out the lasagna. "They've been talking about outages all over the place, and I won't be surprised if it's out for a while."

He places the hot stoneware casserole on the stovetop.

"It's not done yet," I say as all three of us stare down at it, our eyes adjusting to the dusk. Huddled before the stove, we're standing in a proximity to each other that would seem unusually close in almost any other situation. While just a few minutes ago we were all in separate rooms with different things on our minds, now we're elbow to elbow, gazing at the lasagna as if it holds an answer, a magic looking glass of flat, soppy noodles, cheese, and sauce to guide us through the storm. Even Buddy has circled his way over and leans against my leg, panting. Tony and I exchange a glance and wait to see what Summer will say. It doesn't take long.

"Um, Mom, are we going to eat that?" she says more quietly than normal. Obviously, she doesn't see the humor in the entire situation, and Tony and I burst out laughing.

"Sure are," Tony says. "And it's going to be delicious because it's part lasagna, part soup."

It's funny how Summer and I both defer to him, our man of the house, whenever we lose power. He usually keeps the mood light, and I have to say we've played some of our most memorable games of Trouble, Rummy, and Scrabble during storms.

"No, it's not." She says, not warming to the joke, "Can I help light up the candles? Mom, can we make s'mores with the candles?"

"I don't think we'll be here long enough to tell stories in front of a pretend candle campfire," Tony answers before I have a chance.

While he pulls out plates for dinner, I busy about, lighting several mismatched candle tapers and a large Yankee Candle jar, placing them on the counters and the stove to create a circle of light.

"We know how quickly the house cools down without heat," Tony says, less lighthearted now. "A freezing night is not something I want to deal with, and the roads actually don't look that bad yet. Can you text your brother to see if they still have power? If so, we're having a sleepover with Grampa tonight."

After a quick candlelit dinner of soupy but mostly cooked lasagna, we make the decision to weather the roads and head to Dad's for the night. Will and I have been texting back and forth and their power hasn't been affected. The big question is whether to take Buddy. I hate to leave him alone in the house in his condition, but I know it will be an extra level of stress for him to face Elsa and Max.

"Sa, even though your father's dogs are little, there's pack mentality and they'll sense that he's sick. They might not leave him alone."

"I can't leave him, Tone." I bend to scoop him up. "Those little barkers better not try anything on you, huh, Bud?," I say, nuzzling his neck fur. "You'll just round 'em up like you always do."

"Oh, he'll round them up, all right, whether he means to or not," Tony says.

After a cold and tense drive across town, the warmth and light of my father's house does wonders to make us feel settled again. Dad and Will, on the other hand, are shocked to see Buddy in his state, panting and walking in circles and vomiting minutes after we arrive. The good news is that made Max and Elsa want nothing to do with him. They sense he's off and keep a watchful distance, content to have Summer's attention.

"Sa, I'm fine with all of you sleeping upstairs," Will says, "but there's no way I want Buddy up there peeing and puking in the few rooms I have to myself."

"What do you mean there's no way? There *is* a way. He's sick and can't help it!"

"Don't care. That's *my* living space and he's a dog!" he bellows, raising his voice for the first time since he's been home. "He'll lie down when you go to bed, and you'll get a better night's sleep!"

"This isn't about sleep. Don't act like you're worried about my sleep." He doesn't say it, but I can guess what he's thinking: *Why would I? No one is worried about mine.*

These are the types of conversations Will and I have had for the past couple of months, about how hard it is to sleep because of Dad's getting up at all hours of the night. When he first arrived home, our talks were mostly about Dad's condition, prescriptions and routine, the HHA schedule, and the possibility of Will finding a part-time job. But lately, Dad's so unsure on his feet and could easily fall. Will is more and more on guard, and it makes for an uneasy night when you're half listening for activity downstairs.

In search of a solution, I had a conversation with Rhonda about what she's seen with others in our situation. She said some families use a sleeping pill to ensure that their elder sleeps through the night until the aide can arrive in the morning. When Will and I mentioned that to Dad, he thought we were crazy, and it actually sounded odd to me, too, once the idea was out there, hanging in the air. We haven't brought it up again, but there's a price to pay: an exceedingly tired brother who's growing less and less patient with everything—Dad, the situation, and, most of all, the home health aides. He's constantly telling me stories about things they don't do well enough or do too much or do especially to annoy him. The people who were once lifesavers to me are now invaders of his privacy. I try the best I can to mediate and appease.

As Will and I bicker as he fills me in on the latest display of ineptitude on the part of one of the aides, Tony anticipates the end result and sets up a makeshift dog pen, using the dining room table and chairs. His plan is to box Bud's walking circle into a smaller space so he can get settled and either lean on the wall or lie down. Using his walker for support, Dad shuffles down the hall to offer an old, wool army blanket for bedding and a deep metal bowl for his water. The dented bowl looks like it might have done an actual tour of duty, but it's nice to know that Dad considers Buddy worthy of such prized possessions.

"Lay down now, Buddy. You're a good boy," he says gently. "Tone, can you position a chair so I can sit with him for a while? Let's use the dimmer light so we can quiet the room. Sa and Will, why don't you give it a rest? Tomorrow is another day."

"Sounds good to me, Dad," Will says, turning his back to me and rolling up his shirt sleeves to finish a few dishes in the sink. He and Dad have the same quick, mechanical method of rolling up their sleeves, as if they have a secret five-second rule. Meanwhile, the roll-down is one swift motion, half a second tops. But the two men are more different than the same. I no longer try to find any resemblance to my father in Will's features. Where Dad has pointy features, Will's are square. And while they have the same olive coloring that tans very dark very easily, the same receding hairline and the same bowlegged walk, I don't think anyone in a crowded room would figure the two as part of the same gene pool. To make the comparisons of my siblings to Hollywood actors complete, I'll liken Will to *Hulk* star Mark Ruffalo. Of course, I'm talking about the scenes where Ruffalo plays the Hulk's human side, as opposed to the irritable green lug he often transforms into.

Dad gets settled in the chair beside Buddy's pen and reaches down to pat him. I love these rare times when Dad is as normal as ever, the dad he used to be, the one who could take control of any situation and solve all of life's problems. It comes as a great relief. Whatever the medication issue that Will had mentioned on the phone had been, it doesn't seem to be a problem now, and I'm glad for it. I hug him good night before I head upstairs to make up beds for my family.

"I know how worried you are about little Bud," he says. "There's nothing you can do until the morning, so you might as well get some sleep."

"Okay, I will, and thanks for letting us stay here overnight. I told Summer it will be such an adventure."

His eyes widen at my use of one of his favorite expressions. He'd use it when he wanted to coax us kids into doing some odd errand. As in, "We're just going to stop in at Ephraim's Treasure Chest on Franklin Street and maybe trade some coins. It won't take long, and it will be such an adventure." An hour later, I was bored out of my mind, staring at the coins embedded in the concrete floor.

"It's an adventure for me, too, having everyone stay," he says, "and I'm glad to have ya." He smiles, maybe replaying his own memory.

Early the next morning, in an obvious mix-up, three HHAs show up for the same shift. Arriving a few minutes apart from each other, they each register the same surprise and concern when they see the makeshift pen of jumbled dining room chairs with a sickly dog and me sitting in the middle. Panting and leaning against me or the wall, Buddy occasionally lies down and struggles to get back up. I've been trying to get him to eat, but he has no interest. He's had a little water, but not enough, and I'm mad at myself for not checking on him during the night. I'd intended to but slept straight through. It doesn't help that my brother the Floridian and the elderly man living here prefer to keep room temperatures ridiculously high—I think I didn't sleep so much as pass the night in a heat-induced stupor.

Feeling guilty sitting beside my sick boy, with my frizzy bed head and still in pajamas, I try to make small talk with the aides and catch up briefly with these familiar faces I haven't seen in a while. But inside, my mental tap dancing has already begun. At the dining room table, Dad sits staring defiantly at the handful of pills Will has just slapped down in front of him; in the kitchen, Will is banging down breakfast bowls and setting up tea for Dad instead of allowing the aides to assist; and in the living room, Storm Team Five reports the play-by-play on the storm cleanup while Tony tries to divert Summer. "Mommy's busy right now. Why don't *I help you* with breakfast today?"

"School is closed, Mom," Summer yells from the other room. "Do you think we'll have Halloween?"

"We don't know yet, Summer," I hear Tony tell her before yelling to inform me that his company is closed for the day, as is mine.

"You lucky to still have power, no?" one of the aides contributes pleasantly in her thick accent. "They tree branches down, ya know."

I leave Will and the aides to decide which one will stay for the shift, going upstairs to get Summer dressed and put beds back in order. When I come back down, I hear Tony and Will bantering about their favorite subject: the Patriots. I feel no guilt interrupting the bottomless conversation.

"Where are the aides? Who's staying to help Dad today?"

"Me," Will says adamantly.

Not taking the bait, I move on to more pressing concerns. "Tone before you head over to check the house and whether the power is back on, let's call the vet to see if they're open. If they are, maybe Will can watch Summer while we try and head over?"

"Of course I can watch the little trick-or-treater," he replies in a higher-than-normal pitch that I'm sure isn't intended to make him sound like the peculiar uncle that is does.

Thanks for that, Will, I think as Summer directs her panicked expression my way.

I sigh and put the phone on speaker to call the vet's office. We get a recorded message: "Thank you for calling the Park Side Animal Hospital. We are closed due to the storm and will be open again tomorrow during our regular business hours. Be assured our animal attendants are maintaining normal shift schedules for pet observation and care. If this is a pet emergency, please call the Wuff Animal Hospital for assistance."

Tony shakes his head emphatically, "There's no way in hell we're bringing him to Wuff's after what they did to Ruby! Talk about a wake-up call to learn that teaching schools are looking for any opportunity to teach. Don't you agree?"

"Of course I agree!" I say. "I'll try finding another vet and I'll call a few friends to see who they use."

Two years before, Ruby had had a major convulsion on Memorial Day, during a barbecue with college friends. We heeded Park Side's recorded message and, at the insistence of Wuff's intake person, left her overnight for observation. The next day, we arrived to find a network of tubes and wires in her skull, a tube down her throat, and an incision that ran the length of her abdomen. Strapped down and under no anesthesia, she lay there awake and whimpered mournfully when she saw us, like uttering a pained cry for help. It was an unforgettable sound that no dog should ever make. The diagnosis was two-fold: She had a "flipped stomach," a bloating condition that afflicts some large breeds and causes the stomach to twist, as well as a quarter-size tumor on her brain. We instantly doubted the stomach issue. Apparently, the evening attendant had seen her dry retching—something she'd done on occasion ever since she was a puppy. No worse than a quick cough, it was never anything that couldn't be soothed with a treat. For all we knew, it was her clever way of training us to hand out treats. As for the tumor, we didn't doubt the diagnosis, but after hearing the exorbitant cost for the test and the surgery, we wondered who'd authorized the X-rays. There was no guarantee of a positive outcome, so rather than allow the inevitable seizures to continue, we made the heartbreaking decision to put her down.

We insisted that she be allowed to be outside in the natural world for the procedure, so the staff casually removed the tubes. As Ruby bled from unstitched suture wounds, we carried her to the grass in the rear courtyard and said goodbye.

Now, Tony is adamant. "In absolutely no circumstance will we ever take Buddy there to those butchers," he says and walks out of the house.

The day passes quickly, with Summer watching TV in the living room while Grampa reads and dozes and I call a dozen animal clinics in the area. Hearing they're either closed or not willing to accept a new patient in Buddy's condition, I'm relieved to finally talk to a mobile vet who's willing to hear my desperate plea. Normally, I'd be skeptical of someone not associated with an actual facility, but the situation is dire and a home visit is actually the ideal scenario. Brimming with excitement and hope for the first time today, I call Tony, who's back at our house. "Tone, she's agreed to make a house call, except she can't be there until five."

"Perfect, and we're in luck—the electricity just went back on, so I'll swing by after I clear the walkway to pick up you and Summer. How's she doing, by the way?"

"She's been over the moon ever since hearing that neighbor-hoods have the green light for Halloween. Her repeat question has changed from whether Halloween is happening to 'When will it be time to get ready?' I asked Will if he could come over and help to answer the door for the trick-or-treaters. Would it be okay if you walk the neighborhood with her this year? I need to be with Buddy when the vet comes."

"I want to be there, too, Sa. The timing on this couldn't be worse. I've been remembering everything we went through with Rub–"

"I know you do." *If he falls apart over Buddy, I will, too, and I need to stay strong for Summer's sake. Halloween is supposed to be a fun childhood time, not one with distracted, crying adults.* "But can we play it by ear? Summer's been looking forward to this and one of us needs to keep it together. I'll get her dressed and ready. It would be good if you could fill the plastic cauldron with all that candy that I put in the cabinet above the fridge. Please just come and pick us up when you can and let's not talk about it, okay?"

There's a pause.

"Okay, it's just cold."

"What?"

"It's going to take a little while for the house to heat up. See you soon."

Sitting in the backseat with Buddy on my lap for the ride home, I feel his body go limp and become dead weight. Stroking his fur, I can tell he's breathing but unconscious. I tell myself he's just asleep and listen to Summer chatter beside me about the costume she's definitely decided on: Snow Day Barbie. "This way I can wear the long blond wig with a winter coat and hat. Is there any way to keep the wig on without those bobby pins that hurt? Do you think a pocket book will be big enough to carry candy?"

Halloween has never been my thing, and I silently wish the whole ridiculous event would be over. I look at my watch again—the vet will be at the house in less than an hour.

When we get home, Tony helps me carry Buddy up the stairs from the garage, and we place him on his bed with extra blankets underneath. Will arrives soon after. I hear his booming voice as I head to the upstairs bedroom to help Snow Day Barbie get dressed in the most fashionista outfit we can concoct, one that will, hopefully, combine cuteness and warmth.

"Tony Bub, what do you need me to do?"

"I meant to replace the burned-out porch light sooner than this, but it's broken off in the socket."

Turning my attention back to Summer, I can hear the muffled creak of the closet where we store the tool kit and stepladder. It seems we're both glad for busy work as a temporary distraction from our poor Buddy. Even though he's all I have in mind.

The rational part of me appreciates that Will's presence is helping to maintain a semblance of normalcy, but the small talk and soft laughter drifting in through the propped-open front door seem too lighthearted for the occasion. I feel ready to jump out of my skin. Applying more makeup on Summer than I intend, I call downstairs barking orders at Will. "Can you fill the stinking cauldron with candy already, and bring Tony the singing light-up pumpkin for the porch!" Before he has a chance to ask, I add, "I don't really care if the pumpkin works, the batteries are in the top drawer if you want to replace them, it's all on you to decide."

All dressed, Snow Day Barbie looks like one of the made-up child pageant queens. I suppose it's a fitting look for Halloween, a mix of scary and sweet. Thankfully, she doesn't make a stink when, after only one play of "Monster Mash," we shut off the CD player. It isn't appropriate, and I'm grateful she senses that as well.

The vet arrives right on time and along with the first round of trick-or-treaters, the little ones accompanied by hand-holding parents. Will awkwardly greets them all, struggling with whether to use the tone of voice for speaking to children, suppressing a nervous laugh at the same time. Thanking the vet up and down for coming, we make our way into the kitchen to hear the tail end of Tony and Summer's conversation.

"Yes, there's a chance he may go to heaven tonight," Tony says. "We won't know until the doctor examines him. You can say goodbye either way."

She sits next to Buddy, patting him gently, but is too self-conscious to say goodbye in front of the vet. "I said something to him in my mind," she says and quickly heads to the foyer, where Will, allowing us our space, is positioned by the front door.

As Will and Summer open the door together to the second wave of doorbell ringers, and then the third, I sit on the floor with Buddy's head in my lap and Tony watches over the vet's shoulder. Thoroughly checking him, she takes his pulse, listens with the stethoscope, and feels the heat in his hip joints, swollen from his arthritis. I tell her how lame he's become, to the point of relying on glucosamine multiple times a day.

"For months he's been using the dog ramp to go outside, but there have been more accidents lately."

"Especially in the living room," Tony adds, glancing over at the rug.

She nods and concludes, "He's severely arthritic. Keep in mind the winter cold is coming and it might get harder and harder for him to go outside and get around in general. I'm not going to weigh in with a specific recommendation, but want to present you with a few options and possible scenarios."

While she shares her ideas, my mind drifts to walks in the woods with him and laughing at his endless attempts to herd Ruby even when they were swimming, her head high with a stick in her mouth and him alongside, chomping the air in his unsuccessful attempts to grab the stick from her. I know all his silly little ways—that panting smile and side glance that make him look wise, a crafty dog version of Eddie Haskell. The smell and feel of his thick coat when he would curl up beside me on the bed and make that soft little grunt when lying down. *How much I'm going to miss him.*

"Unfortunately," she finishes, "I realize none of these hold any guarantee that he will feel better."

"He's an old boy, Sa," Tony says gently. "I think it's time to say goodbye."

With tears streaming, I can only nod in agreement. Tony somehow musters the strength to not lose control of his emotions. With Ruby, I had been the one to keep it together while he fell apart, and the reverse is happening now. It's funny how one of us always manages to be strong for the other. He kneels to hug Bud and kiss his head, and then goes to take Summer by the hand out into the cold to walk the neighborhood. While the vet injects him, I stroke his fur, talking for his sake, trying to let him hear my voice, that he's going to be okay and will have the chance to be with Ruby again. I'm grateful for Will, who squats down by my side, and for the quiet prayer he says.

Afterward, getting up with shaky legs I force myself to get moving before Tony and Summer come back home. I thank the vet and Will walks out, leaving with her, carrying Buddy so she can make arrangements for his ashes. Exhausted from the day's constant flow of adrenaline and last night's poor sleep, I lie down in our bedroom with a pounding headache and cry. Soon, though, Tony and Summer come in from Halloween and I'm grateful that they occupy themselves and allow me time to myself. On the edge of drifting off to sleep, I answer the bedside phone.

"Sa, I'm sorry to bother you, and I wouldn't if it wasn't important," Will says.

"Is everything all right?"

"Ahhh, not really. I came home to learn that no aides have been here to help Dad for the evening shift. Can you believe that?"

"I don't know. I wasn't there to hear what you told them this morning when you sent them all away."

"I didn't say anything about changing the schedule for tonight! Just let me finish. Dad ate an entire jar of grape jelly and he's covered in it. He's a complete mess. It's crazy town once again over here and I'm cooking now because he's starving. I'm tired of these aides, Sa. We need to let them go, and you should be the one to do it."

"Okay, Will, I'll do it tomorrow," I say, too tired to be the mediator anymore. I know this means more on me now, to give Will the breaks he won't be getting from the aides anymore. "Thanks for your help tonight. Good night."

In the quiet darkness of our bedroom at night, Tony and I are finally alone. Given everything that's happened in the past twenty-four hours and the fact that we slept with Summer between us at

Dad's house last night, it feels like ages since we've been side by side under the covers.

"Can we talk about what happened today, Sa?" he whispers. "I can't believe our little Buddy is gone."

I know he'll tell me I'm not to blame if I tell him what I'm thinking, that I should have called our usual vet at Park Side sooner, to give an update and ask about a stronger antibiotic. He was dehydrated—I should have found a way to make him drink.

"Sa, do you want to talk?"

I roll onto my side. "No. No, I don't. I just want this all to be over. When is it all going to be over?"

I fall asleep too quickly to hear whether he answers.

The temperature the next day is unseasonably mild. Clear blue skies and bright sun begin melting away all evidence of the storm, as if it had all been a surreal dream. The standing Tuesday staff meeting is on my mind as I go through the motions of getting myself and then Summer dressed and ready. *I need to be there on time.* There's no time to process the loss of my beloved precious friend. Nowhere near recovered from the chaos of the weekend, there's only one thing to do: push the feelings aside, compartmentalize and go to work.

When I get there, I glimpse the newsfeed in my in-box—

> Historic October Snow Struck Northeast Before
> Halloween—A historic storm hammered the Northeast
> with record snow on the last weekend in October,
> knocking out power to more than 3 million people
> and damaging thousands of trees. Topping the snow
> totals ...

I have zero interest in the details and click the ESC key in the upper left-hand corner of the keyboard forcefully to escape the factual commentary that bears no resemblance to my experience. The tears catch in my throat at the thought of Buddy, and of seemingly always saying goodbye. It feels like an endless process of letting go. I shift my attention to returning calls, answering emails, and the matter of calling Pinnacle to convey Will's request to let Rhonda and her HHA crew go.

> *Though he fall, he shall not be utterly cast down;*
> *For the Lord upholds him with his hand.*
> Psalm 37:24

Spinning 10

Work continues to be the best part of my day and is going well. Or so I think. I have in mind the image of an archer shooting a bull's-eye, from one of Summer's old bedtime books. The visual serves as a reminder for me to stay focused on tasks that will really make a difference—that will deliver "results," in corporate speak. Granted the archer was a tiny blue fairy, but who cares? The point is, she's not at all intimidated by the giant sunflower.

My sales-related activity has become the only area of my life where I feel competent and in control. It used to be that I would dally and procrastinate when it came to making calls, but something about not having a lot of time has made me more efficient about the time I do have, and my workday is down to business. I'm also more selective about where to direct my time, and I focus on potential accounts that have a greater chance of panning out, namely large organizations with the greatest possibility of hosting a graduate-level program on-site. It's not a stretch as I try to make clear the convenience of a high-caliber education brought right to their sizable workforce.

"Ha, how do you like that?!" I say to myself as I hang up the phone. I just had a great call with a new contact at a prospect account and got the green light to schedule an appointment in person. My calls are getting through to the senior levels I'm pursuing, and voice-mail messages are being returned. There's something empowering about this mind-set. I have too much to do to mess around, and this straightforward approach seems to resonate with people on the other end of the line. It's not just about cutting to the chase faster—it's as if my BS radar has been fine-tuned. My dealings with my father, my immediate family, HHAs, nurses, doctors, and bill collectors are lessons in clear, direct communication, and now I'm having authentic conversations with prospective clients. Connecting.

It's an entirely different story though, with my immediate colleagues in our small department. No how-to business book will ever tout the merits of working heads down. Nor will one ever warn that being a member of the Sandwich Generation has the potential to cloud years of Workplace 101 knowledge. For me, basic tips like "manage up," "dress for success," and "be friendly—share a smile!" have been replaced with an internal mantra to "tune out office chatter, produce, and don't cry!" And I'm assuming my actions will speak louder than words—of course everyone can see I'm committed and busy.

After my call, I report for my one-on-one meeting with the newly appointed manager, who's new to sales but the department rock star nonetheless. She's representative of the bull-by-the-horns millennial generation, and there's something about her steely über-confident gaze that unsettles me and knocks me off my game. And, need I add, she has perfect hair. Poised, pretty, and probably about twenty-eight, she's Anna Kendrick to my unfunny, less confident Melissa McCarthy with not so good hair. Her office, like all of them in this renovated brownstone, is set up nicely for comfort and collaboration—unlike so many traditional corporate environ-ments and cube farms, the overall office environment here is, well, homey—except I feel the opposite of at home as I sit with her at the small round table next to her desk.

The purpose of our meeting is to talk about what my strategy and sales targets are, now that I'm officially in my new "hunter role." The team was recently divided into two groups: account manag-ers who can mine existing accounts for additional programs and business developers who can open new doors. I'm proud to be part of the latter camp but don't underestimate the challenge. Always well-prepped, I've created a few, possibly overdone PowerPoint slides to depict possible courses of action. I love models and charts and have worked up four-quadrant diagrams, screen shots, and tables to depict very simple points, but that's my thing, my security blanket—to always be prepared and, perhaps at times, overboard. Then again, it seems to me the nature of business to overengineer most things.

After minimal small talk, we get down to business. "I could target low-hanging fruit and promote traditional programs in our sweet spot, which could mean faster revenue, but I think it's a gamble to keep tapping the same geographic defense sites." I flip to the next slide. "Or we could take the longer road and begin priming the pump in the cybersecurity space, and as you know, I've begun by making inroads with the following target compa-nies." Next slide. "I realize we also need to support our budding health-care program; another option is these steps I've outlined as a way to start gaining university exposure. The thing is, I would like prioritization of where to focus."

Silence, as we stare down at the slides, I'm sure thinking quite different, if not totally opposite thoughts.

The conversation that ensues dances around the question of why I can't do *all* of this. Talking slowly, as if to someone who's a little slow on the uptake, Twenty-Eight seems annoyed with my slides and the position I've put her in. I realize that my weak, stammering, nonsensical explanation of why I can't do it all—"to maximize my time and focus"—is lost on someone who *can*.

The reality is, it's a fair question and it's appropriate for any manager to encourage the stretching of goals. Not to mention the soundness of not putting all the eggs in one basket. But I'm overwhelmed. I want to do well in this new role for the sake of both career growth and department growth, but I can't confess my genuine fear that if I'm stretched any thinner, I'll break. I'll fail on all fronts. Had I been in a frame of mind to have a confident, square-shouldered conversation, I would have been able to express concern that it's risky to dilute our efforts by chasing three new market segments and recommend that we instead focus on saturating one really well. But I'm stuck in an anxiety-ridden pattern of overapologizing to everyone (and generally falling short of my own high expectations) between fleeting moments of coolness where I find the words and look the part. With Twenty-Eight, I've become so expert at building a brick wall of professionalism, of business-only conversation, that revealing the smallest glimpse into my personal life will cause my shield to crumble. So rather than articulate my concerns and look for middle ground, as I might do in a less-pressured, well-rested frame of mind, I shut down.

No one understands what I'm going through. Sitting in the awkward silence, battling the fight-or-flight response, dying to cut and run, dragging myself along the road to burning out, I get it for the first time. *Truly—no one understands.*

"We're all busy, you know," Twenty-Eight says with all manner of certainty and assuredness, and begins to stack a few papers nearby, indicating that our meeting has ended. "You aren't extended any more than anyone else in this team."

My ears actually begin to ring. It's my own personal version of the effect used in war movies after a bomb is dropped and a soldier stumbles around in the aftermath, seeing the action but through a haze. I hear a high-pitched hum and then nothing else.

I nod in submission, which I suspect she interprets as agreement, and fumble to collect my slides and notes. Like a schoolgirl who's failed a test—or worse—I flee.

During the dazed walk back to my office, I flash to the night before, in my father's living room, taking my eleven-to-seven shift to help him pee in the night, our concern being the risk of his falling in his weakened condition. Lately, he's dizzy and leans against the wall when trying to go from room to room, and he refuses to use a bedpan, as his dignity is tied to an ability to stand up and pee like a man. He turns a deaf ear to our pleas for him to take a sleeping pill so that he, and all of us, can rest at night. In his fight to keep control of his diminishing independence, he won't accept "staying wet all night," no matter how much we beg him to stay in bed.

I sleep in the newly purchased recliner, which extends out to a flat-bed position, and situated next to the hospital bed that Pinnacle had delivered. In light, interrupted sleep, I could sense when he was rousing every two hours like clockwork (a side effect of his increased Lasix dose): midnight, 2:00 a.m., 4:00 a.m., 6:00

a.m. After standing up too quickly, I'd fight the lightheaded, dizzy feeling and room spins while he leaned on me for support. With the room spinning, I would hold the portable plastic urinal (the medical device company called it a "male portable-potty pee bottle"). While I suppose positioning a flaccid penis in the pee bottle is a routine part of the job for those in the medical field, for me it was the extreme of uncomfortable and embarrassing. In my wildest dreams, I would never have imagined I would be helping my father in this way.

Since letting Rhonda and her team go, overnight help from an HHA is an option only when Will and I really need a break. And then I pay out of pocket for that luxury of a full night's sleep, which is the case in this instance. My night shifts are nothing in comparison with Will's, though. He takes the brunt of the night duty. While on his own path of sleep deprivation and burnout, he's become an expert at helping our father change into a fresh, dry Depends while standing up and showed me how to do the same. What once would have seemed an absurdity has become just another part of life.

When the HHA arrives at 6:30 a.m.—my angel of the morning—I bolt home to be there before Summer is up to help her get ready for school and safely on the bus, as if it were any other day. The delight in seeing her again and being together always makes it easier to muster a good face. And even though I know my day will be spent in a mental fog, I'm grateful for the uncharacteristically mild winter that's allowing me to drive from my house to my father's home with just pajamas beneath my winter coat, back and forth like a hamster in a wheel, all the while wondering how I can jump off.

Stepping back into my office I'm deflated but relieved to be safe in my own space again. I do what I always do, dive into work.

It doesn't even occur to me that there may be an alternative. Not having shared with Twenty-Eight the actual circumstances of my personal life, I continue on this path, head down and focused. I pull up a target account list in Excel and add two new columns, typing quickly, banging the keys harder than necessary: "HealthCare, Cyber." *Just make inroads however possible,* I think to myself. Ingrained in my DNA is the Finnish notion of *sisu*—a term that translates loosely as perseverance and determination—and the echo of childhood lessons about what to do if at first you don't succeed.

A few hours later, typical lunchroom banter among the primarily female staff is about going to the gym after work. "Who's going to spinning class?" I smile politely and laugh ruefully, knowing that I have my own version of a spinning workout to get to.

Oh yes, we're all just as busy, you know.

God is with you in all that you do.
Genesis 21:22

Fatigue ... Emotional, Mental, and Physical

11

January 2012

I'm always making mental notes to tell my husband things. Not just daily details from the honey-do list like "Can you pick up bread on the way home?" but important things like how to tell him I'm not myself, I'm on the edge. But how do you say that and when? I try one morning before work, when we're up early.

We're up even earlier than Summer, who has radar for whenever I turn over in bed, let alone get up. Other than during my commute, I never have any time to myself. Even in the bathroom. In my prechild days, I would hear mothers complain about their lack of privacy in the bathroom and always think they were exaggerating. Now I get it. Because she's an only, there's that added pressure to play the role of companion in lieu of her not having a sister or brother. So many times I've said, "Summer, honey, Mommy needs some privacy in here for a little while," and closed the bathroom door.

"Yep, I'll just play out here in the hall," she'd say. Then, literally seconds later, she'd ask, "Mumma, you almost done? Can I just come in?" She'd open the door with a sheepish smile and make herself right at home, no matter what I might be doing—putting on makeup, taking a shower, being generally indisposed.

I'll never understand the magnetic power I seem to have while I'm on the toilet. Even Buddy used to squeeze his way in and find a comfy spot to lie down. I suppose they know when you're trapped and can't do anything about it. I often wonder when kids finally stop following you around. When do they turn into loungers who stay in bed late? As preteens? Teens? I suppose I'll take issue when that time comes, yelling for my little Banana Nut Bread to "Get up and outta bed," but for now I'm always glad for even a few minutes alone with hubby.

Here in our bedroom, with the sun just starting to break through, I sit on the edge of the bed, watching silently as he pulls on running shoes, getting ready for his morning workout. His morning discipline is impressive. He loves to run even though his isn't a wiry build—more stocky and muscular. He's developed the pear shape, with junk in the trunk, while I've got the gut. Yesiree, every woman's dream—to have the apple figure instead of the hourglass. Even in my best shape, I've always been one variety of apple or another. When we met during our college years, I was a certified fitness instructor and he was voted "best buns" on campus. Honest truth. But I digress. He's aging well. Although his once-thick, curly brown hair is receding, it doesn't bother me as much as it does him and he always looks good.

The depth of what I'm feeling almost seems too monumental to say. I've just woken up and already I'm fighting the urge to cry. Round-shouldered, I'm wondering how I'll find the energy to begin the day. I force a tight-lipped smile, with tears just about to spill, and assume he can sense or hear my inner thoughts. *I'm weary. I'm hurting. Can't you see?*

I believe Tony is higher on the emotional IQ scale than most men, but I'm not sure if he really sees me. Then again, we've been together since we met in 1985—maybe he does. He's no dummy and probably just wants to get outta Dodge and away from the looming waterworks. I suspect he's not as relieved as I am for the time alone. Not to paint myself as the martyr and him as the goat, but he has his own agenda, namely running on the treadmill and getting to work on time.

He's dressed in record time and walking down the hall to the stairs, en route to the basement and the treadmill. "Just let me know how to help, Sa," he says without glancing over his shoulder to look at me or waiting for a reply. I could be passed out cold or poised in bow-and-arrow stance aiming for his head, but he'll never know.

Before he's even to the bottom of the stairs, I fall apart. Lying back on the bed, crying silent tears. Nowhere near well rested. Not able to think straight. *I don't know how I can continue. I don't know what will help.* The sound of movement in Summer's room down the hall is the cue that I'll soon need to generate some movement myself. I click on our bedroom TV to fill the room with familiar, conversational sounds of morning news and weather as if trying to absorb a little energy from the jocular *Good Morning America* crew. *Pull it together.* Time Square crowds are all bundled up and I notice how easily the weatherman interacts with the crowd, hugging people and laughing. *They look happy.* Slowly, I regain composure and get up, careful to avoid looking in the mirror. *I can't stand how old I look.* I stare blankly into my closet, at the rack of clothes hanging there. *I wish I could have a hug from that kind Sam Champion.* Similar to looking for something in the refrigerator even though you're not hungry, I search for something to fill the void. *Just pick anything to wear. It doesn't matter.*

While I stare transfixed, the wave of self-pity eventually passes, morphing into sarcasm and seething. *Fat chance—I can't even get a hug from my sweaty husband, never mind from a stylish, friendly gay man.* My tears have dried. *What kind of nonsense comment is that? How the hell do you think you can help when you can't spend five minutes to talk to me? You always had time to chat and make plans with the daycare lady though, didn't you?* Familiar pain from years past is still there, buried, and I struggle to once again look past the hurt and carry on.

My newfound "must be nice" line of thought begins. *It must be nice to be Joe Healthy. He's never looked better and I'm a mess.* I grab the black chunk-heel boots and brown wool skirt and toss them onto the bed. *It must be nice to cruise off to work every day, never having to get Summer ready in the morning and on the bus.* I yank a brown, short-sleeve, crew-neck shell off the hanger, stretching the neck line in the process. *It must be nice to get to work and actually focus on work and nothing else.* I reach for a black cardigan sweater, for the extra layer. *It must be nice to have a long commute and never, ever have to* plan—*scratch that*—make—*scratch that*—pick up *what's for dinner!*

"Good morning, Mom," Summer says standing doe-eyed in the hall just outside the bedroom door. "I was thinking we could have waffles and sausages today. Do we have time?"

Inhale, exhale.

"Mom?"

Inhale exhale—*just breathe.*

Slowly, I begin to feel like myself, but Summer has turned to walk away. I had glimpsed the sadness in her expression and furrowed brow. Somehow I'm reminded: *This is the child I prayed so hard for after our miscarriage. A blessing.*

"Wait. It's okay, we have time—we'll make time! I could use waffles and sausages today, too, Sum." Off we head to the kitchen, both still in our pajamas, and like so many times before, the simple needs of my little girl distract and temper my mood.

The reality is that though I could use help with so many things, I have not married an uncaring goat. Just an Italian man who has good days and bad, tender moments and rushed, like anyone. He's just as unequipped to handle everything that we're juggling as I am. I know he's willing to help, but I need to break it down and take time to make a written list of to-dos, with categories, deadlines, and numbered priorities. But not color-coded, I've yet to go that far.

And what's one more list? I already make mental lists and conduct status checks on countless things, as if on a military schedule, striving to squeeze every second out of the day. I'm a multitasking maniac, paying bills for our household, our tiny cottage on Cape Cod *and* Dad's house, and tending to all the duties that accompany maintaining our lifestyle. Running the race that all working parents know well, I always have a litany of to-dos—groceries to buy and laundry to be sorted and washed, doctor and dentist appointments to make for Summer, birthday parties to plan and attend (and gifts to buy and wrap), teacher conferences and school events, car maintenance to schedule, interest rates to watch and mortgages to refinance, potential Cape-house renters to correspond with, extended-family obligations to meet (well, sort of) and friends to disappoint (*"I'm sorry, I can't make movie night. I need to spend more time trying to get organized at home." "I'm sorry I don't have more time to talk." "I'm sorry I never called you back." "I'm sorry, I'm so sorry. . . ."*) Some friends understand or say they do, but who really knows?

How could they? In time, it's easier to dodge friends altogether to avoid another apology.

Alas, although I have help cleaning tubs and toilets every other week, I'm still losing the daily battle to keep order. If I'm really being honest, and Lord knows I am, all my dutiful task abilities are a far cry from what they used to be, let alone what I *want* them to be, which adds to my anxiety.

Having grown up in a cluttered mess, I learned at an early age how important organization was to me. That was well before the trendy movement of professional organization coaches and books. Even as a child, I made sure my few pairs of shoes—brown Earth Shoes from Thom McAn, kangaroo tennis shoes with the cool side pockets, and hand-me-down boots from a sibling—were neatly lined up in my closet. Never mind who else's clothes and shoes were strewn throughout the house—my neat ways helped me to think clearly and be "one up" on the rest, ready to go on a moment's notice.

Now, not so much. There are always dishes in the sink. Perpetual paperwork piles up on the kitchen table. I try to look past fingerprints on windows and toothpaste splatters on bathroom mirrors. It's a feat if clean laundry makes it out of the basket and into drawers, and it's a miracle if it remains folded. Junk-mail piles have become the bane of my existence, and decorative baskets are chock-full of papers, from nonstop incoming mail and catalogs to Summer's sweet but limitless schoolwork and drawings. Our docile cat, Meadow, has his own way of getting my attention, protesting his overfull cat box by relieving himself on the floor right beside it. Smart cat. This chore would be a perfect one for hubby except he never seems to remember or notice until I become the crow. "How can you walk by the cat box every day and never *see* it!" I've asked on more than one occasion. In easier days, I used to save myself (and him) the grief and just clean it myself, but those days are gone.

Summer and I are finishing our breakfast at the counter island as Tony emerges from his workout, dripping and obviously feeling good from the endorphin rush of exercise. "Med went on the floor again," he says on his way up the stairs to shave. "What a shitty, shitty kitty." He chuckles with delight at his juvenile rhyme.

As my house falls into disarray, so do I. My priorities are always in flux, shifting among managing my father's health-related matters, managing new accounts at work, and managing to keep up a good face for my daughter. I schedule and make appointments for everything from teeth to eyes to ears to heart, and either take him myself or arrange for transportation with a family member or a paid HHA.

Mind you, these aren't always just busy chores that require more doing than thinking. There are things that take me far outside my comfort zone, especially managing prescription medications. I'm nervous every time I fill the "days-of-the-week pill box" with Dad's meds. These aren't the bear-shaped gummy vitamins I'm used to dispensing to someone who is excitedly, joyously hopping on one leg, pleading for "just one more?" These are serious medications that alter and affect mind and body functions. Conscious of TV commercials with announcers who rattle off a stream of inconvenient and possibly life-threatening side effects in a pleasant professional manner, I check and double-check to make sure there are no errors. I've taped the prescription printout from the doctor to the inside of the kitchen cabinet door and made notes in the margin so that I know every pill by its clinical name and brand name. Furosemide = Lasix, a diuretic. Metoprolol = Lopressor, a beta-blocker. Klor-con = potassium, a banana in big pill form.

Before Will came home and took over pill administration, there had been moments of terror: "Hello, Pat, I just dropped the pill box on the floor and everything spilled out. I can't remember what days he's already taken, I can't tell some of them apart, and Max just ran off with something in his mouth." When Will took over pill patrol, most of our conversations were about whether Dad was consistently taking them. He took the brunt of the day-to-day battles, as my father would recognize familiar ones, calling them "horse pills," and often question what they were for. I can't say I blame him either. Neither did Will, who was in the position of forcing meds that he didn't believe in. An advocate of the doctrine of Dr. Schulze, a well-known nutritionist, and of eating clean super-foods, Will lamented the damage that these prescriptions were doing to our father's internal organs. The doctors know, too, that the toll on the kidneys and liver is a trade-off in the balance of managing CHF.

In general, it was a drain on my nerves, as were many of the conversations with medical staff, namely Dad's doctors and nurse practitioners. I would write down keywords and phrases so I could accurately share with my siblings what had actually been said. Similar to the phases of learning a foreign language, I could understand it better than speak it, and though I learned to hold my own, I was always out of my element. Even though I could sound-board details with siblings so that medical decisions seemed as if they were never 100 percent on me, I still felt the heavy weight of being health-care proxy every day.

There are infinite calls to make and paperwork to fill out on his behalf. For benefits from the state and to clear his record with the IRS, who'd been docking his pension check for unpaid taxes that, in reality, had been caught up. I laugh now, in the aftermath of the exposure of the corruption at Veterans Affairs, to think how foolish I was to even imagine that assistance from the VA was possible. Because Dad never took advantage of any of his earned benefits, I thought that there was a chance for help, that the VA would agree he was better off at home and allocate the money we desperately needed for round-the-clock care. I completed application upon application, with diligent follow-up that included letters to our local and state government officials. On top of that, factor in hours, even days, wasted navigating through automated phone prompts, holding interminably and awaiting return phone calls that sometimes put you right back to square one. As I listen to swanky telephone Muzak, I channel the persistence of Paul to get anything accomplished.

And then there's my *own* household. I've arranged a network of help, paid and unpaid, from dear friends, neighbors, and college students, to all of whom I'm forever grateful.

"Hello, Ella?" (calling from work). "I just want to let you know my sister Pat will be picking up Summer this evening because I have an after-work reception to attend up on campus." "Hello, Joy?" (leaving a message in the morning rush before leaving for work). "Quick reminder that Belle (another neighbor, college age) is taking Summer to her theater group this afternoon. Can you have her dressed in her reindeer outfit?"

"Hi, Merida," (while deep-breathing during the evening commute). "I'm sorry I'm running late. I'm touching in to make sure all is well with Summer. Would you mind popping chicken tenders and fries in the oven and I'll be there as soon as possible?"

These people were there for Summer when I was not. They got her off the bus, made her snacks, chauffeured her here and there, and listened to her accounts of fun times at school functions, friends' houses, and the occasional Brownies meeting.

At the home of my closest friend, Ella, there are many requested afternoon favors that stretch well into the evening. It's always fine with Ella, though, and certainly with Summer because she's so at home there. I met Ella at my first job out of college. A cross between Meg Ryan and Nicole Kidman, she's beautiful on the inside and out. She left the corporate world to focus on her family and owned a daycare business for years before becoming a grade-school art teacher. She's one of those people who somehow magically attract children, forest animals, strays, and animated talking birds, enough to rival any Disney princess. When I quickly drop Summer at her door, she communicates an ocean of empathy with a warm smile and sincere eye contact, as if to say, *She's okay. Do what you have to do.* Everyone should have such friends.

But even with this network of help, I'm falling behind in managing it all. Scattered. I have work responsibilities that involve long car rides and day trips throughout New England to present at information sessions or to welcome students to their first class— almost always in the evening. Not to mention networking events, breakfast meetings, and after-work hours. Though this is far from a stint in the Peace Corps, I've lost sight that I'm being paid to sip wine and nibble shrimp cocktail. It would be a dream job under any other circumstance, but I'm always acutely aware of my family responsibilities and my father's schedule, making mental note of messages I need to leave, to check, and to follow up on.

On one of these working evenings at the Worcester Club, I make one last attempt to reach Tony on my mobile from the parking lot before heading inside. The university is hosting a cybersecurity-related dinner discussion that I've been working on for weeks, calling to invite CEOs and executives of major defense and technology companies in the area. Talking fast, I leave a message. "Hi, Tone. I was hoping to catch you in person to remind you about setting up Summer's humidifier before bedtime. All you need to do is rinse and refill the tank. It's been running on the high setting all week and seems to be helping her throat. Or maybe it's because I swapped out her pillow, just in case she was allergic to the down filling. Who the heck knows? In any case, I'm waiting to hear back from the specialist about checking her adenoids. She can't get sick right now, and neither of us can be out of work, so anything you can do to help would be great. I'm heading in, so I'll see you later. Figures I don't have an umbrella and it's a complete downpour. Anyway, have a good night and give her a hug from me, please."

Sprinting from the car to avoid getting soaked, I realize that these same people who I'm trying to politely dodge and skirt around are the ones I'll be chatting up in minutes. Shaking the drops off my tan business raincoat and straightening my suit jacket in the foyer, I hear the muffled sound of my phone ringing in my pocketbook and fish it out. The glow of the screen blinks—"Home." *Tony must be returning my call.* "Hi," I answer softly, mirroring the hushed vibe of the historic building.

"Sa, I can barely hear you. I'm calling you back."

The slowpokes I ran past outside are filtering in, wiping off the rain and glancing my way.

Great, I'm the less-than-ladylike runner in the rain who's now rudely on a cell phone. I try smiling what I hope will come across as friendly and apologetic. The thing is, I know well the power of first impressions. I turn and walk casually down a long offshoot hall where I face a wall of black-and-white portraits depicting proud and stodgy patrons, all of whose legendary status is lost on me, and hiss into the phone. "Did you bother listening to my *message*? I'm at the event now!"

"No, I didn't yet. I figured I would just call back to talk. Why are we whispering?"

"It's not funny! I can't talk. Can you please listen to my message?"

"Yeah, sure, but I thought you might like to know a doctor's office called and left a message saying they can see Summer tomorrow afternoon."

"Tomorrow?"

"I guess they had a cancellation. They want you to call first thing in the morning to let them know either way."

"Tomorrow I'm going to have all of the follow-up from this event, not to mention another appointment for Dad's denture-fitting. Maybe I can ask Colette to take him."

"I can't stay home either, Sa. There's a Licensee meeting that I can't miss. In fact, yesterday—"

"I'm not doing this right now, Tony. Our daughter sounds like she has marbles in her throat, so one of us has to find time!"

Spotting other people from my department, I can see that everyone has his or her game face on, welcoming attendees with a charming smile and drink in hand.

"Gotta go, Tone. I'll figure something out." Smoothing the front of my suit jacket and securing my name badge on my lapel, I take a deep breath before joining the mingling crowd.

It doesn't take long to change gears, networking and making introductions between top faculty gurus and industry giants. Finding common ground in this preliminary phase means simply beginning dialogues to define the issues. It's all very interesting even though, at times, the vernacular is over my head. During breaks in dinner conversation, my mind naturally wanders to tomorrow's challenge of being in three places at the same time. *I hope Tony remembers to set up Summer's humidifier. She can't get sick again. I can't miss work.* Sip, sip, chitchat, chitchat.

My days and nights are turning into endless checklists to get through. I'm not really living. The feeling of accomplishment and the endorphin rush that's supposed to accompany the checkmark of a task completed never come. Instead, I feel as if a tidal wave is building.

Most days I have a reserve of adrenaline to fuel my to-do list, moving in high-speed and wondering, *Why does everyone drive so slow?* Followed by the occasional days when I crash. On those days, I'm supersensitive and tired beyond belief. At work, I tread on tenuous ground. I'm fine as long as I stay on work-related topics, but it's like a switch—as soon as my thoughts or conversation turn personal, I get a lump in my throat and fight the urge to cry. Even though my immediate concern is for my father and my family, memories of my sister's final days randomly come to mind—for example, the image of her lying under the crisp white sheets in the hospice bed with her skeletal body and gaunt face, her head tipped back and her mouth open, like a robin nestling waiting to be fed. It catches me off-guard these days, months after her death. Maybe it's just the exhaustion, or maybe it's a natural part of the grieving process, but it didn't affect me as much at the time, standing by her bed, squeezing her hand as she passed away. Now I dissolve and crumble at the most unexpected times. It's like I have a hidden scar. *My sister is gone.*

And gone are the days of merrily cooking up a storm. Instead, various takeout options come to mind on my way home from work, when I review what we've already had that week. I weigh the health benefits of pizza over a Happy Meal and McDonald's over Wendy's, as if thinking about it will compensate for the nutrition shortcoming. The convenience factor of Ted's Pizza drive-through, now on speed dial, wins out most of the time.

Inevitably, my pace is slowing and becoming more deliberate, like a metronome. A simple mantra of "Just be there for family" plays incessantly in the back of my mind, ordering one foot in front of the other. That's sometimes how I get through the day, consciously telling myself to keep going. Forcing it. I try to see the humor in it and call some activities my own personal "Get up, Trinity" moments, alluding to the *Matrix* movies, except that *she's* running to escape cyber agents whereas I'm running to fix myself another cup of desperately needed coffee.

I'm not okay and I can feel it. Especially when I wake up in the morning, I feel heavy. Not the forty-pounds-overweight heavy—that, too—but I mean soul heavy. Something is lost—my joy, my feeling of being in control and excited for the day. I feel as if I'm aging exponentially. I've never been this unhealthy, and it doesn't help that I stay up late to try to erase the stress of the day, eating anything in sight, having a glass or two of wine and watching late-night TV. I'm stuck in this routine and look forward to those few hours spent wrapped securely in our tan micro-fleece blanket on the leather recliner. I need the time alone. When I finally head upstairs, I collapse into bed and pray that I'll sleep through the night—not be awakened by Summer's recounting of a bad dream or, worse, my own ridiculous, worried thoughts.

I suppose when you're in really good shape, you can tell when you're not feeling great. Your energy is off and you're less likely to do that little hop when you click heels together like a leprechaun. When you're run-down, every day is another day of weariness, and it's hard to tell when you become really, really run-down. But our bodies, thank God, have this way of sounding the alarm to finally get our attention. For me, it begins as a heavy period, as in menstruation. No big surprise there, just another thing to ignore, like the fact that I need to take about a dozen steps when I first get out of bed, before my feet stop hurting and I can fully straighten up. I see myself in the mirror, leaning on the bathroom counter, with my left forearm and hand flat to stay steady while I brush my teeth, as if I were hung over, or on a cruise ship experiencing extremely choppy conditions. Seeing my reflection and chronic slouching posture, I consciously remind myself to try to stand up straight.

The bleeding continues. To the point where I'm annoyed and *have* to notice. Not to be gross, but the enormity of some of the clots is something I'd never seen. These are primal, meaty Rorschach ink blots of blood. Sitting on the toilet, changing into a fresh clean pad, I rip the soiled one from my underwear and call out "Look, honey, you gotta see this one. It's like a little pony!"

"You gotta call the doctor, Sa," Tony says, recoiling. "That's not normal."

I take to using the super-duper, extra-long, mattress-size pads, and stash plenty in my purse so that I can change "the situation" when I'm at work. As luck would have it, though, even super-duper absorbency can fail.

"Can you believe this, Bethany?" I say, standing in my colleague's office doorway with my old-standby office sweater tied around my waist. It's basic black and comes in handy in a pinch. "I'm living out every schoolgirl's worst fear that you'll get your period and stain your pants. I need to run home and change, but I'll be back."

"At least it's not during gym class," Bethany says. "We can be thankful they haven't made us climb the ropes yet."

"Although that wouldn't be a surprise. Can't you picture that as our next team-building event?"

We laugh.

"Seriously, though, have you called your OB/GYN? Is this normal for you?"

"I did call a few days ago. Apparently, anything goes at this stage in life, and chances are it will correct itself. The nurse practitioner said it was common in premenopause and something about a woman's forties being a time of trial and great upheaval. At least that's what I heard. I'm going to call again though and ask to be seen. I know something's not right."

"Good. You *should* call, and make sure they do blood work, too. In the meantime, you'd better not let your great upheaval cause you to miss our afternoon staff meeting. I'm hearing there's an announcement to be made."

"Oh? No one would miss me anyway, but I'll be back in time."

After the mad dash home—about thirty minutes door to door—I am indeed back in time for the meeting. As it turns out, there's no announcement. Too bad—it would have been nice to have a juicy bit of news to infuse excitement into the rest of the day. I feel so weak, sometimes even lightheaded if I stand up too fast. I add an extra cup to my usual afternoon coffee crutch to get me through, but caffeine never seems to help much anymore.

A week later, heavy periods become the norm, and the exam and blood work show that I'm anemic. The doctor prescribes multivitamins and iron pills, but because things aren't likely to correct any time soon, I insist on a D&C (dilation and curettage) to assess and clean out "the situation" once and for all.

The day after the procedure, Bethany is nice enough to swing by my office to see how I am.

"It sounds pathetic, but it all seemed like a day at the spa," I confide. "Not at all what I expected. It was pampering, rest, and relaxation. Tony took the day off to drive me, and you should have seen how nice he was, with concerned eyes and opening doors. The nurses were so kind, all dolled up in those colored scrubs attending to me, asking, 'Would you like another heated blanket while you wait for the doctor to come in?'"

"Wow, that does sound nice." Bethany seems to be holding back laughter. "But it's not like any of the spas I've been to. I usually just get a facial and they clean out my pores, not my—" She's laughing so hard she can't finish the sentence.

It does seem funny, and I know she's not being insensitive. She is one of the few people who are fully aware of my double-duty lifestyle, Bethany has seen me fight the urge to bawl on many occasions in her office.

"And after the procedure, it was more of the same," I say. "More heated blankets, kindness, and compassion, but with drugs"—I make air quotes—"to ease the discomfort and allow me to rest. Imagine that—permission to rest!"

Still recovering from her fit of laughter, she wipes her eyes. "Did they find anything that would cause the bleeding?"

"That's the weird thing. I was almost hoping that they would, so it wouldn't seem like I'm a big baby, but there was nothing conclusive. I think the doctor called it menorrhagia. Anyway, the solution that she proposed, and I accepted, was birth control pills to help regulate and reestablish a normal cycle. An added benny when you're on the pill is that periods are much lighter and shorter in length."

"So that's that? Just another day in the life?"

"What do you mean?"

"Should you even be here today?"

"Oh, the doctor suggested I take a day or two to recoup, but aside from being a little sore, it's not worth the worry of not doing what I have to do."

And, yes, that's that. Rather than taking the time to reflect and recover, the day after the procedure, I go back to work. As usual,

I fetch Summer afterward and stop in to visit with Dad. Back on track and didn't miss a beat.

Actually, I'm making light to avoid a little of the reliving. The truth is that I've never been so physically weak in my life. And that's saying something, having been through several health scares, including an emergency appendectomy, a battle with campylobacter (compliments of a business trip to Thailand), severe gallbladder attacks that went undiagnosed during nine months of pregnancy, and removal of said gallbladder a week after giving birth via—no surprise—a C-section!

Even though there was no medical reason for the bleeding, I know it was caused by extreme chronic stress. The same stress that compelled me to go back to work the very next day. The stress of having bills to pay, a professional persona to maintain, a husband and daughter content and wearing clean clothes and serving as your father's keeper. The enormity of the self-imposed psychological weight I was carrying had already presented in many physical ways, and hemorrhage-level bleeding was just the icing on the cake. It had been foreshadowed by months' worth of other bodily ailments and annoyances, like overnight teeth-clenching and a misaligned spine, and varying degrees of fatigue and insomnia that contributed to daily digestive tract issues. And my coping mechanisms left a lot to be desired. The pounds went on from the late-night eating, the alcohol, the fast food, and the lack of sleep. Also affected was—you guessed it—my hair. It went from gray-streaked to pure white in the dreaded, most noticeable way—framing my face.

I can imagine the "tsk, tsk" of readers who will call me out for whining. "It's your own damn fault," they'll say, and they're right. Intellectually, I completely understand how ludicrous it is to allow your health to suffer. But when you find yourself in a family caregiving role, while already working full-time in a highly visible, pressure-filled position, caring for your family *and* your parent, self-sacrifice kind of sneaks up on you. You think you can handle it, telling yourself, *Toughen up and get through the day—the next will be better.* I know the adage that "no one can help when you can't help yourself," but when you're in it, judgment is clouded. That's what it comes down to—your judgment just gets clouded.

> *For God is not the author of confusion, but of peace.*
> 1 Corinthians 14:33

Heart to Heart

12

March 2012

To: Pat@verizon.com;FLWill@hotmail.com;Col@gmail.com

From: S.Persiani@university.edu

Date: March 22, 2012 8:45AM

Subject: Reminder-Dad's Status mtg. w/ Pinnacle

Good Morning my dear siblings,

I hope your day is off to a good start. Just a quick reminder—we have the meeting this afternoon with Dad's medical team at Pinnacle (4:00 at the Grafton St. facility). I scheduled it at the end of the day, so hopefully leaving work a little early won't be a problem. Have a good one and see you soon. Love, Sa

I hit "Send" and head down the office hallway to the kitchen to pour my first cup of the day. Getting that email out first thing was top of mind on my ride in, knowing that if I didn't, I'd run the risk of getting distracted and forgetting. I'm deep in thought as the Flavia machine takes its good old time making my espresso roast. *Thank goodness Joy can get Summer off the bus today. I should bake banana bread or something for her tomorrow. Oh, there's that sales process meeting tomorrow. I need to spend time today to prep my portion of the flow chart.*

"I'm sorry, what?" I say, noticing Bethany waiting politely for her turn to get coffee.

She laughs. "I said, should we try and head out for lunch today? Maybe a little change of scenery?"

"Hmm, can I let you know later? I want to, but I shouldn't, you know? I might just eat at my desk. If I do, maybe we could run across the street together to grab sandwiches and bring them back?"

"Sure, that would be fine, too. Let's play it by ear," she says warmly. She's always a shoulder, propping me back up and into action with her dry sense of humor and stories about raising three boys. We've had the best laughs swapping stories about our kids, whether concerning vacation antics, infatuated, preteen texting gone wrong, or the overenthusiastic kookaburra in a school play.

As I head out of the kitchen with my mug in one hand and a stale muffin in the other, left over from an open house the night before, she adds with smiling eyes, "Hey, S. B., it's no big deal and maybe even something you planned, but check your pretty sweater when you get back to your office. It looks like you might be rockin' the 1980s asymmetrical style." Sure enough, as I walk back down the hall and look down, my cardigan buttons aren't aligned. Not just one but two buttons are misaligned in my "it's all about comfort," eggplant-plum, Lands' End sweater set.

It's official: I'm losing my mind. *Ugh, I hope no one else noticed.* I cringe at the possibility, but I work through it quickly. *Oh well, at least Summer looked like a doll for school.* I set my sights on the calls I plan to make.

Buttoned up, the rest of the workday passes in a blur, and at 3:58 p.m. I rush into the Pinnacle lobby to find Pat and Will already waiting in the stylish wingback chairs. Pat is still dressed in her scrubs, having just come from her job in the UMass Lab, and I can tell Will must have been at work, too, because he's dressed in jeans but in more layers than the average New Englander, especially for this unusually warm winter. He took a part-time gig at a seafood distributor just down the street from Dad's house and spends most of the time in cold storage. An ironic choice for a guy from sunny Florida.

"Hey, hi. Has anyone heard from Colette?" I ask, out of breath.

"Does she know about the meeting?" Pat says.

"Well, yeah, she was included in the same email that I sent both of you."

"She can't come," Will says flatly, and does that thing he does to clear his throat.

"Why's *that*?" Why do I have to ask?

"Dunno. She told me, but I don't remember."

Pat and I shake our heads and *tsk* at the same time.

Just then we're greeted by Julie, Dad's case manager and social worker. "Well, look who's here!" she says, smiling broadly and looking past us.

We all turn to see Tony, rushing in with his face flushed from his mad dash to join us. We're all glad to see him, but none more than me because I know the effort it took for him to get here from his office in Pawtucket, Rhode Island. Plus, he tends to lighten the mood among us siblings with his knack for puns and his readiness with a sports score.

"The meeting may now commence," he says, clapping twice in what I know is his Yul Brynner "I am Ramses" impression, making us all laugh instantly.

We file into the pleasant conference room for the adult day program that Dad attends three days a week. It's on the opposite side of the building from where he spends most of his time in the nicely decorated activity rooms and the large dining area lined with windows. I'm pleasantly surprised to see his entire team seated on one side of the long oval table: the nurse practitioner, his physical therapist, his occupational therapist, his caseworker, and his kind geriatric doctor, Dr. Schafer, at the head. I'm used to interacting with them individually, so seeing them all together in this way feels daunting and official. They're ready to give a full account of our father's status from an objective, clinical perspective, and though I'm smiling politely, my stomach constricts in worry. *This is really happening. Please don't let them have bad news.*

They begin with friendly banter. There's no doubt the team has done this before, probably hundreds of times with families in similar situations, so they know how unnerving it can be. Emily-Anne, the petite, friendly nurse practitioner, shares a quick anecdote about our father's flirty wit.

"Your dad was here for his regular scheduled day earlier this week and I changed his bandages on his shins. I always ask first if it's okay to take a look at his legs, and without missing a beat, he said, 'You bet. I'll show you mine if you show me yours.'"

We all laugh, well knowing that side of him. A side that during the course of our childhood could be either awkward or inappropriate from our point of view. He would chat up everyone from waitresses to schoolteachers to checkout clerks. But it's harmless and part of his very essence. We all know he loves the ladies. With a twinkle in his eye, he's either a charmer or a dirty old man, depending on how you want to look at it.

It crosses my mind that we're lucky to have this bighearted team of health-care providers who take time to know the person, not just the patient. They know his eccentricities and have witnessed firsthand his charm and his exceptional love of Mrs. Dash.

Then it's time to get down to business.

"Your father is very ill," Dr. Schafer says.

You can feel the mood shift in the room. It's suddenly very quiet, and the air stills as we brace ourselves. A manila folder is open in front of her.

"His physical body shows every indication of kidney failure, as is typical with long-term use of ACE inhibitors (blood-pressure medicine)." She explains in layman's terms how the kidneys are crucial to removing waste products, and help balance water, salt, and other minerals in the blood. "When kidneys stop working, waste products, fluids, and electrolytes build up in your body and pose quite a risk. It will be only a matter of time before he will be sleeping more and eating less."

Until she explains it, I hadn't been aware how even the simple pleasure of eating is a chore for congestive heart failure patients, as the motion of chewing and breathing concurrently is a complex function. A minor detail that healthy people take for granted is an exhausting hurdle for CHF patients.

"He will become unable to ambulate on his own and will likely need a two-person assist to lift and get out of bed, to toilet and bathe."

Dr. Schafer paces the discussion slowly, allowing us time to process the information. Her words are thoughtful and deliberate as she continues to lay out his prognosis and the decisions to be made.

"Creatinine has been found to be a fairly reliable indicator of kidney function. The creatinine levels in both urine and blood are determined and compared. Elevated creatinine level signifies impaired kidney function. Based on his low blood count and kidney functions, he is a candidate for a blood transfusion and dialysis." She thoroughly explains the process, benefits, and risks associated if we decide to go in this direction. "We feel that he is of sound mind to make his own decision and want to talk with all of you about that step. We can have the conversation together with him, or you can talk privately with him as a family."

After we all weigh in with ways it could play out, we decide it should come from me, as the health-care proxy. And so as not to put him on the spot, we'll have the conversation at home rather than during his visit to Pinnacle. I'm not at all sure how to have the conversation and wonder if Colette will be able to help.

Next we hear brief status reports from the physical and occupational therapists that concur that Dad is slipping on all fronts. "Our functional assessment notes several impairments from when he began in our program just a few months ago," the physical therapist reports. She goes on to share observations of his declining ability to overcome physical constraints (such as doors and stairs), using measures of mobility expressed in clinical terms of basic activities of daily living (ADLs) and "functional independence measure" (FIM). "He loses balance and fatigues more easily but has such determination to push through and try to show us that he can perform the activities."

I chime in to add that he's not well-rested. *Like me but for different reasons.* "He's up every few hours to go to the bathroom because of his current 80 mg Lasix dosage."

We talk about ways to try and manage his bladder urge reflex and are assured that we'll continue to have the supplies we need, such as bed liners and the higher commode that we use by his bedside. He's already stopped wearing his usual button-down pants in favor of elastic-band sweatpants, which are easier to pull up and down. Will doesn't say anything, but I know he's far from well-rested, too. In dealing with Dad's incontinence and occasional dementia behavior, he's learned how to manage it with various reassurances and uses short, simple instructions to help him navigate to the bathroom.

At this point the team stops and asks if we have questions. The clock ticks audibly for a few seconds that feel much longer. Patricia is the one to voice the question on all our minds.

"With someone at this stage of decline, can you tell how long he has?"

For the first time during the meeting, I notice that my brother's normally straight and composed posture is slumped, and I'm surprised to see how much this is affecting him. Tony slides a box of tissues toward Will and takes one for himself. I know this is hitting close to home for Tony, as his own father died just nine months before from the same disease, the day after Father's Day. He and his sisters had to make the gut-wrenching decision about pulling life support when their dad's lung capacity diminished beyond repair. Carmine was no longer able to breathe on his own. It was both heartbreaking and a blessing that they were all at his bedside when he passed. When our eyes meet, I know that's the scene playing out in his mind.

We reach for each other under the table and he gives my hand a squeeze. There's nothing worse than seeing my strong, capable husband cry, and I feel the sting of tears as well. I don't even try to hold them back and accidentally let one of those stupid snorting sounds escape. We all laugh, breaking the tension.

"Ya know, he would love that you're all crying over him," Emily-Anne says.

We laugh harder, knowing that he would. We hand tissues to each other and console with arm rubs and half smiles through teary eyes. Pat's not crying, but she has that type of highly sensitive skin that gives her emotions away. Her face and neck are blotchy red. It's obvious that she's on the hairy edge with the rest of us, but I'm awed by her strength, my sister who has endured the greatest loss of all: her beautiful, gentle son. Our Jared, gone so young in a freak skiing accident, and now he's forever young and beautiful in our memories. It seems fitting that she, the eldest, voiced the hardest question.

Dr. Schafer gives the only answer possible. "It's hard to know, but anywhere from six months to a year is reasonable."

We pass the tissues again and this time a couple of people from his team join in.

Eventually, Julie facilitates the close of the meeting. "As you know, it's our philosophy to help you keep your dad at home for as long as possible. But when the time comes, you may need to consider moving him to a nursing facility. We have several area nursing homes in our network, so we can continue to offer treatment and support."

We all agree that Dad has become accustomed to his familiar team and that we don't want to lose consistency of care. Dr. Schafer reminds us that she'll want to hear back in the next couple of days about his decision on dialysis, and I nod. Still quiet, Will takes the nursing home list awkwardly from Julie, and the meeting ends with hugs and assurance that the team will be there with us until the end.

Pat, Will, Tony, and I gather in the parking lot before getting into our cars, and it's a different scene from the one after the meeting with the lawyer a few months earlier. There's no hostility or apathy. In this together now, we talk easily and breathe a collective sigh of relief at being in the crisp evening air. I'm quiet, though, thinking of the best way to have the talk with Dad. Tony picks up on it.

"He's not going anywhere any time soon, Sa," he says. "And whatever his decision is, that's what we'll do."

"That's right," Pat says. "Remember the tough stock that we're made of. Just look at Lou-lou as a good example. She beat doctors' projections by far." She laughs. "We're the lingerers."

"At least you're not the Langoliers," Tony says, referring to a Stephen King movie about monsters who eat everything, including time. I think I'm the only one who gets it, but the others chuckle anyway, appreciating his effort to lighten the mood.

Later I call Colette to ask if she'll help with the conversation with Dad. I fill her in on the meeting, and even though I don't use the clinical language, she seems to understand the depth and meaning of the discussion as well as the consequences of dialysis.

"Sure, I'll meet you there tomorrow at noon," she says. "Can you get away from the office for lunch?"

"Yeah, I have to, but I'm not sure I'll be able to actually eat. Thanks for your help with this. See you soon."

I wake up several times in the night with the kidney conversation on my mind. Knowing how the loss of his driver's license changed him, I'm worried that this will do more of the same. Another chip away from who he used to be. More proof of age beckoning.

Using ingrained presentation skills training 101, I try to simply visualize the conversation. I try to convince myself that this will be even easier because it's family and I can just read the medical terms and figures from my notes. Falling asleep, I remind myself *not to forget my notes. . . .*

As Dad and I sit at his dining room table, Colette brings in tea and doughnuts. She has a knack for making the mundane lovely. Whereas I would use paper plates for quick cleanup and rinse a mug already in the sink, she pulls out the blue-and-white, porcelain miniplates and matching tea cups. I pass on her offerings, my stomach in a knot with the familiar initial stir of indigestion.

Trying to be casual, I recap the meeting with his team. "You know, your team really likes you, Dad. You should hear how much they enjoy your sense of humor and notice how much you put into the physical therapy."

I have my notes with the lab results Dr. Schafer gave me so I can provide details that he'll want. I use them as a crutch, continually glancing at the day planner open in front of me. I keep talking, not able to look at him directly, praying I don't lose it and cry.

"So, it seems that your body is doing all it can to keep flushing your system of the water and the medication. But it's taking a toll on your kidneys. The latest lab results show that your creatinine ratio is 3.7 and a month ago it was 2.4. They gave another figure called your BUN level, which stands for blood urea nitrogen, it's another indicator of kidney function. . . ." Finally looking up from my notes, my voice trails off. Based on his blank expression, I can see there's no need to continue to rattle off figures in decline. I pause to give him a chance to take it in. Apparently very taken with their doughnuts, he and Colette continue chewing quietly. It doesn't help my nerves in the least, but I continue anyway.

"A suggestion that they have is for a transfusion and dialysis."

"It would mean you have a stent, Dad," Colette says matter-of-factly and resumes chewing.

He finishes a sip of tea and clears his throat. "Naw, that's okay, girls. I know what it would take to have a stent and the schedule of appointments. That's not what I want to do."

"Are you sure, Dad? Don't you at least want to try?" I ask, my voice breaking. Perhaps he's already come to terms with how he wants to live his final days, but I haven't, and I want him to fight. I'm fairly sure this is the first time he's hearing that his internal organs are failing and yet he's made the decision, definitively and without a second thought, not to undergo the transfusion and the tedium of dialysis.

This life-and-death discussion over doughnuts is too much for me and I begin to cry. I completely lose my ability to speak. Thank God my sister doesn't. For all the times when I thought she's sounded phony and superior with her medical jargon, she shines in this moment. Casually picking at her doughnut, she directs the most difficult conversation of my life. She restates the options a few times, in different ways and varying the scenarios, to be sure he knows the consequences, allowing him to change his mind if necessary. He doesn't.

I'm not sure how I look when I return to the office, but I do know the adrenaline surge that carried me through the conversation has passed and, with shaky legs, I need to sit. Weak from crying and not eating, I have no energy left and still no desire to eat. The weight of his decision is unbearable. Knocked down, I retreat to my desk to try to work.

Over the next few days, with coaxing and hand-holding from my brother, we begin touring the nursing homes in the Pinnacle network. I like the one nearest to my home even though it doesn't have bells and whistles. A fancy foyer and marble stairs aren't what matter to me. I want him as close as possible and envision making evening visits after Summer is in bed.

> *Fear not, for I am with you; Be not dismayed, for I am*
> *your God. I will strengthen you, Yes, I will help you,*
> *I will uphold you with My righteous right hand.*
> Isaiah 41:10

Just Breathe

13

Early April 2012

Ideal workdays are when I have a client meeting off-site or a networking event, and as luck would have it, today I'm attending a two-day information technology conference in Boston called Health IT Insight, which is targeted at CIOs in New England. The morning scramble is underway with the typical banter.

"Can you put my hair in a high pony but with no bumps?" Summer yells down the hall. "You know I hate when you make bumps!"

"You can always start trying to do it yourself if you don't like my way!" I holler back. *She's far more fashion-savvy than any first-grader I've ever met.*

In bra, camisole, and undies, I'm standing in the opening between the bifold, bedroom closet doors, scanning the mix of clothes that hang color-coded from dark to light. My overall organization around the house is slipping, but this is the one area that I still have under control. It's essential—organization speeds efficiency, and I have to be focused. There's no time to dawdle or mull. In a matter of seconds, I decide on the black suit, mindlessly pull on the teal mock-neck sweater, and step into the pants. In the background, the weatherman confirms my choice as sufficient.

"Mostly sunny and breezy with a high of forty-four today. Winds remain from the north-northwest, and expect gusts of up to thirty-five miles per hour. You may want to bring any potted plants inside or protect them with plastic."

Plants? That's one more thing to do—water the plants. As I reach into the back corner of the closet for my knee-high black leather boots, it occurs to me how much I love these boots. They somehow infuse strength, power, and confidence, and these days I'll take any help I can get. I don't even care that they're dated. Everyone but me is in stilettos these days. I had the chunky square heels reglued at Carbonneau's last winter because it seemed easier than taking the time to shop. I used to be at least somewhat stylish, but now I'm glad if it's comfortable and clean.

"... as there is a chance of a hard freeze tonight, with wind-chill temps in the single digits at times."

Forget outdoor plants—how long has it been since I've watered the indoor plants? I add it to my mental checklist, along with a note to add some egg shells and coffee grounds to the watering can like our grandmother, Ma, used to do.

As I back out of the closet in the hunched position necessary for the slanted dormer, Summer and I collide. Stunned, we stop in our tracks and stare at each other. This could easily go south and we'll both end up crying and ranting, but amazingly enough, we don't scream "Owww" or, in my case, spew (and then try to retract) the curse that's imminent on my pursed lips.

Summer just rubs her shoulder. "Sorry, Mom."

I toss the boots onto the bed and hug her longer than I should. Harder, too, as if I'm trying to pour in my apology for all these crazy, rushed mornings, for all the times I've coerced her into going to school on days when I knew she'd be better off resting at home, for every time I've screamed for her to *Hurry up!*" so I wouldn't be late (or, actually *later*) to work. I feel her little body squirm, signaling it's time to release and reminding me that it's okay, that I'm just wound a little too tight.

She hands me the brush and a purple, elastic hair band. Biting my lip and holding my breath, I do my best to style the most amazing high-pony do in her first-grade class.

I thank my lucky stars as I drive into Boston for what's shaping up to be an easy commute. Traffic is moving on the Mass Pike and I'm past the dreaded slow spot near Exit 13 in Natick. From Worcester to Boston, it's about forty-five minutes, and I'm on track to arrive in under an hour. Granted, I'm on the road early enough to miss the heavy traffic, and that reminds me: I need to pick up something special to thank Joy, our neighbor, for allowing us the occasional early morning drop-off. *What would I do without Joy?* It's such a help to have someone put my daughter on the bus when I have these morning networking events.

As I enter the illustrious Harvard Club, I'm comfortable and looking forward to learning the challenges of the industry, getting familiar with the lingo, checking out the players, and networking, all with the goal of assessing how the university can support this space. I've attended so many of these venues that I have no nerves or trepidation about being here even though health-care topics, per se, are new to me. One of the things I enjoy most about this position is the exposure to so many diverse industries.

I admit to having felt proud and superior a few years back when I would pick up Summer from preschool at our local Montessori, yawning at seeing the stay-at-homes picking up their kids after having just come from a workout, still sporting their yoga pants and toting fashionable water bottles. *Can't they go a few minutes without a sip of water? And, what's up with the same shorter-in-the-back bob style on almost everyone?* In contrast, my day would have consisted of meeting with people ranging from, say, a chief engineer at the Naval Undersea Warfare Center to a senior VP at UMass Memorial Hospital, or attending an event sponsored by the Massachusetts High Technology Council, conversing with the who's who at both established multinational companies and up-and-coming hotshot start-ups. How smug and self-important to have had that mind-set when, in fact, the benefits of healthy living and the joy of attentive, focused parenting weren't lost on me, just swallowed and pushed to the side in my delusional quest to have it all.

As I sip coffee from the gold-rimmed porcelain china, I scan the room to decide which table round looks most promising. I've done my homework in preparation for the event by placing an advertisement in the program flyer, which is riddled with sponsors' colorful corporate logos. The purchase of an ad to promote upcoming health-care-related, graduate-level courses not only provides context for why a university representative such as myself is among the esteemed IT practitioners on hand, but also allows access to the list of registered attendees. It's a common practice in most industries—the event host secures revenue and vendors get the dual benefits of advertising exposure *and* a tangible list for preevent perusal and follow-up purposes.

In short, I now have a roster of attendee names, titles, and companies, so I can easily navigate the crowd to make introductions. As at so many other events I've attended, I'll direct conversations that will allow me to assess interest in on-site graduate programs and partnership potential. Similar to the color-coded wardrobe, the list is another means of achieving efficiency and maximizing time.

As the agenda gets underway, I'm delighted to find that the speakers and panel discussions are relatively interesting. They speak primarily in the context of business (benefits and challenges) and secondarily in a tech-insider context. The speakers frame the discussion in terms of impact on patients and hospital bottom lines and touch on a slew of possible technological solutions. For the IT attendees at this event, an ideal world would use technology to simplify the workload of inundated medical professionals. Technology enables physicians to see more patients per hour. Technology enables better insights and minimizes unnecessary tests. Technology helps to itemize fees so that everyone can make sense of it all!

With every euphoric possibility of IT as the answer comes the downside and reality of the complexities of health care today. Many discussions underscore confusion and unanswered questions about storing and sharing medical data, questions such as who owns or is ultimately responsible for the patient's medical records. The patient? The hospital? In these times when identity theft and individuals' right to privacy are leading issues, what are the risks involved when lab results or someone's surgical and prescription history end up in the wrong hands?

As you'd expect from an IT event, the focus is on understanding issues from a systemic perspective. One speaker in particular, Dr. Martin Kohn, chief medical scientist with Care Delivery Systems at IBM Research, speaks to the fact that it's not just about reliance on technology. *Wait, what?* I think after several presentations of hard-core technology fist pumping. *Who let this guy in?*

He goes on to explain how Watson, the supercomputer that played on *Jeopardy*, was programmed to gain intelligence. He explains how Watson could be used for greater good than entertaining families with trivia game shows, could use data to predict who may be at risk for diabetes, or strokes. That said, he shares an abundance of statistical evidence to illustrate how other countries have it figured out. Apparently, the goal should be to keep people in their home, healthy and active, and penalize hospitals whenever patients have to be readmitted. *Ha, imagine that!*

We are all "agents of change in health care. . . . Change will not be precipitated by technology," he says.

Ahh, now that makes sense, but what about elderly people with congestive heart failure?

As the day progresses, I find that I'm relating to the information from an increasingly personal perspective. If I understand Dr. Kohn's message correctly, he's saying that truly transformative change comes from people—caring, kindhearted people like those who breeze in the side door of my childhood home to take my father's blood pressure and expertly change the leg bandages on the open wounds of his shins.

Somewhere on this spectrum of health-care topics, with privacy and innovation at either end, lie people like my father. Real people in need of personalized care.

I continue to listen to planned innovations of virtual doctor visits and dial-in medical stats—that "with the ease of making a phone call, you could send blood-pressure figures and pulse ox, easing the burden on medical professionals treating vast numbers of elderly people." But it all seems so clinical and removed from the reality that I know. I try to envision the team of HHAs who helped my dad or, for that matter, my sisters and myself figuring out the complexities of a remote home-health system as a replacement for in-person health care.

I smile, eat the fancy lunch, make small talk, shake hands, and otherwise network, but I don't really engage, and I certainly don't voice questions or opinions during the Q&A sessions as I normally would. I have a lump in my throat and know that my voice, my professional façade, would break. I keep thinking of Dad in his living room recliner, with all of us revolving around him, trying to keep him comfortable and in his own home in spite of the mounting challenges. The reality is that he's losing his balance more often, winded and dizzy from breathing difficulty, and his leg wounds aren't healing well or fast enough. While I look forward to the innovations and medical promises of tomorrow, on this particular windy day in April, I'm not able to detach from my own personal, tangible experience.

Normally charged and motivated after networking events, this time I drive home in tears.

I could recount many morning-rush scenarios and days at work that don't end in tears, but who am I kidding? Many *do* end in tears. And the absolute worst days are when I'm too tired to cry, just weary and mentally flat, without the capacity for any kind of release. It's an understatement to say this is a stressful time. These are days spent in constant motion, highly scheduled. Once I'm out of the house and at work, at least things settle into a predictable routine. Thank heavens for polite colleague interactions and the organized construct of the workplace.

The real work—mental, physical, and emotional—begins when I leave the office, hauling my daughter, my munchkin, around to check in on Dad or run errands to pick up his prescriptions, adult incontinence products (I should buy stock in Depends), and a surprise treat when she'd much rather be home playing after her long day at school. I get that. I want that too. But I also want her to have empathy and understanding beyond her seven years. A driver's license wouldn't hurt either. As it is, I hold open the backseat door while she hops out. As we walk across the parking lot toward the Rite-Aid where my father's laundry list of medications awaits, she realizes where this is all leading: to the intended "quick stop" at Grampa's house.

"Why do we *always* have to visit Grampa?" she whines. "I don't like how it smells, and the dogs jump on me!"

"Summer, stop the baloney. We're going and that's that. It'll be a quick visit anyway. Do you have a book or homework?" I try to sound as matter-of-fact as possible, hoping my conversational manner will somehow diffuse this familiar scene that usually escalates to yelling, or worse, crying by at least one of us. Something is different this time, though.

"No, we don't have homework tonight," she says quietly. "And you always say it will be quick and it never is."

I register the resigned tone and have no words. Constant is this feeling of being squeezed and conflicted. Of wishing I had more time to spend with my immediate family but knowing how essential it is to be there for my father. He's failing, and these are numbered, precious days. In some strange way, I'm tuned in to his CHF, and more and more, I find that I'm unconsciously holding my breath.

Summer's tired, I'm tired, but I won't allow it to break my resolve. I keep step, holding in the tears, and a passing memory of my own childhood comes to mind. During the years when my father moonlighted with his janitorial business to make ends meet, we would help clean in office buildings, banks, and the occasional dance studio after school and on weekends. Even though my childhood self would have preferred to lounge the hours away, eating Slim Jims and Funyuns in a seventies-TV-induced coma, those everyday moments and time spent together bonded us forever. Like Summer, I did my share of complaining, but in between there were conversations about school projects, our shared interest in science-fiction stories, inventions of old, and innovations to come. I cherish those times. They were pure gold, simply because we were together.

In my mind's eye, I glimpse the motion and rhythm of his figure-eight mopping technique, and the memory provides a calming cadence to this walk across the parking lot with my daughter. For the moment, I'm able to quiet the perpetual conflict in my head, knowing that being together, even if it's a rushed errand to the pharmacy, is always what matters. I do the only thing that I know to do and reach out for Summer's hand, and without missing a step, she puts her hand in mine. I dread the day when she's "too big" to hold hands in public.

For now, it's still okay. We're okay. I exhale and remember to breathe.

You enlarged my path under me; So my feet did not slip.
2 Samuel 22:37

CRAWL

*H*ydrangeas had been a focal point in our wedding. Some brides fixate on finding the perfect dress, planning the sumptuous menu or honeymoon. I deliberated music selections for the string quartet and went overboard with flowers. The pale, oversize blossoms adorned the end of every church pew, banquet room chair, and vase in sight.

Deliberately now, I tap into cherished better days to steady my walk past desk upon desk of heartlessness.

All Fall Down

14

Late April 2012

The weekly staff meeting is breaking up and everyone is leaving the conference room in their usual style. The meeting has run over—it's a little past 11:00 a.m.—and a few people are rushing out to either make another meeting or get started on the day's work. Others are lingering to chitchat or pay compliments for well-made points. As I put away my notes and consider my action items, my thoughts are interrupted by the sound of my cell phone's ringtone in the distance. I bolt across the hall to my office and answer in time to hear the panic in my brother Will's voice. "Sarah, Dad was really bad this morning. He was on the floor beside his bed when I came downstairs."

"Is he hurt?"

"No, I helped him up, but he was really out of it. The congestion in his chest sounds so heavy. He's wheezing again and they'll probably increase his Lasix."

"Where *is he?*"

"I brought him to his day program. He was such a mess."

"*What?* Why did you bring him? Why didn't you just let him sleep? We could have asked one of the nurses to check on him this afternoon."

"Well, *you* weren't answering your phone and he needed to be seen by someone! Look, if you want to resume your sleep-shift schedule or sleep here every night, go right ahead. But I can't stay up anymore during the night, I just can't. I'm not taking the guilt trip either. He wouldn't stay in bed, and this was bound to happen."

"Hold on, Will, I need to get the other line. It's Pinnacle."

I switch to the other call.

"Hello, Sarahbeth? It's Ramona." She's one of the nurse practitioners. "Have you spoken with William today about what's going on with your father?"

"Yes, we were just on the other line. Is he all right? It sounds like he spent a portion of the night on the floor. We're not sure how long. He was probably getting up to go to the bathroom. I wish he would just stay in—"

"Honey, I think you need to come here right away."

"On my way."

I send my colleagues and management an email—I don't recall the exact wording, but I'm pretty certain it includes the bare-bones information that I have to leave, written in my rushed, panicked state. Through the entire ordeal of my father's decline, I've made the consistent mistake of trying to maintain a stoic and professional work persona. *Be the person you were when they hired you years ago, not this crumbling, anxiety-ridden, working mom,* I would think to myself. *Don't play on sympathies—hold your head high. Compartmentalize, do what needs to be done to get through the day, just to get through. . . .*

I hit "Send" and race down the stairwell to the side-door exit. All thoughts of the morning meeting and action items dissipate and are replaced by my now-familiar caregiver's anxiety. On the ride over, I think about the past few weeks that have led up to this and about Will's growing exhaustion. I don't have any right to be upset with him, but I can't help it. Why couldn't he just try my baby-monitor idea? He insists that he sleeps too deeply and won't hear it. He keeps telling me I don't understand how difficult it is to live there with my father's growing confusion. And he's right. As much as I check in, I still have the consolation of retreating to the solace of my own home, if you can call it that. Then again, even when I'm not with my dad, I can't just switch off angst, worry, and back-of-mind thoughts about him. I need to be available at all times. Even when I'm not physically with him, I have conversations about him with my sisters, my husband, my husband's sister, nurses, doctors, and bill collectors. Endless and ever-present is the feeling of a looming crisis, a tidal wave silently building.

When I *am* at my father's house, it's almost impossible to help him in the evening anymore. He's agitated, and even though we have conflicting medical reports as to whether he technically has dementia, he's demonstrating "sundowning" behavior more and more. A common symptom of dementia, sundowning is a state of confusion that occurs at the end of the day and into the night. The cause isn't known, and it prevents people from sleeping well and may cause wandering. As you might imagine, sundowning is a common cause of caregiver burnout.

Dad now argues over the most minor details. Worse, he'll become confused and occasionally panic and freeze in the middle of a routine motion—getting off the toilet, for example. My brother and I have had to talk him through it, detailing the steps of how to keep going, or in some cases to just stand there. "Just hold on to the grab bar, Dad. We've got you," we say while we maneuver around to change his Depends. Even more difficult are the motions required to change his clothes or get him into pajamas at night. It's a significant challenge for us untrained caregivers, but it's the role we play. Some nights it's exasperating and I get through it by yelling for him to do his part. But I've learned that turning up the volume doesn't help. It just makes me cry with shame afterward for losing my composure. I never imagined I would be helping in this way, so very hands-on. And all of us are doing our part. Even my husband has had sleepover shifts.

My last thought as I pull into the Pinnacle parking lot is that Dad's tiny dogs were probably lying right beside him on the floor last night. Will didn't mention it, but I know they're as protective of him as he was of them in his better days. In their own way, they've been his caregivers as well. Through all the chaos, their watchful eyes have been observing vigilantly. Max and Elsa play silent witness to all the down-on-our-knees moments.

I remind myself to breathe as I step through the automated doors into the cheerful Pinnacle lobby. I'm getting used to the transition from rushing around to making a full stop. It sounds like stating the obvious to say that everything around the elderly (time, movements, conversations) is slower, more deliberate. To be with them in their space is to leave the restless, fast-paced world I know and step into a mire of sorts. In time, I'll come to appreciate the still moments, but for now, I settle for deep, conscious breathing.

Familiar with the setup of the facility by now, I peek into a few of the exam rooms and find him resting in one of the beds. I take a seat next to Ramona, the nurse practitioner, and see right away that he's lethargic and full-on hallucinating from lack of sleep. The lights are dimmed and he's picking at the air in front of him, eyes closed.

"He's comfortable anyway," Ramona says. "He had some broth and toast when he came in, and if you want, we can try a popsicle."

I nod and raise my voice just enough so he knows it's me. "Dad, do you want something else to eat, a popsicle?"

He smiles when he hears me but keeps on picking. "Nah," he murmurs, "I'm O. . . ."

We sit there while he dozes, drifting in and out. He occasionally chuckles aloud and motions as if he's eating something. Ramona says gently, "We're arranging for a room at the nursing home that was your stated preference," carefully adding, "we should keep an eye on him for a few days and give you and Will a break."

The conversation is careful for my benefit, and I know what it means to move him into the nursing home. That familiar lump is in my throat, but I'm not going to lose it. I need to make good decisions, decisions about his health and his best interest. Obviously, he's no longer safe at home. I reason with myself that maybe it will just be for a few days. Maybe with him out of the house, we can use that time to sell some of his collections and raise enough money to pay for the round-the-clock coverage that we now desperately require.

An ambulance is arranged to transport Dad to the nursing home, and I stop at his house to gather a few of his things. While I'm there, I call Colette to give her the update and ask if she can take the dogs to her house.

"Of course," she says. "Hang in there, Sa. You're doing the right thing."

"Yep," I say brusquely and hang up more quickly than I'd meant, to quell the rising emotion.

While we'd been talking, the phone beeped to let me know I was getting another call. Will left a message saying he's already on his way to the nursing home.

In the quiet of my father's house, I take stock of the rooms. They look different without the energy of all of us coming and going, Dad the center of attention, a frail fixture in his electronic, button-controlled recliner. Though we'd bought the recliner to help him in these feeble days, it's been confusing to him no matter how often we've demonstrated it and spoken in that cloying, louder-than-necessary manner: "See Dad, you just push the button, like this!" I sometimes wondered—hoped, actually—that he was just playing a part. *How could this impostor be our dad? Once so competent and now so easily confused.*

The living room, in particular, has morphed into a hub of sorts, now the heart of the home. Resembling a makeshift hospital room, it's quite a different scene from the earlier shabby-red-couch days. There's an actual hospital bed against the wall, under the portrait painted from my mother's 1952 high school picture. Wearing pearls and a navy velvet shawl, she half-smiles down, ready to alight. The portable commode is at the end of the bed. On the opposite wall, under the picture window, is the coffee table, now serving as a holding area for bandages, Depends, bed pads, and wipes. The only "normal" living-room object on it is the TV remote. On the far wall is the oversize entertainment system wall unit, chock-full of knickknacks, his treasured pair of Asian fishermen figurines he picked up while stationed in Hong Kong, dozens of books from science fiction to herbal remedies, stacks of *Popular Science* and *Popular Mechanics* magazines, and the usually blaring TV. Most of the time, his Fox News companions are shouting in the background, but today is an exception. The TV is off and the house is eerily quiet.

His other companions are there, though, at my feet and looking at me expectantly. I squat and pat the dogs. "He's going to a place where they can help him more," I tell them quietly and wish they understood. I give them a treat and reflect on how this setup had initially been ideal for all of us, including the staff of home health aides who also kept him company here for the past year. With his failing health, it all unraveled. *At least we'd cobbled together a year of borrowed time for him to stay in his home,* I think, trying to fool myself and rationalize that we did the best we could.

I grab toiletries, pajamas, and enough clothes for a few days, and as I leave and lock the door behind me, I say a quiet prayer asking God to help me through the rest of the day.

Once again, I experience a heightened awareness as I step deliberately over the threshold into the nursing home. I can't help but notice the foreign, antiseptic smell of this unfamiliar environment. His room is on the ground floor, nearest to the nurses' station. His roommate, whose name I will later learn is Pedro, sits in his wheelchair, just outside the door. He looks vague and disinterested, and I feel vulnerable and out of place.

I've never been comfortable in medical settings. It's not for me, never has been. I never wanted to be a nurse or played doctor as a child. Even though this is far from being a hospital, it has that medicinal atmosphere. Unlike Pat and Colette, who have worked in hospitals and labs, I'm completely out of my element in a place like this. I take in so many new sights and sickly smells—dispensers of antibacterial hand sanitizer hanging outside every door, the med cart parked just behind the nurses' station, equipped with ice chips, applesauce, plastic minicups, and a medley of soft drinks to disguise and ease multiple prescriptions into the patients. It doesn't take much for me to feel queasy, and my head is already spinning.

In his room, my father lies on his side in the fetal position, still loopy and not fully asleep. He looks so old. Emily-Anne, the nurse practitioner from Pinnacle, had accompanied Will to the room to help get Dad settled and gives me a warm embrace before she leaves. I pull the covers around him and rub his shoulders. Scanning the room, I'm unsettled that it seems so small. *Why did I pick this facility? Did I make a mistake?* Nervously, I fold and stack clothes in the set of drawers on his side of the room. I keep busy, opening bathroom and closet doors to explore.

"Hey, Sa, look—they have a schedule with the activities for the residents," Will says in an obvious attempt to distract me. Even though I know it's his way of making polite conversation, I can't bring myself to join in. Sitting comfortably in the chair beside the bed, he's perusing the brochures. "They also have the menu all printed up for each day of the week. I think he's going to like some of the—"

"Oh really, isn't that *wonderful*, Will!" I burst out. "I'm sure he's going to be *thrilled* to be here for the activities and meals!"

This must be Will's lucky day, I think sarcastically. *No more night duty.*

Compounding my anger is the fact that I've yet to talk with anyone from the facility. I can see the nurses' station just outside of the room, but no one has stopped in since I've been here. "Do we know the nurse's name?" I ask. A littler louder: "Has anyone even come in since you've been here?"

He shakes his head. I can see in his countenance that he's not returning my anger. He just sits quietly in the chair and begins to thumb through the brochures again.

Just then a stone-faced nurse comes in and, without so much as a hello, introduction, or explanation, puts a syringe into Dad's mouth to knock him out! Determined to make eye contact, I step into her personal space.

"What *was* that?!"

"Morphine. Doctor's orders," she says, clearly unaffected by my emotion. "He'll sleep now." She turns casually and leaves the room.

Morphine was also the last thing administered to both my mother and my sister Louanne before they died. I learned then that it's a common end-of-life practice to help smooth cancer patients' transition from body to spirit.

Can this be happening?

Dad goes slack, and I sit slowly on the edge of his bed, dazed.

In Will's concerned expression, I see now that he's fighting his emotions. Choking up, in almost a whisper, he says, "Go home, Sa. I'll stay with him now. Everything will be all right."

During the drive home, it hits me that the dreaded day has finally come—don't need to worry anymore about how I could ever admit my father to a nursing home. It's done. As with so many others in similar situations, a simple fall was the straw that broke the camel's back and sent him there. After months of wearing his fall-monitor wristband and having practiced using it and assuring us he would use it, he didn't.

The tidal wave is crashing down around me. I can hear it and feel it. I'm dizzy as I crawl into bed. Completely drained, I fall asleep immediately. It's not an escape, though. Throughout the night, the same harsh words play over and over in my head . . . *betrayal, failure.*

> *Come to Me, all you who labor and are heavy*
> *laden, and I will give you rest.*
> Matthew 11:28

Seeking Strength

15

Early May

*I*t's a familiar stretch of road. *On my commute home, I'm in the giant bend of the I-290 off-ramp to the rebuilt section of Route 146, heading south. I notice the newly painted maroon overpass and modern streetlights. But something is wrong. I can't slow down. My car is accelerating and about to touch the bumper of the black SUV in front of me. I'm panicking, my heart racing. It's hard to breathe. I'm pressing the brake pedal, but there's no resistance. It goes straight to the floor. I swerve to miss the SUV and spot the blur of the new Walmart plaza to my right. Then I see the Olive Garden restaurant whiz by. I downshift, but it makes no difference. An automatic reflex, I pump the brakes and push down hard, but I'm still accelerating. Now I can't breathe at all. It feels like my heart will explode out of my chest. I'm straining to pull back, pulling the steering wheel and pressing my back into the seat and my head into the headrest.*

Oddly, I hear the sound of galloping hoofbeats growing louder. Thump, thump, thump. *I'm afraid to take my eyes off the road.* Thump, thump, thump. *Out of the corner of my eye, I see a brown horse running alongside, eyes wild, straining. . . .*

"Mom, can I turn on the TV in your room?"

I wake and see Summer standing beside my bed, with tousled hair. She bends in closer and asks again, whispering politely. "TV?" As the dream fades, I register the familiar sound of Tony running on the treadmill downstairs. *Thump, thump, thump.*

I wish I could say that after leaving my dad in a nursing home, I was filled with new resolve and courage, ready to face whatever lay ahead. But it wasn't like that. Quite simply, as it tends to do, the next day arrived and I got back into the flow. But less enthusiastically now. Before, I'd been so busy with all the running around that my predominant disposition was tired and annoyed. Nothing less than overextended to the point of exhaustion. Now I notice something for the first time: sadness. I'm really sad. *Empty, like there's a piece of me missing that no one can see.* Thankfully, there are the details and distractions of my own family's needs to attend to—making breakfast, tying shoelaces, loading the dishwasher. They don't offer peace, though. I feel as if I'm in mourning.

And I realize that I am. It's no longer self-pity about missing personal time and worry that I'm not around enough for my family. It's sorrow. Deep sorrow that my father is among strangers and not home with his dogs at 19 Cliff Street. Even though he's still with us, there's been a shift, a loss. A pall has silently floated down, covering me, blocking out the vibrancy of life.

The phone messages left for me fill me in on what's happened since I left last night.

"Hi, Sa, it's Pat. I'm here visiting Dad, and you would be so glad to see him up, all clean and shaved, sitting in his chair having breakfast. A good one, too, waffles with the strawberries and whipped cream—wait. Do you want more fruit, Dad? I gotta go, Sa, I want to make sure he's set with a little extra before they take the cart away."

Similar calls from Colette and Will reassure that he's getting great care and help and visiting with people his own age. While he was out, a catheter was put in, so he had a respite from the perpetual bathroom march that comes with Lasix. The updates bring me some comfort, and I start to consider the possibility that I've been in denial about the level of care he requires.

Maybe this is the best thing.

Sunday's church service is the motivation to leave the house, and I'm ready. I'm planning to stop up at the nursing home to see Dad after the service. It's been two days, the longest I've gone without seeing him in months. I needed the mini-break to sleep, cook healthy food, and simply have time for myself and Tony and Summer. Though I'd intended to do some cleaning, too, I mostly watched TV, more or less comatose.

"Bye, Mom," Summer yells down the stairs as I button my coat in the basement entryway. "Don't forget you said you'd bring me back a chocolate sprinkled doughnut—you promised."

Tony and Summer have been engrossed in the *Super Mario Bros. Obstacle Course* on Wii all morning, and I don't want to be the killjoy who ends their special time together. "Okay, my peanut butter cup. Tone, you want anything?"

"Nope, I'm havin' Summer's leftover scrambled. Take your time, Sa. He'll be okay, and you will, too."

On the ride to church, my mind wanders. I think about how many times I've gone to church alone since grade school and how

I never seem to mind. I remember standing beside my parents' bedside on Sunday morning and whispering, "Dad, can you drive me to Sunday school?" and he always would. Sometimes Louanne would come, but most of the time I would be dropped off in front, on Greenwood Street, and picked up later at the side door, near the hallway that connected the Sunday school classrooms. Back then, the appeal of songs, crafts, and, of course, the chocolate doughnut after service during the fellowship hour, was too much to pass up. These days, it's a gift to be alone with my thoughts, and I cherish the private time to worship and reflect. And today, feeling anxious about visiting Dad afterward, I'm relieved that Tony and Summer aren't here to see that I'm not quite myself.

Thinking back to one of my earliest, best memories of church, I recall the Christmas tree we made out of pine cones. Mr. and Mrs. Bergman were Sunday school coteachers for that memorable Sunday. I remember it so clearly, right down to fingers sticky from Elmer's glue. A piece of plywood cut into a triangle provided a base for us to secure the pine cones. The bottom row had three pine cones, the middle row had two, and one went on top. We could choose from colorful yarn as garland or glitter to wrap and sprinkle as minidecorations, but I liked mine simple and plain.

While Mrs. Bergman helped with the mechanics of the craft, Mr. Bergman read aloud a story about the birth of Jesus. The lesson was that our Lord was sent to be born in this world to live among us. So as we decorated our pine cones, we learned the meaning of our church name—Emanuel. In my best printing, I wrote "God With Us" and drew a smiley face on the back. That pine-cone craft kicked around the house for years, sometimes popping up in a box of Christmas decorations, sometimes in the middle of July under the couch, covered in dust balls and cat hair. God With Us. Smiley face. It's odd that it should just come to mind like that.

I walk from the parking lot into church with a shy smile on my face, my head filled with the memory. *God With Us, God With Us.*

"Good morning," I say to the usher and take the bulletin that outlines the service hymns and Bible verses. I find my familiar seat on the right side of the church, at the end of the pew near the wall. Our Lutheran congregation was founded mostly by Swedes and Finns, but like many community churches, it has evolved over the years to include all ethnicities. While I've always liked the quiet, modest nature of our worship service, I developed a deeper appreciation for it during an extended business trip to Finland many years prior. I was there to provide soft skills training for technical professionals, and in the course of things, I witnessed a reserve similar to the notion of "saving face" in Asian cultures. Pleasant but private. Relating to the people in a way I hadn't expected, I came home feeling a kinship with my mother's Finnish heritage for the first time. And now, though we all wish our small congregation would flourish again, like it did in its seventies' heyday, I love the intimacy and closeness of our service. I can look from pew to pew and see familiar faces and enjoy a sense of community, knowing some families' backgrounds just as they know mine. Absent is any notion of pretense or who's who—it's just "Here I am, Lord."

Pastor begins the sermon with her familiar greeting. "Grace and peace to you from God our Father, and our Lord and Savior Jesus Christ. Amen."

While I've heard this line hundreds of times without really considering it, today it makes me bawl. I suppose it's because I want the grace and peace.

Suddenly self-conscious, I try to hold back the floodgates and look normal. I don't hear a word of the sermon opening; instead I'm preoccupied with my panicked self-talk.

Oh dear, please help me stop crying. I'm tired of crying. I'm tired of being tired.

The tears stream as I search in the bottomless pit of my over-stuffed pocketbook for the packet of tissues. It's a small victory to find it and I pull myself together and take a deep breath.

"When Jesus calls his disciples, he doesn't spend time building up their egos or enticing them with promises of success, power, prominence, and wealth," Pastor explains emphatically. "He doesn't even tell his would-be disciples what their goal is going to be or how they will achieve it."

I try to tune back in to the sermon, but I can't stay focused. It's like being underwater. I can hear the muffled words, but my own thoughts are louder. *Don't cry, just breathe, don't cry.* I close my eyes and pray. *I surrender. I cannot do this myself, Lord. I'm weak and need your strength. I need your guidance. Please help.* I try to muster a prayer that's worthy, but simple and repetitive is all I can come up with. A child's plea. *Please help.*

I hear the pastor again. "Jesus simply invites them to follow him and promises them a new twist on their old occupation: like him, they will become fishers of people. Jesus lets faith and the Holy Spirit do the rest."

Until now, the main tenet of my prayer life has been thankfulness and gratitude for the blessings in my life. It seemed acceptable to ask for help for people who are sick or in need and for the troubled world as a whole, but not really for personal help. Having traveled to many countries early in my career, I've seen glimpses of real poverty and despair—real need for help. I've walked crowded markets in China and seen what people there consider acceptable to eat. I've driven by hundreds of cardboard-box homes in the slums of São Paulo, gagging from the sickly smells of filth. I've wept to see elephants beaten and crying in the busy street markets of Thailand while distracted tourists busily shop for bargains and steals. In my mind, these are people, places, and animals that are deserving of prayers. Not me, an educated, middle-aged, white American woman who had the dumb luck to be born in this country. Even though my family life was closer to an episode of *Mary Hartman, Mary Hartman* than *The Brady Bunch*, I had the good fortune to be raised in a house filled with love. Unconditional love. In light of that great gift, I should be able to handle a little extra running around. I feel ashamed for being weak. But the fact is, I've come to my breaking point, and my simple heartfelt plea is the admission—*I cannot do this on my own.*

"When Simon Peter and the first disciples were called, they did not question God's will. They knew it and accepted it," Pastor continues. "You are also able to know the will of God if you are able to seek it. When you are willing and committed to doing the will of God, He will work the circumstances in your life."

The service continues and, finally, she offers the familiar closing line, and I'm fully present again. "And may the peace of God, which surpasses all human understanding, keep your hearts and your minds in Christ Jesus. Amen." Just as with the opening message, I've heard this a hundred times but today it sinks in. *God, whatever you want, that's what I want.*

The sending song, "We Are All One in Mission," is a simple folk tune from Finland, and its familiar melody touches my heart. It's a little thing but somehow seems fitting.

When the service is over, I'm sure I must look a fright, red-nosed and puffy, and I make a beeline back to my car. Gone is the childhood reverie of an hour ago as I try to find my spare tube of mascara among a bunch of wet tissues in the mess of my pocketbook. On my way to the nursing home, I stop at the Dunkin' Donuts at the foot of Providence Street to pick up Summer's doughnut and something for Dad and me. It feels eerily similar to the days when Dad would bring Table Talk pies to Louanne in hospice, and it occurs to me that this is probably the start of a ritual of bringing *him* endless treats. The tune of the sending song loops in mind and softly I hum the repeating melody.

At the nursing home, I notice that smell again as I cross the threshold, a complex product of utilitarian cooking and disinfectant cleaning products that don't fully mask the odor of urine. On the main floor, just around the corner from the lobby, I glimpse my father sitting in a wheelchair in the hallway lineup of elderly, and I stop dead in my tracks. Frozen. It takes my breath away to see him there, one of the bunch. They're lined against the wall, most of them either asleep or hanging their heads in boredom. Behind the desk, the nursing staff seems oblivious.

My mind reels. *Please help, please help.* I take it all in as I walk slowly down the hall. I won't put on a phony smile—I couldn't if I wanted to. I owe him my true guilt-ridden self.

As I get close, I see that he actually looks good. So much better than the last time I saw him—perfectly shaved and in his navy blue pants, light blue button-down and navy fleece sweater vest. He's dozing and doesn't know I'm there.

Suddenly, I know this isn't about me. *I can do this for him.*

I kiss his cheek and rub his arm to rouse him a bit. "Hello, sleepy Daddy. It's me."

He awakes easily, not with a jolt as I feared. "Hey, honey, whatcha got there?"

"I brought you a chocolate-covered. Ate mine on the way."

"That's okay, as long as you didn't eat mine."

I'm a little shy talking in front of the other patients and say hello to a few of them. Some reply with eager eyes and smiles, some don't.

"Let's find a little place to visit. Can you hold my pocketbook and coffee on your tray with yours?"

We wheel down the hall, whose beige walls are hung with bright-colored art. There's a section where the patients' handiwork is on display. I head for the TV room but end up passing it by when I notice there are a few dozers in there. *On the bright side, at least there aren't many people alone in their rooms. It seems only residents visiting with family are in their rooms.* I decide to try Dad's room, but his roommate, Pedro, is there visiting with *his* family. We end up at the farthest end of the hall, in the all-purpose room. Windows line an entire side of the room, but there's a half wall, so you have to stand to see the view. Inconvenient for residents, say, in wheelchairs. There's a nicely decorated oversize hutch, like something you might find jammed into one of the bedrooms at his house. Displaying delicate china teacups and a porcelain-faced Victorian doll, it's the one homey touch in the room. Otherwise it's table rounds and chairs and, taking up one corner, a bulky metal weighing station equipped to handle wheelchairs. I park us near the windows.

"Wow, Dad, we're higher up than I thought. Is this the west side of the city? I feel like I can see all of Worcester." While I chatter on about the view, he eats his doughnut in silence. "Didn't you used to live in this neighborhood when you and Mommy first got married? Wasn't it a three-decker on Marion Avenue where Uncle Henry used to pretend to shoot at people passing by from out of the window?" I chuckle.

He just barely nods in the affirmative.

"I remember how many times Mom mentioned her shock when she first met your youngest brother, in his Elvis wanna-be phase. Although I'm not sure he ever really grew out of it, did he?" Colette had reminded me that this building is on the same block as the home where my parents started out together fifty years before.

Its grounds actually cover the exact spot where the house had stood. The painful poignance of his being back in this location in the sunset years of life isn't lost on me, and in the face of Dad's neutral expression, I blush with shame at my comments. Sighing, I pull up a chair beside his and hold his hand. "Sorry, that wasn't nice."

He changes the subject and pats my hand. "What's the plan, Sa?" he asks, sounding upbeat.

"Do you remember coming here and what happened?"

"They told me I fell, but so what? Ya pick me back up."

I nod in agreement but don't say anything right away. I want to make Will the scapegoat, to say he can't do it anymore, throw him under the bus completely, but I can't. It wouldn't be fair. So I say something less definitive, a half-truth. "Dad, you know we've been asking you for quite a while to stay in bed during the night. Having to sleep by your bed on pee duty is taking a toll on all of us. We don't have the money for round-the-clock care. Not to mention that they need to get the congestion in your lungs under control and your Lasix at the right balance. You were exhausted and right out in left field when you were admitted." I pause, tears in my eyes. "I don't really have a plan as much as knowing that we need a break for a few days to figure it out."

He nods. He has tears in his eyes, too.

We move back into the hall, where the action is, and I spend time just sitting beside him, chitchatting with the other residents and getting to know the nurses and aides. I sign various forms and make plans to take his laundry home to wash it myself because it seems another tangible way to care for him. After a couple of hours, I leave with a heavy heart and promise to return again soon.

In the car, the Dunkin' Donuts bag on the passenger seat reminds me that Summer will probably be upset that I've taken this long. *That's okay. I'll promise to do something special with her to make up for the time spent away.* I stop at the grocery store to pick up what I need to make her favorite meal for Sunday dinner. Even though I'm weary from the emotional roller coaster of the day, I know I need to keep pushing, for my family's sake. *The least I can do is cook for my family.*

Being in my kitchen and slipping on my smock apron is a comfort in itself. I choose the one with the tiny yellow rosebuds and off-white rickrack trim. I have a few of these cherished aprons in the hand-towel drawer. My mother and grandmother made them for themselves from McCall's patterns, and my sisters and I each have a few. Before I start cooking, I set the television music channel to Classic 70s.

"I love, love, love that we're having pork roast today, Mom," Summer says while making up her own version of a modern/ballet/lyrical dance routine in the great room, twirling gracefully one minute and dramatically sprawling on the floor the next. Our open floor plan allows the convenience of satisfying her unspoken desire for me to watch her while I prep dinner. "Can we have mashed instead of the roasted potatoes?"

"You bet, my little green bean."

"Oh no, you're not planning *those*, are you?" she asks while simultaneously doing jazz hands and taking large sumo-wrestler steps in what I assume is an African interpretation of the song playing in the background, Gerry Rafferty's "Home and Dry." Careful not to laugh out loud, I give her an impressed expression.

"Well, I guess I won't now. What's your idea for a vegetable?" I ask while slicing onions, running the knife under cold water every few cuts to dampen the tear fumes.

"Onions. Let's smother onions on the pork roast to cook, like you do. I could help chop up a cucumber, too, for a cucumber salad and no lettuce."

Even during this easy exchange with my cheerful girl, my thoughts are with Dad. *He loves pork roast, too, especially any charred onions in the drippings.* Summer doesn't seem to notice my distraction.

After a dinner during which I'm quiet but grateful for this relaxed time together, I head back to the nursing home and bring Dad a chocolate ice cream shake from McDonald's. Hanging out in the TV room, we mostly sit in silence watching the news and commentary about Trayvon Martin and rising fuel prices. I stay to help the aide, Benita, get him ready for bed and notice little tricks she uses to smooth the process. With simple directions and gentle ways, she changes him completely while he's still in the wheelchair and helps him to stand and pivot into bed.

I'm relieved that he's in good hands but can't help tearing up as I overthank her. Not saying anything, she just smiles and kindly pats my arm.

He's out as soon as Benita clicks off the humming fluorescent light mounted on the wall at the head of the bed. Glancing back as I leave, I realize that even though he's tucked in and comfortable, it doesn't make it any easier to leave him there. It never gets any easier.

Draw near to God and he will draw near to you.
James 4:8

Driving Blind

16

Late May 2012

A snappy jingle plays and fades. "And we're back," says Matty, star of the "Matty in the Mornin'" talk show on Kiss 108. "For those of you just tuning in, we're listening to Billy complain even though he gets everything free and does whatever he wants."

The Monday morning commute is on, and just like in my dream, I'm in my car on Route 146, but this time I'm headed in the opposite direction, northbound, going to work. Unfortunately, I'm wide awake.

"Okay, here we go," Billy replies. "As if you don't get to do what you want."

Matty replies in typical fashion. "Don't forget, I'm married with a dog, so I get what I want to do less than half of the time." Their sidekick lady laughs.

It's like any other day of banter between radio personalities, but today I can't see the humor. I'm tired and ornery from my schedule in general, and now there's the added layer of worry about Dad's new living arrangements. I didn't know I would feel such torment about whether he was being helped, by whom, and how were they treating him. In the few weeks that he's been in the nursing home, I've stopped by as often as possible, sometimes before work but mostly afterward. While I'm able to put on a good face and stay upbeat when I'm around Dad and the staff, I usually fall apart when I leave.

Tony had picked up on my humorless mood this morning and was good enough to make a pot of coffee before heading out for his long commute. Filling the whole house, the aroma of the fresh brew was a small blessing and just what I needed to start the day. I wished I could take a pass and play hooky from my "be all things" lifestyle for just one day, though I know that if the wish *had* been granted, I probably would have spent the day worrying about everyone anyway.

As I drive, I daydream about how it was when Tony and I were just starting out, living in Framingham. I loved the time with our dogs. For the most part, Ruby and Buddy were our dog-children. I miss them and the vibrant lifestyle of walking with them, off-leash, on the leaf-covered trails at Callahan State Park, trail bikers sometimes whizzing past and the occasional horse and rider meandering along. I used to stop and rest on an oversize flat-top rock where three trails intersected. Filtered light through the trees would make everything look magical—my own real-life enchanted forest. The dogs would stop exploring to lie by my feet if I sat too long, content to also take a break. When I got up to continue along the trail, it was always with a sense of peace, contentment, and clarity.

The chatter between Matty and Billy pulls me back.

"Don't let these people make fun of you, Bill. I think you're adorable. . . . A little selfish, but that's fine."

"Why am I selfish?" Billy asks, amazed.

"I'm not having this conversation, because it will end up in a hurtful place, and then people will get mad at me for being mean. I get two kinds of tweets, one making fun of you and the other are people mad at me for making fun of you."

I'm only half-listening, but the radio show still finds a way to annoy me. The provoking banter is getting to me. No longer wandering sun-dappled trails, my thoughts turn to how little time I have to myself. *I guess I'm selfish too. Not moving him in with me— what kind of person am I?* As I've done a hundred times, I imagine the scenario of moving him home with us. *How would we manage in the night? What if he wanders and falls? With my bad back, how would I be able to lift him and help him walk? I'd have to stop working. How would it affect Summer? I barely have time for her now. His dogs aren't house-trained, and what about our cat? Dad really just wants his own house anyway. I wish I had a break from it all. God help me, I'm so weak.* Despite my guilt, I rule it out—until the next time that it comes to mind and I mull it all over again, weighing the pros and cons, hoping Will comes to the rescue, somehow, once again.

My dependable "must be nice" line of thinking kicks in, and I replay jealous memories about former and present colleagues who seem to have it made. I've had several female managers with healthy parents living across the street or in the in-law apartment downstairs. *It must be nice to have a mom who works out at Curves in the morning and then picks up your kids before you leave for work.* This in contrast with my severely arthritic and pain-riddled mother who went and got cancer just when it was my turn to have "Gramma help." *It must be nice to have dinner ready and waiting for your entire family when you get home from work.* If I had a dime for every working mother I know who brags about how they hate to cook and don't have to because either Mom or hubby does the cooking. . . .

I never used to compare myself with others. I had my own "live and let live" kind of vibe going on. Now I'm fully invested in my own slant on "mommy wars" and hate myself for it.

Matty continues his whining rant. "You think I want to walk around the reservoir in Weston, filled with mosquitoes in the summer and freezing in the winter? All weekend, that's all I do. Run around with the dog and go to the dump." (More sidekick laughter.)

Why did I ever think these guys were funny? I can't stand another minute! I slap at the radio console to change the station and accidentally switch it to the AM band. Tony and I never listen to AM radio unless we're in a pinch, en route somewhere, when a pivotal Red Sox or Patriots game is underway. On those occasions, the old-fashioned play-by-play and scorekeeping are novel and fun.

Before I have a chance to change it back to FM and "scan the band," as we say in my family, changing stations up and down the radio, I hear the pleasant sound of a piano playing lightly—*dingle, dingle, doo*—as if it's a preview excerpt of the program about to start, and the voice of a man with a distinctly southern accent. "A storm in your life can destroy you, or it can develop you. It can build your strength, your wisdom, your knowledge, your understanding, your commitment, your devotion, your faith, your serenity, your peace, your joy."

Then a deep, resonant announcer's voice overrides: "Welcome to *InTouch* with Dr. Charles Stanley." And the peaceful piano chiming fades out.

Now this *should be interesting.* What catches my attention are the word choices: strength, peace, joy. *Yeah, right, I used to have that.*

Dr. Stanley continues: "How do you ride out the storms in your life, because we all have them? Do you quit and walk away?

Or do you fight to endure them? How do you respond? Storms are inevitable, our anchor is immovable. Say it out loud with me."

I don't say anything, but I'm listening intently.

"When God is working in your life, you are so much better off. There's more serenity, more peace, more joy, because you know you're in the center of the will of God. God's Word is an immovable anchor in the difficult times you may be going through."

It seems a little melodramatic, but I decide I want to listen. Even though I've arrived at work, I sit in my car in the parking lot across the street from the office just to hear a few more minutes. I realize it means I'll be a few minutes late, but I need to hear this.

The message is comforting—that the eternal God is our refuge, with everlasting arms, and that I'll have the strength to bear whatever each day brings—and although I want to hear the entire program, I know I need to get inside and start the day. As I get out of the car, I laugh a little to myself. *Uh-oh, next thing I'll be dragging Tony and Summer to a southern revival.* Though I don't have a song in my heart as I walk in, at least I'm much less angry. It seems as if for the first time in a while, I have clarity about what I need to do. It's time to take action about my situation.

After snapping on my office light, I begin setting up for the day. Top of mind is to make a call to the benefits person in Human Resources. I click my laptop into the docking station, and rather than wait for the system to boot up, I use the automated phone system to find the extension and dial the number. I speak his name slowly for the automated voice prompt, "Evan Burnanskey," while Windows chimes awake in the background. "Edmond DeChancey," the female robotic voice offers, so I try again, louder and more deliberate. "Evan Buurnannskeeey." This time the system gets it right and I press #1 to connect the call. My urgency turns out to be for nothing, but I smile to hear Evan's pleasant voice-mail message. He's a genuinely nice guy and perfectly suited to Human Resources. I remember liking him from the start, noticing that he was always approachable but professional, with a unique sense of style and self.

Beep.

"Hello, Evan, it's Sarahbeth in Corporate Continuing Education. I'm sorry to bother but wonder if you could give me a call when you have a chance. I would like to find out about using the Family Medical Leave Act benefit, umm, to care for my father. I'm at Extension 4105 when you have a chance. Thanks."

The message sounded much more confident than I feel. I'm worried about how this is going to look. I know, logically, that my request is fully warranted, but still I sense that there will be a likewise warranted "Here we go again" response. Ever since my mother died during my first week on the job, I feel as if it's been one type of tragedy or another. I try not to be a Debbie Downer and have learned that the less I talk about my family situation the better, although I suspect I overcompensate by talking more about the bright spot in my life: Summer. If I recall correctly from my days without kids, this is annoying for colleagues without children. There's one particular coworker, around my age, who unabashedly shares her "I don't like kids" sentiment. It always makes everyone laugh. For some, it's the kind of nervous laugh that tends to follow the voicing of something un-PC, but for others, primarily those without children, it's a confident howl in solidarity with her brazen pronouncement. I usually giggle as well because it makes me think of Wanda Sykes's comedy bit where she says, "Kids are a lotta work, they a lotta work," sounding dead serious, but then she adds with a sarcastic wink, "But they're worth it."

Regardless of how they're received, my occasional breaking-news updates are reports of Summer's above-average, darlin' ways.

This, I figure, is much more acceptable than discussing how many times my sisters and I found cigarette-burn holes in my mother's pajamas or my sister's bed linens, from both of them having taken to regularly falling asleep while smoking in their opioid addicted, later days. The opioid crisis was not commonplace and certainly not discussed.

I would swing from seething anger at my mother for the mess her home had become and from the cigarette smoke stench that clung to Summer's clothes and hair, to heartbreak over how cheated I felt for not having my mother's healthier, younger version as Pat and Collette did. Most of the time, it was better to hide how much I missed her.

When Evan returns my call, I request FMLA time off in a shy, almost apologetic way. I spell out the various scenarios in which I might need the time. "You see, we don't know how much longer my dad has, so I don't want to use up more time than is necessary and not be there for him at the end. Plus, I don't want to let our sales team down and not make my number, so I will still be working. Then again, I've been doing sort of a second shift, caring for my dad for a long time, and would like to just be with him while he gets settled in the nursing home."

Evan is patient while I pause to collect my thoughts and then resume my thinking-out-loud monologue.

"I've been handling his appointments with the help of my siblings and home health care workers, but to be honest, there are a lot of little unplanned things that pop up every day. You would be amazed at how many phone calls I have about him. I've been trying to get his dentures refitted for months and wish the dentist would just go to him. I can't tell you how many appointments there are where either we make arrangements for someone to take him or I take him myself. Most times that's actually easier. He's become a regular part-time job. I would say a portion of every day is on his behalf, but I don't really know how to split the time."

I'm a geyser of extraneous Dad details, but Evan finally gets a word in. "Let me explain the benefit that you have available. The Family Medical Leave Act is a federal law requiring covered employers to provide employees job-protected and unpaid leave for qualified medical and family reasons. It was put into effect under the Clinton administration and intended for situations exactly like this. The act allows eligible employees to take up to twelve work-weeks of unpaid leave during any twelve-month period to attend to the serious health condition of the employee, parent, spouse, or child, or for pregnancy or care of a newborn child, or for adoption or foster care of a child."

"Yes, I've used FMLA before, when my daughter was born. But I used the full three months in one lump sum to be home with her. Is there a going rule for how to use it for eldercare?"

Evan makes it clear that I'm on my own to figure that out. There are no best practices or suggested schedules to build from. It's like an open checkbook of time, albeit unpaid, and all I have to do is determine the amount and the frequency. Simple, right? Actually, it presents another high-stakes decision for me to make in my already overwhelmed state.

"You don't have to figure it out today," Evan says. "Take some time and talk about it with your family and make a plan that works for you and your manager."

What I don't know how to articulate is that, unlike maternity leave with its easy-to-determine timeframe, eldercare is often unpredictable and crisis driven. Or that even if I'm not sitting bedside for every second of the time off, doing things for my own family or well-being is just as important.

Back of mind is growing anxiety over Will's impending return to Florida. We're at odds about whether Dad will ever return home, and despite my pleas for Will to stay, he's made up his mind. It's only a question of when. His absence will mean there's one less family member regularly checking in on Dad, but I'm more upset about how Dad will feel knowing that Will is leaving.

A few days later, I email Evan to share that I've decided on a four-day workweek, with Monday off, as the best way to extend the weekend care routine. It's also the least disruptive to the workweek. I know it's not the perfect scenario, but it's something, and from the informal conversation I had with my manager, I trust I'll be allowed time as necessary for midday calls and appointments that come up.

With Will's decision to go back to Florida, I have to step it up. *If only I knew how long Dad has. . . .*

For we walk by faith, not by sight.
2 Corinthians 5:7

Velcro and Laces 17

June 2012

For my first Monday using the FMLA, I've scheduled a meeting with Dad's new team at the nursing home. Once in the car, I tune to the AM radio station. I've been listening to "Life Changing Radio" regularly now, on the way to work and during lunch errands, and I'm consistently amazed that no matter the message, it's exactly what I need to hear. There's a new program every half hour, and the pastor speaking now has a strong authoritative voice. I'm not even to the end of my driveway when he asks, "So you may be asking yourself, I'm a good person, I'm a Christian, where did my joy go?"

I laugh out loud. I've seen parodies of this scenario, from Jim Carrey movies to *Candid Camera*, where a voice from above seems to be speaking directly to you through the radio.

Okay, you got me again, I'm listening.

I'm still grinning as I roll down my window to say a quick hello, ironically to my neighbor Joy, who's out strolling with her grandson and has paused at the end of our street. It's rare that she sees me in a good mood. She usually sees me at the end of the workday, when I rush in to do the grab-'n-go with Summer, disheveled and on the fly.

"Are you heading up to visit your dad?" she asks.

"Yeah, it's the first time I'm meeting with his entire care team and I'm dying to hear if his white blood count is better since his last blood test. I almost passed out the other day. There was blood in the tube and in that bag—I forget what you call it, but you know what I mean, from the catheter. I guess he has a urinary tract infection. They've removed the catheter since then, but it makes me queasy to think about it. I can't believe I put him through that. I should have told them to take it out right away. I just thought it would help him to sleep through the night, but apparently he gets up to try and go anyway."

She's pushing the stroller back and forth to keep the toddler in motion. "I think it's just called a drainage bag. You didn't know, so don't beat yourself up. Maybe *they* should have taken it out sooner as well. How's his disposition? Sometimes UTIs can really affect the elderly."

"So I've learned. It's been awful. They said he's been combative. Can you imagine?! My dad has never been combative in his entire life. With me he's just quiet or confused, asking the same things over again. They asked if I would approve a temporary low dosage of Haldol, but that leaves him so lethargic. I'm sick about it."

Joy stoops down to help her now-squirming grandson out of his stroller so he can move around. Immediately, he picks up little pebbles and squats down to toss them into the sidewalk gulley drain. He imitates the sound they make when they reach the bottom. "*Plunk, donngg.*" We watch him for a few minutes in silence. He's totally amused by the pebble drop, and I'm deep in thought about Dad's medications. My pillbox duty at his kitchen table seems like child's play now. The ante has been upped, and I'm way outside my element once again. *What do I know about these medications and whether this is the right thing to do?* My mind had raced when the nurse on duty informed me of the doctor's new orders, but I talked myself down: *She seems so matter-of-fact, so I must be overreacting.* And so I signed. But then what I found out about Haldol's side effects during a late-night internet search made things worse. The only consolation I can come up with is that it's only a temporary arrangement, until they can get the UTI under control.

Joy breaks the silence. "How's your little Student of the Month doing? I'm planning to get her off the bus today. Are we still on?"

"Yes, that would be a big help. I'm not sure how long the meeting will run, and it will be nice to spend some time visiting afterward. Isn't it something that the school recognizes excellent effort? We love that and are so proud of her! She's getting so independent too. Seems like it was just yesterday when we were having our stroll around the neighborhood and now she's announced that her spring shoes *cannot* be from Stride Rite. She wants *real* laces, no more Velcro!"

We laugh, but only briefly.

"It hurts in a way," I say. "I guess it's bittersweet to see my little peanut thriving and stepping into her independence while I watch my dad moving in the opposite direction, both right in front of my eyes."

Joy smiles politely, and it dawns on me that these aha! moments of mine aren't unique. So many others face circumstances so much worse than mine. She's surely witnessed the same heartache, if not more, but is too gracious to say so.

"Ah, well, I should be grateful for the days when I remember to put on my own shoes," I say. "Now *that's* a good day."

We laugh again.

"Hang in there," Joy says with kind concern. "You're doing the best you can, and they're both okay."

"Thanks, Joy." I wave to the little plunker, who's now thoroughly engrossed in his drain game. "Bye, honey!"

He looks up. "*Plop.*"

I pull away and turn the radio up to hear the closing words.

"So, that's why. In those difficult times, remember, God needs to turn the soil, till the earth, sometimes with tragedy or strife, to open the ground (your heart) to God's grace. Your joy is tied to your salvation, and you can never lose your salvation. Until we meet again, this is Dr. David Jeremiah with *Turning Point.*" Even though I've missed almost the whole program, I'm not disappointed. I know I can always look it up online if I really want to hear it. But I'm really appreciating this process of fellowshipping with the Lord where I just hear a few key passages during small windows of time, giving me succinct direction just when I need it. It's difficult to explain but wonderful to experience.

I arrive at the nursing home and find the conference room just in time. Two people are already there, and we have to wait only a few minutes for everyone else to arrive. Unlike at the Pinnacle meeting months ago, I'm the only one representing our family, and there's no friendly banter. The team is chatting, but only among themselves.

I'm alone on my side of the table, and on the other side, are new faces in familiar roles: the head nurse for the floor, the occupational therapist, a physical therapist, a case worker, and an activities person. This time, there's no kindhearted doctor at the helm. Dr. Schafer has transferred to another practice, and although we've been assigned an interim nurse practitioner, she isn't here for the meeting. Apparently, she's doing her best to handle the added caseload, and attending this type of status review meeting isn't always possible. So we're in transition until a new doctor is hired.

The head nurse, Helga, opens the meeting, and once again it's clear from the start that this is a routine process for the staff. "Since your father's admittance in April we've had a chance to assess and get to know him. The first thing—"

"Um, I'm so sorry to interrupt," I say. "I realize we're just getting started, but hopefully it's okay to chime in?"

Helga nods but smiles with pursed lips.

"I just want to add that I'm not sure you know my dad just yet. Because of the UTI, he's been disoriented and not actually himself. I'm hoping the infection is under control?"

"Yes, we'll definitely get to that." It's obvious she has a clear agenda to follow, and I get the sense that it's better to wait my turn.

The meeting is run efficiently, and all the bases are covered, from clinical/medical topics to day-to-day care. I'm relieved to learn that the antibiotic seems to be working and his white count is coming down. At one point, she casually informs that he's being considered for relocation to a floor for dementia and Alzheimer's patients and quickly transitions to a review of his daily schedule. I shift in my chair, cross my legs to reposition and roll my shoulders just slightly, trying to shake off the tension I can feel building in my neck. The news makes me uncomfortable because that means a lockdown floor, where exit stairwells require a key and a four-digit code is necessary to board the elevator. My rational mind understands that it's for safety's sake—to prevent wandering—but still, it makes me shudder, conjuring notions of psychiatric units of yesteryear. *How can I be doing this to him?* I fear I'm missing key details of the report about his daily schedule and hope I appear calm as I try to tune in again and catch up.

"… and of course, effective enhanced care is achieved with family support and regular visits," Helga concludes, sounding a little too practiced. I'm reminded they've probably been through this a million times, and from their perspective, I must seem yet another overly worried daughter passing through.

When it's my official turn to raise any questions or concerns I might have, I reference notes in my brown-leather day planner. "It probably seems a little over the top," I say as I flip the page, "but I make quick notes to myself after some visits, in the parking lot, so I won't forget anything." It's dead quiet, and as I scan my notes, I imagine that a few eyebrows are raised and eyes are rolling. I clear my throat. "Um, it will be nice to take advantage of your podiatry services. Can we schedule him for an appointment?"

"Of course," Helga says. "Not a problem. We also noticed that your dad's feet are in dire need of nail care and have him scheduled already."

"Great, thanks. I know that you're concerned about the bulging carotid artery in his neck, but he would like to be able to shave himself. He says, 'I've shaved for more than sixty years on my own. I think I can handle it.'"

"I know," Helga says, chuckling along with the rest of the team. "We've heard the same."

It's agreed that he'll be able to shave himself, initially with someone present to be sure he's safe.

"It was noted for him to be on a soft diet when he first arrived," I say, "until you could assess his eating with broken dentures. I brought in a backup pair, so he should be all set. I would like him to have the regular, low-sodium meal plan now, and I've made the request several times, but it doesn't seem to happen. Is there something else I need to sign?" I notice that the pitch of my voice is rising, making this sound like a plea.

"Oh, boy, the poor guy," Helga says. "Absolutely. I'm surprised they haven't switched him sooner than now. We'll take care of that right away." She makes a note in his chart.

I take a deep breath before my next one. "I'm not sure who in particular, so I don't have any names if it's one person or more, but he's told me that he often feels like just a sack of potatoes when he's lifted and moved." I'm trying to keep my voice level, but I'm losing the battle to nerves. "Is that how it is?" I don't want to come across in this first meeting as accusatory or complaining but need to know that he's being heard—more uncomfortable territory for me. I press my hand to the back of my neck and massage in little circles to relieve the stiff-neck twitch that's settled in. It usually happens when I inadvertently hold my posture too tensely.

During my visits, I've met a few of the aides, mostly the evening crew, and have seen an efficient, fluid, two-person technique of lifting him from his wheelchair into bed. How am I to know if this is standard practice or has been only for my benefit? I'm trying to be open-minded, wondering if the onus is on my father to get used to these different but capable hands. This uncertainty comes with the territory, and it's impossible to know the real truth because I'm not with him all the time. The psychological torment of this huge unknown can drive you mad if you let it. I'm just getting to know the staff members, and I want to give them the benefit of the doubt but not be naïve and too trusting.

I can feel my face flush as I try to verbalize a conflicted message. Panic is creeping in.

Suddenly everyone has an opinion, talking over each other but all trying to reassure me.

"I don't think that's how it's been at all" says Sandra, the occupational therapist.

"We make it a point to respectfully move our patients," the caseworker chimes.

"Well, it's not out of the question that they might move faster than Benny is used to," the physical therapist acknowledges.

Helga, still running the meeting, interjects with the final word. "Of course, Sarahbeth, we'll talk to the aides who have your father and ask if they could give him more verbal cues when he's going to be moved. We can always use the reminder to handle with care, and I appreciate your telling us this. Please know everything will be okay."

Based on their replies and concern, I do feel better. *I've been heard. They do understand.* I breathe easily again.

It's time for one last update. "So far, your father has declined coming to any of the scheduled activities, but that's to be expected for new residents," the activities representative casually begins. "He likes to sit next to Mrs. Mendez, whose husband is also a patient on the floor. Mrs. Mendez gives him all of the news, so we have him join her table for meals as well."

I nod along, knowing the back story for this couple. Mrs. Mendez made the decision to live at the nursing home to be near her incapacitated husband every day. She's healthy and well and a living example of selfless love.

"We notice he asks to leave the most during the late afternoon, asking people walking by to drive him home, so we want to give him more things to do to distract him. Are there any particular activities that he likes, such as listening to certain music?"

I wasn't prepared to hear this, let alone hear it posed so nonchalantly. Apparently, the activities director is desensitized to patients' requests to go home. The whole team is. But I'm not. I have a physical response, similar to the feeling you get before public speaking when your chest constricts and there are a few minutes of nervous breathing that you try to keep quietly under control. None of this is familiar ground. *He asks to go home?* I take longer to answer than is comfortable, just staring down at my notes on the table. *An activity?* The scene of him contently reading at his kitchen table, coffee mug in hand, comes to mind. The notion of a lifetime spent in his home, surrounded by the energy of his five children coming and going—that was his joy. *We were his activity.* I'm almost in a state of shock and know I shouldn't try to say what I'm thinking. I'm done and don't want to talk any more or hear any more. I realize I'm biting my lip.

I clear my throat. "I'll have to give it some thought." This time no one comes to the rescue with assurances that it can be fixed and that everything will be okay.

The meeting wraps up and I thank everyone quietly. Pushing my chair away from the table, I swallow familiar worry and guilt.

I compose myself in the bathroom before going to visit with Dad. As I walk the hall looking for him, my mind races with ideas for how we can bring him back to his home. Having called several home health agencies, I know that the cost for round-the-clock care is about $7,000 a month. And that's factoring in shifts from both Will and me to keeps costs down a little. *Maybe there's still a chance Will won't go.* I wonder whether Dad's treasures and collections will be enough to cover the expense, and I plan to find out.

I spend the rest of the afternoon visiting. During the day, the energy is much different from the energy during my usual evening visits, a definite lively bustle of activity. Passing by are colorful people wearing colorful scrubs who, for the most part, are happy and friendly. Sitting in the hallway beside my father, I can appreciate why the patients like to park their wheelchairs along the corridor wall, taking it all in and being in the flow of life. Old-school reality TV. I chitchat a little, but mostly this is an exercise in just being there with him, side by side, and still with my thoughts, which are now filled with renewed determination to cobble together enough money. *For starters, I'll follow up as much as possible with the VA. What if I stop in again at the center near Lincoln Plaza?* Then I begin to mentally catalog collections that may have value—the coin collection, cameras, violins, miscellaneous stock certificates, gems. The challenge is that none of them are organized and in one place, but Will and my sisters will help. Maybe there's hidden treasure buried in the piles after all.

Of course, I always have an eye on the clock.

"Dad, I need to go now and pick up Summer. I asked my neighbor to get her off the bus for me and it's almost time for your dinner. It's corned beef and you'll be able to eat the regular meal. It's all set now."

"Okay, honey, sounds good. Tell your little one I said hi."

"If you don't mind, I want to say a quick prayer before I go. I kinda feel like I want to."

He shrugs. "Okay."

I scoot my chair closer and, taking my dad's hand in mine, drop my voice for just me and him to hear.

"Dear God, help my father to be safe and happy here. Help us to trust the care that they provide and give assurance to him and all of the patients who live here that they are in good hands.

Strong hands that won't let them fall. Help the people who come to work to have a happy heart and knowledge that they are making a difference in the lives of people who need their help. Amen."

As I finish, he gives my hand a squeeze.

Therefore comfort each other and edify one
another, just as you also are doing.
1 Thessalonians 5:11

Final Jeopardy

18

July 2012

Save the Date for Annual Health Services & Wellness Fair ~ Qualified Exhibitors: Reserve Your Tables Now!

If your organization offers community-based health and wellness programs and services, consider exhibiting at our upcoming event. This year's fair will showcase our many collaborations with leading health-care providers and vendors.

"Hi, everyone, thanks for coming, and for bearing with me as I rescheduled this meeting several times to accommodate changing schedules." I say over sidebar conversations to indicate I'm ready to get started.

We could be a living poster titled "Women: Generations at Work," wearing fashions representative of our age demographics, from sleek, pump, pencil heels and perfectly pressed Anne Taylor separates to professional yet funky Chico's styles and smart shoes worn for the practicality of walking a hilly campus. And then there's me, in the Lands' End sweater set du jour and in need of serious hair-smoothing products.

Sitting around the conference-room table, we comprise a Millennial (Twenty-Eight), two Baby Boomers (Rhoda and Brenda, who head up the health sciences initiative and the marketing department, respectively), and a Gen-Xer (me). Of the four of us, I'm the least senior, but that's okay—I can always breathe easy around Rhoda and Brenda. They have a straight-talk style that I understand and respect. This as opposed to my interactions with some of the younger members of the team, where meaningful public discourse is obscured in favor of being politically correct and, above all, syrupy sweet. Surface nice. As usual, I'm hyperaware of my shortcomings under the confident scrutiny of Twenty-Eight, but something about being around the vibe of Rhoda and Brenda bolsters me.

This is great—everyone is here on time. Given that we only have a thirty-minute window, this should be a quick meeting with, I hope, a quick decision. I'm eager to get the green light for what I expect will lay the groundwork for inroads into the health-care arena and subsequent new business. Glancing around the room, I'm forced to wait as Brenda wraps her sidebar conversation with Twenty-Eight, which involves typical congratulatory praise for our young leader.

Passing out a three-page handout, I get right down to business. "As you know, I've called the meeting to discuss the level of participation the university should have at an upcoming health fair event. You'll notice the first page is the event description and an overview of the three tiers of sponsorship. As usual, there are different price points corresponding to increasing levels of marketing exposure—bronze, silver, and gold package options. Bronze is the bare bones of an exhibit table, with visibility in the program guide and online, and gold is the Cadillac of coverage, with more of everything. That option, granted a bit pricey, includes the opportunity for collateral in the attendee handout bag and to speak at a sponsored breakfast or luncheon breakout session. All of the levels include access to emails of the attendee list, which is worth the price of admission in and of itself."

Everyone is studying the first page of the handout, so I continue. "I have no idea or insight into what kind of budget we could spend on this, but clearly there is value in each tier." Pausing to encourage discussion, I add one more point to note. "This is an ideal platform to attend in some capacity, for name recognition among the other suppliers and vendors attending—"

"Which is . . .?" Brenda asks, not looking up and absently twirling one of the beads in the chunky necklace she's wearing.

"Good segue," I say, flipping the page in my own handout. "Page two has the list of companies attending . . . at least so far. There is another month before the deadline, but already we can see we'll be in good company. This could be a nice way to test the waters for interest in our health-care offerings for this market."

"Which is what? Specifically, what offerings?" Rhoda asks, and everyone looks up expectantly from the handout to me.

I wonder if they assume I'm jumping the gun. We're all aware there are new courses in development, but none are ready for prime time. *Typical sales mentality, right? To go ahead and sell what's not available. But that's not me. Don't they know that?* I decide not to make a joke about it—there's no time and it would probably sound defensive.

"Yes, good question. On page three, I took a stab at language for a generic flyer. You'll see it's basically a high-level description of several existing courses that may be of interest in this space, with heavy emphasis on our ability for customization. It's nothing new to us but I think worth floating in the market." I shift my gaze back to Brenda. "Of course, it goes without saying, I'll loop in someone in marketing to help create the final-version collateral."

"Well, of course," she says, with raised eyebrows and a kind smile, still twirling the brownish bead. It's no secret I have a preference for making my own flyers. With the success and growth of the team, the task of collateral creation, I've been reminded, is now part of a defined job role in her group.

No longer reviewing the handout, Rhoda removes her glasses and wipes the bridge of her nose, looking a little fatigued. "But, the reality is that we don't have any set offering as yet, and my concern is that this may be too premature given faculty bandwidth."

I glance at Twenty-Eight and pause, allowing her the chance to explain and underscore our sales model. She doesn't, but smiles encouragingly in what I interpret as a "this is your meeting" expression, so I continue cautiously, somewhat annoyed at having to voice what I'm sure we all know.

"I understand your concern, and there's really no promise or commitment at this point. It's just that, as you know, our approach is that we're not selling off-the-shelf solutions. It's never about being prescriptive in assuming a client's issue and proposing a solution, as much as prompting to understand the need and collaborating on a solution. We can decide down the road if there's a business case to design a graduate-level course or a seminar or something else depending on the request. The real question for me is what kind of budget we might have available."

I'm attempting to shift the discussion away from the issue of resource constraints.

"Since I don't have visibility into how this prioritizes in terms of overall initiatives and new markets, I defer to you."

"Ha! What budget?" Brenda says. And a fleeting thought is whether the necklace is something she bought on a safari vacation or picked up at a yard sale. The bead she's absently winding appears to be teak or some type of wood. "I could list a half dozen things on our immediate radar, including a priority on web redesign, and this is not on any of my lists." She slides the handout to the center of the table. "Isn't it possible that you simply go as an attendee, as you would normally?"

"Sure, definitely possible, but having a presence casts a broader mes—"

"There is no bandwidth for delivery," Rhoda says, also sliding her handout across the table in my direction after glancing at her watch. "Not now or, from what I can see, in the near future. I just don't think we should take too much on at this point."

It's to be expected that Rhoda feels this way. Just as our sales-model approach is common knowledge, so are the challenges of working with faculty who have maxed-out schedules and egos to boot. Even so, I didn't expect this much pushback. For the past five years, the one constant, consistent message that all sales reps have been drilled on is the notion that we're not selling off-the-shelf solutions. It's a given that we don't have a range of offerings developed yet—we haven't landed enough business to justify it!

There's an uncomfortable pause in the room as I wait for someone else to speak. I'm guessing Brenda feels the same because the bead is now held in her fist, with her right hand over heart, as if saying a prayer or the Pledge of Allegiance.

It's dawning on me that having a table in this event doesn't look promising, which will make it that much harder to attain my sales quota. I'm frustrated and don't bother to hide it, tossing my handout onto the table. From my perspective, a decision not to invest anything is an indicator of the level of commitment to drive new business in this space.

"Hey, ladies, I have to run," Rhoda says, pushing her chair away from the table. "I have to be up on campus for another meeting, and I think you all know where I stand. Keep me posted on what you decide." She pats my shoulder as she breezes by. "Chin up, S.B. It's still important to be there even if you and I end up going as attendees." With Rhoda's quick departure, there's a change of energy in the room and the chunky wooden bead is back in play.

For the first time Twenty-Eight speaks up. "If we do exhibit, and I'm not saying we will, I'm curious to know which package tier is your recommendation, S.B."

"Honestly, I don't know if I have one as much as knowing that we should have a table—I'll take any," I answer hurriedly, aware of the clock and leaning forward to reach for the handout again. "I've talked with the event organizer and gave a heads-up that we may be interested. The good news is that because this is our first year at the event, she's willing to offer an additional 15 percent off whatever option we choose."

I shift in my chair, sitting up straighter to match Twenty-Eight's perfect posture. "It's worth repeating that we'll have access to attendee contact info, which would be a great boost to our distribution list."

"How's that list coming along anyway?" she asks, her eyes smiling, and with that seemingly reasonable question, she cuts me to the quick. With my focus spread among three industries, health care is the area most shortchanged. It's nowhere near as far along as my perfectionist self would have it. I'm not quick enough on my feet or confident enough to make the argument for why my bandwidth is legitimate reason for the investment. Unfortunately, somewhere along the way, I've become mesmerized by Brenda's twirling bead, distracted and staring.

"Well, it's coming from mostly online research and outreach calls." I sigh, dragging my attention away from the hypnotic bead. "Slow but sure."

With the hint of a smile, as if amused and privy to some secret I'm not, she prompts again. "But if you did have to pick, is there an option you like?" Shifting in her chair, Brenda stops twirling. Quickly I stare down at the handout. On the spot, I'm searching the medal-tier options as if there's a right or wrong answer. In the noticeable still of the room, this feels like a definite pop-quiz moment, a game-show scene from hell, and I'm dead certain I won't be leaving with the new car, ceramic cat, or any cash prizes.

A less exhausted version of me would have been able to deftly navigate multiple agendas, multigenerational differences, diverse personalities, and a twirling bead. The nonburned-out version of me would have argued passionately to make the investment in the high-end package to allow optimal exposure for the budding program. My Sandwich Generation version does not. No longer thinking about the levels, I conclude that the decision to not invest is an indicator of the commitment not only to this space but also to me. *That's okay, I have more important things to worry about.*

My surprise and annoyance have turned to concession. Feigning what I hope comes across as ambivalence rather than embarrassment, I shrug with a polite smile. "I would be fine with the bronze level to minimize our cost and still have the visibility that we're playing in this space, but given that we don't yet have enough health-care offerings, we should probably shelve it for now."

"That's my vote!" Brenda says a little too fast, clearly relieved, and collects her notepad and cell phone.

Twenty-Eight does the same and nods in agreement. "I might even be interested in joining you and Rhoda to scope it out as well," she says over her shoulder as they leave together. "So let me know when you're registering, as an *attendee,* and I'll decide for sure."

As I straighten the deserted conference room and toss the handouts into the basket, my thoughts immediately shift to my family and my father. For some reason, a bedside brochure comes to mind that the care team at the nursing home had given me during the last visit. I hadn't wanted to accept the plain blue booklet titled "Gone from My Sight," but I flipped through it eventually and now I realize that I've just experienced a speed round of the five phases of grieving: disbelief, anger, bargaining, depression, and acceptance.

> *If it is possible, as much as depends on you,*
> *live peaceably with all men.*
> Romans 12:18

Sharing the Sun

19

August 2012

Monday

As the elevator sluggishly pulls to the fourth floor and the doors slowly open, I can already hear her grating voice, singing at the top of her lungs, "And it's one, two, three strikes you're out at the *old ball game!*" Of all the luck, Dad has been moved to the floor with the resident ex-vaudeville girl, Daisy. Daisy is wispy thin, with translucent skin, but she has a voice so deep and raspy from years of smoking and singing that it's almost painful to hear. Today she's wearing a light pink ball cap, a dark pink "Go Sox!" T-shirt, and bright pink lipstick. In the background, somewhere down the hall and out of sight, another patient shares an opinion: "Shaddup, and stop your lousy singing." Another voice yells out,

"I can't take it. Stop it, stop it, stop." And someone's moaning "ahh, ahh," perhaps to block it all out.

This scene has become familiar, and I know how it plays out. Daisy will carry on, in full show regalia, until one of the aides talks to her and escorts her to an activity or to the smoking area downstairs. Sometimes the moaning continues nonetheless.

Daisy stops singing as I approach and looks sternly at me. She's serious business when she's performing and, I've come to notice, friendliest during dinnertime.

"Hi, Daisy!"

"Where's that little girl of yours who always looks so scared?" she croaks. And she's right—when Summer is in tow, she usually squeezes my hand for dear life when Daisy wheels up to us.

"She's with her dad and I'm here to have lunch with *my* dad. Is he in his room?"

Before she has a chance to reply, legless Trudy appears in her electric scooter. "He's already down the hall eating," she says as she whizzes by. Trudy makes the rounds all day long and is one of the happiest seniors on the floor.

I've studied the people on Dad's floor—the quiet ones, the yellers, the scowlers—and I've learned to appreciate their little ways and see that they're doing the best they can, just like all of us outside these walls. This is its own minicommunity. Just like Summer, the screamers used to scare me to the bone, but their outbursts don't make me jump anymore. In fact, I view it as an affirmation of lungs and breath to bellow whatever their choice comment or sound, as if reminding themselves and everyone in earshot to, "Deal with it—I'm still here!" *Good for you, Old Yellers,* I think now, and appreciate that they are the ones with spunk and life. They're the seniors who are able to meet your eye. With a smile or with a glower, it's one and the same: expression, signs of life.

That isn't the case with my father. His eyes are either closed or downcast most of the time. His right hand rests just above his right eyebrow, partly shielding his face. I can't always tell if he's sleeping or turning inward. As a result, I'm on my knees more often, kneeling beside him to talk and look up into his face. Once, when Colette and I were visiting, she asked, "Dad, can you open your eyes?"

To our surprise, he answered, "Why? I can see just as good with them closed."

"You can? Well, then,"—she couldn't resist—"how many fingers am I holding up?"

No answer.

She made mock punching motions like Curly from the Three Stooges and then mimicked strangling him.

Still nothing.

"I suppose, then, you can see the Russian black bread and pickled herring that I brought you from Water Street?"

We sat dead still and waited. A few seconds later, nodding his head from side to side and with a crooked smile, he slowly opened his eyes to see us grinning and giggling.

On this day, I find him in the lunchroom at his table with Jeb, who's been his roommate for a few months now, since he was moved to the third floor. I don't think he notices or cares much one way or the other who his roommate is or whether he has one. If anything, after Pedro was released to go home and he was between roommates, he seemed glad to no longer have the language barrier to overcome, or to have to hide his Hershey's minis.

Jeb was admitted to recover from a stroke and can't talk. One side of his face and body are slack, so he's always propped up securely in his wheelchair. He's pleasant and perfectly lucid and seems quite interested in our family visits. With his eyes and a nod of his head, he conveys concern or joy to indicate whether my dad is having a good day or a bad one. Colette, Will, and I refer to him as our own private Captain Pike, the fleet captain on the original TV *Star Trek* who's rendered mute and communicates with light signals. Never a Trekkie, Patricia always asks, "Who???"

"Hi, Jeb. Hi, Dad. I brought you some American chop suey from home. It's regular hamburger, 'cause I know you don't like my turkey-meat version. I boiled the hell out of the macaroni for you too." I kiss his head and pull up a chair next to his. "Do you want to save it for later or have it instead of your tuna sandwich?"

He reaches for the Tupperware container and pushes away his plate. "You got any vinegar for it?"

"Yep. You have your own stash in the residents' fridge, and so far no one has touched it." I leave to fetch the vinegar and make a wide arc across the room, being careful to avoid being spit at by Ol' Berko as I pass by. As Mrs. Mendez explained to Dad and me one evening, months ago, "Ol' Berko's sight is very bad, and he believes spitting wards away demons."

"Hmm, a free benefit for us," Dad had responded. "They don't tell you that in the brochure."

We all cracked up.

Lunch passes quickly and then it's time to head out and get a million other things done while I can. The walk down the long hallway back to the elevator offers glimpses, dioramas of life within these walls. Depending on the room, there are wheelchair silhouettes of elderly people with heads bent asleep. There are rows of smoothly made beds with TVs droning in the background. There are aides bending to help lift someone here or readjusting a fallen slipper there.

"Thank you, God, for the blessing of these patients in our life," I whisper. "Daisy, legless Trudy, Jeb, Ol' Berko, and all the others who, in their own way, look out for each other. Please look out for them. Amen."

Wednesday

It's around three o'clock and I'm at my desk at work, reading the email that just came in from one of my contacts at the army base in Natick. It's a thank-you message and acknowledgment of my preparedness at a recent meeting. Not many people take time to write such a nice note and it makes my day. *Should I forward this along to Twenty-Eight or will it look too self-serving?* I've never quite mastered the art of sharing kudos for myself. *Actually, it wasn't just me at the meeting. We all did a good job.* And with that I decide to instead share it with the rest of the team members who attended. Before I have a chance to hit "Send," though, I get a call from one of the nurses at the nursing home.

"Sarahbeth, it's Bryn. Can you stop up for a visit by any chance?"

Bryn is one of my favorite nurses. I love her little pixie haircut and that she's always ready for a laugh, not to mention that she gushed over my spaghetti sauce during one of the Sunday family dinners that we set up for Dad in the all-purpose room. (I try to bring a little something extra for the staff.) I picture her sitting behind the large nurses-station desk making this call. "Is every-thing okay?" I ask as knee-jerk reaction, but I'm a little confused because I can sense enthusiasm in her voice.

"There's nothing to worry about. Your dad is just having a really good day. He's joking and making everyone laugh. I thought you might want to see him when he's not out of it."

"Really, he is? I *would* like to see that. Thank you for thinking to call me. I'll see you in a few! Oh, wait—I'm going to swing by McDonald's and pick him up a milkshake. Do you need anything?"

"No, we're all set, but thank you for always asking and bringing us things too. It's not necessary, you know. We love your father anyway. Just hurry to come up!"

Another quick prayer comes to mind as I hang up the phone. *Thank you, Lord, for the blessing of the people who notice and care for us.*

Knowing that the rest of my day is quiet, with no scheduled meetings, and that we're on summer hours, I tell myself I can always log in from home in the evening. I hit "Send" on the team thank-you email and quickly pop my laptop out of the docking station.

I arrive to find Dad in tip-top shape and with a twinkle in his eye. We decide to wheel outside to the patients' patio for our visit and choose a spot that's far enough from the smoking area but still in the sun. It's a beautiful day, and colorful umbrellas are up on the white, plastic patio tables.

"Hey, Dad, it was nice having lunch together Monday and then dinner with Will yesterday, wasn't it?" I say mainly to see if he remembers that we'd been there.

He sips his chocolate shake, looking contemplative. "Sometimes I don't feel like myself, Sa. I guess I remember, but you know, these days are a blur."

"I know, Dad. I wonder if it's because of all the medications you're on too. You seemed tired. I actually stopped up last night after Summer was in bed, but I didn't want to wake you."

He nods. "I seem to miss half of my visitors from sleeping."

"Yeah, and the other half you don't remember came!" I joke, and we have the best laugh we've had in a long time.

After a moment, looking at me with a smidge of a smile lingering on his face, he asks, "And how about you—how are you?"

It's been such a one-sided relationship for so long that it's a shock to have my familiar old dad back and asking about me. It takes me a moment to reply, fighting emotions. *I've been here all along, but it's as if he's awoken from a dream. I don't want to wreck this time together with tears and make him feel bad.* "Um, it's been hard. I mean good days and bad days like anyone. To use an old-timer word, I'm not as spry as I used to be, but I'm getting by. I do what I have to do."

He thinks for a while before responding. "You know, Sa, I always hoped all of my children would find their life's work. Some people are lucky and know right away, and some struggle with it. In any case, life is to be lived, not just endured."

"I know, Dad, and I agree," I say quietly. "I will." Looking away, I quickly wipe a tear, determined not to cry. We leave it at that.

It's a good visit and I stay for a few hours, not wanting to rush in and out. We talk about some of the characters on his floor and I give him news about the dogs. Even though he's glad they're with Colette, running around in her big yard and being loved up with attention from her girls, I sense on that subject that he's the one determined not to cry. We're glad for the occasional interruptions from other patients or visitors who stop on their way past to chat for a few minutes. They can't help but comment on the perfect weather, and we move our spot a few times to keep up with the sun. "Let's get our vitamin D," Dad says.

When we finally say goodbye and I return to my car, I make a note in my day planner capturing our laugh and his wish for his children. There was also something else he said, something so ordinary and so special at the same time that I want to have it in writing. After the last time I moved his chair, he said softly, almost to himself, "We're sharing the sun." So bonded, that time we both teared up.

Getting Summer settled for bed is always my favorite part of the day. Sometimes she gets hit with the silly bug and we have our best laughs and closest talks just before lights out. Although tempted, I didn't ask Tone to cover the bedtime routine for me tonight. I wanted to keep our time together even though I know it means I now need to dig deep to find the energy to work.

It's after nine-thirty, and the overhead light in my home office is a stark contrast to the dim and quiet of the rest of the house. Its harshness illuminates the unkempt stacks of magazines and bins of unsorted junk mail on almost every surface. I opt instead for the elephant desk lamp from Pier 1, and the room softens in the glow. Now it seems easier to block out the disarray and concentrate. For the third time this week, I'm reviewing a five-hundred-plus-page document regarding our bid for a government contract. I don't bother to use a highlighter or yellow sticky notes to mark the sections that are confusing; I know the topics that are potential issues and can speak to each one specifically.

I shoot Twenty-Eight a meeting invitation to provide the status and a proposed next step. It's clear to me that I've taken the bid as far as I can, having already held several meetings with the appropriate contract representatives and written up program definitions in the sections that call for our input. There's a lot at stake with this contract, and if we should be awarded the business, it will secure a longtime on-site program at a local army base. For the final review before submission, I know I need to involve the university's legal review team and ask for help. That's okay, though, and I switch off my desk lamp, remembering the affable dean—the initial manager who hired me—with his deep resonant voice, and how he used to say with a broad smile, "If you need help, just ask for it!" I seldom did, though, instead pointing out what was lacking—lacking in process or, worse, in other people—especially during my initial years on the job. It was partly a product of arrogance, of having come from an über-confident corporate culture with mostly male role models who didn't apologize or ask permission.

But it was more a product of ingrained childhood lessons of self-sufficiency. Being a good girl meant not being a bother. It meant not needing anything, emotional or otherwise, and to the detriment of my professional persona, I know I alienated many a colleague and sales-support assistant with this façade. I rationalized it by telling myself it's better to be well-respected than well-liked, though that's debatable in any corporate culture, of course, and definitely at odds with the kind of close-knit office workplace where I find myself at this point in my career.

Even though the dean's still around, I miss him. I also miss Penny, the team manager who preceded Twenty-Eight, and those early years in the department when it was less formal, less structured. Being mindful of the reporting structure, I don't think it would be appropriate to schedule time to catch up with them. And being constantly on the run leaves little opportunity to casually connect.

There's a dull ache in my lower back, and my neck is stiff. I'm surprised to find that a couple of hours have passed. Glancing at my calendar for tomorrow, I see there are several meetings with various colleagues on the docket. Kind advice Penny had once given me—"Try to invest more time in your colleagues," which I understood to mean paying attention to how I make others feel, building on others' ideas instead of dismissing them in favor of my own approach—has been bubbling to the foreground again in these watchful days of caregiving. In step with Dad's slowing pace, I'm increasingly comfortable with saying less and listening more in meetings. While once I would drive the discussion and push my own opinion, it now seems fitting to sit back a bit, still engaged but not out in front. I'm changing inwardly. Paying little mind to how my colleagues might perceive the change, if at all. Just like Dad among the other residents in the nursing home lineup, I've become comfortable being on the sidelines. Doing my part and showing up every day, I trust that actions speak louder than words. And that I'm just as much a part of our "office family" as anyone.

Friday

With a printout of the directions to Concord in hand, I'm getting ready to leave an hour early at the end of the day for what I hope will be a rewarding errand, when Twenty-Eight stops by my office on her way out too.

"I have some concerns about your pipeline, S. B.," she says, standing in the doorway. She's weighed down by the laptop messenger bag and pocketbook over one shoulder and several bags of gifts she received, from who knows who or why, in both hands. She's referring to my list of companies with weighted potential to actually book on-site education.

"Oh?" I say. "Do you want to talk about it now?" I sit at my guest table, hoping she'll do the same.

She doesn't. "I can't right now, but we should set up some time."

I nod and change the subject to something more exciting, "By the way, about that conference-panel invitation." I'd emailed her a reminder earlier in the week but never heard back. "It's a great venue at Disney in Orlando, with a lot of industry leaders and dozens of breakout sessions to choose from. It'll be nice visibility for our university name to be in the mix, and I'm thinking it sounds like a great opportunity."

"I've always wanted to do things like that," she says with a distance in her voice, as if the concept isn't quite concrete. "I'll let you know." She repositions the shoulder bags as she leaves. "Have a good weekend."

"You, too," I reply, unsure if she heard me as the side door to the stairwell closes.

I gather up my own belongings and laptop bag, sure that we'll schedule a meeting to review my pipeline activity soon enough and that'll be that. But as I head to my car after our drive-by "meeting," I can't help but tally a mental list of activity: *Our fiscal calendar begins in July and we're only one month into the year. Check. I'm updating the database with call activity and I have several promising new accounts lined up. Check. I have the rest of a full year to make my number, and if the previous five years are any indication, I know I'll do fine. In fact, she knows I'm pretty far down the path with a government contract that will lock in multiple years of prepaid courses. Check. I've used about six days of FMLA time out of twelve weeks allotted, so that can't be it.*

Confident that I'm in the clear, I sigh with relief and settle in behind the wheel. I've been carting around about a dozen violins in the back for days, and today I'm single-minded about making my way to the appraiser to find out their worth. I call Colette and end up leaving her a message thanking her for picking up Summer so that I can have this time. I also ask how her lunch with Dad went. She was taking him out for lunch and a ride today, and I was as excited as if it were me. I appreciate that she's brave enough to go on what seems like such an adventure, and as I pass the miles during the long stretch of Route 495 North, I reflect on everyone's attitudes about the present situation.

I wouldn't label Colette as blasé so much as relaxed, with a "we're doing the best we can" attitude. Pat shares the same sentiment but with an added edge. I'd be rich if I had a nickel for how many times she's said, "He didn't plan and has himself to blame," all the while, making regular, frequent visits, and bringing him treats and goodies along with the rest of us. Will knows quite definitively that this is in God's hands and it's not for us to worry. I'm trying to get to that place and have had thoughtful moments and new insights in church to help me, along with radio ministry lessons that have brought new meaning to life's trials. But my courage seems to fade every time I say goodbye and leave him there. The others make time for me when I call to share a good moment or a worry, but I suspect they think I'm in denial about the idea that he's in the nursing home to stay.

I'll show them, I think as I drive.

I also mull our ability to blame Louanne. There's no more convenient scapegoat than a dead sister. On any given day, any one of us could be the one to say, "If it weren't for Louanne, he wouldn't have blown through his reverse mortgage," or, "If it weren't for Louanne, he wouldn't have spent so much on antiques." And we all jump in for a rousing round of the blame game, adding nitpicky details about the sorry mess it had become. Our other favorite conversation starter is "How selfish." "How selfish of Louanne never to think twice about how Daddy wanted to spend his money," any one of us might say, not considering our own roles in failing to keep a safe watch over his nest egg or help him to plan. Sure, Will and I helped him with paperwork to secure the reverse mortgage, but then we dutifully backed away. I assumed it wasn't appropriate to keep a hand in or that it would look dubious. I trusted the capable father of my youth to know what was best. Here we are instead, after the fact, playing a much less fun grownup version of "pig pile" on our sister. I push thoughts of blame away and decide to stay positive and focused on my immediate goal, selling the violins. *By the end of the day, I'll have money in hand!* High hopes fill the car as I drive the rest of the way to the appraiser's home-based shop.

Over the next hour, though, they're slowly dashed as he opens each case and deems its contents worthless. With the exception of a petrified mouse carcass, nothing out of the ordinary is found and there are no ancient finds worth thousands. In fact, the violins are worth less than street value because of Dad's tampering with the varnish and their storage in a damp basement. After paying the appraiser's thirty-dollar assessment fee and the gas expense for the hour-long drive, the trip has been less than worthwhile, literally.

What a waste, I think on the silent drive back, preferring not to turn on the radio. *What would Louanne say to this?*

And it comes, clear as day. Teasing me and laughing, with one hand poised close to her ear, the ten-year-old version of herself rubs a thumb to her forefinger and says, "Listen to the world's smallest violin playing. My heart bleeds for you." I know it's not meant to be mean-spirited, just funny. She made that motion on so many occasions, and it was never as apropos as it is in this moment. Here it is—closure, served up Louanne-style—and it makes me laugh.

Finding the buried treasure isn't going to happen. I swallow my disappointment and decide there's no use crying anymore, no more blame game. It doesn't solve anything or help anyone. We're still in the same situation and I need to constructively handle it however I can. I say a prayer and thank God for the moments of clarity I'm receiving. I don't want to look back anymore and wish it were different. I need to deal with the reality of the situation and take it one thing at a time. *I'm not finished yet. I still have a goal to accomplish with these violins.*

I stop at one of the local antique shop/auction houses that Dad and Louanne used to frequent and where he'd bought many of the violins. I've never met the auctioneer, but he definitely remembers the spending duo from my description. I don't need to say much for him to see that I'm the crazed one in the family, on a mission to peddle back a boatload of violin loot. Having knocked loudly on a door open to the public and marched up to a messy desk in the corner of a deserted room, I ask if he or someone in charge could join me in the parking lot. He follows me out, and I suspect he knows as well as I that this exchange is more than about the pile of musty-smelling violins in the back of the car.

I can't help but think if this were a movie, the trip to Concord and this moment here in the Gina's Antiques parking lot would be presented in a montage laid over with music, the conversations unheard but understood. There's an element of sadness, given the back story of the frustrated protagonist, but there's also something darkly comical as she crosses the line into behavior she wouldn't normally dream of. The auctioneer makes legitimate points and puts up a good argument—"They aren't even nice enough to hang on the wall at a restaurant for decoration!"—but it doesn't matter. I'm on a mission. With chin firmly set, I slowly take the cases from the back of the car and stack them neatly on the pavement, and then the viewer reads my lips as I say, measured and steady, like something out of an old western movie, "And I'm not leaving until you pay me something back." I accept the auctioneer's one-hundred-dollar offer without negotiation, glad to be done with it. Clint Eastwood would be proud.

I put the money in our joint account along with other meager purses that have been cobbled together. Altogether, though, it's far short of what's necessary to bring him back home—a few hundred versus several thousand. Ultimately, I use the money to thank the nursing home staff with the occasional pizza dinner and treats from Dunkin' Donuts and, for Dad, a series of massages, albeit initially unwanted. My hope is that these small tokens of gratitude and respect make a difference to the host of people helping to care for him. It feels good to be able to do something tangible in a situation where so much is unfolding out of my control and out of my hands.

I'm quiet, more still, when I visit now. More often down on my knees beside his wheelchair, trying to engage him. Helpless as I watch him slip into himself.

> *That each of them may eat and drink, and find*
> *satisfaction in all their toil—this is the gift of God.*
> Ecclesiastes 3:13

Shape Up or Ship Out   20

Late August

Tuesday

E ven though the days are still warm, the back-to-school vibe is in the air, making it no longer seem like summer vacation. The final days of August are excruciating for Summer, who's counting down to the bliss of school. The sprinkler lies on its side in the backyard, abandoned, gone the appeal of running and whooping loudly through the tickly spray. Her bathing suit drawer is getting fewer visits, and I now serve as a watchdog to keep new school clothes fresh and clean.

While she's filled with expectation about the wonders of second grade, I feel like I'm crawling to the finish line. It's okay, though. There's that industry conference coming up in October that I'm hoping to attend, and my own sense of expectation fuels the daily grind. It's nice to have something to look forward to and a possible few days away, in Florida to boot. The best part is that I've been asked to be part of a small panel discussion about ways that learning departments within companies (also known as "corporate universities") can better work with traditional universities. It's feel-good recognition for me, and has the benefit of added exposure for the university.

I cashed in every possible favor to get neighbors to watch Summer while I was at work for all of the prior week, after the Y summer camp ended. School begins tomorrow, and yesterday was Monday, my weekly FMLA day off, leaving today to find someone, anyone, to watch Summer so I can go to work. The last day of the dreaded summer-vacation childcare challenge and I struck out. My request to work from home was denied without much conversation as to why, so I'm using a vacation day to work from home. It doesn't occur to me to 1) use it as an *actual* day off, or 2) feel angry about it yet.

I have several calls scheduled, the first being the weekly staff meeting, which begins promptly at nine. Even though I'm squirreled away in my home office with the door closed, I can hear Summer in the living room merrily singing the jingle for Target's back-to-school commercial. It's a snappy list of school-related supplies to the tune of the Go-Go's hit "We Got the Beat."

Summer and the TV blare, "Pens and markers, paper, wide-ruled. . . . Putty, sneakers, tape, sticks of glue. . . ."

I stick my head into the hall for one final stern reminder. "Sum, don't forget what I said. I need to be on this call, so please pipe down, okay?!"

She nods, smiling a devilish grin while doing her special jig, and whisper-screams the finale, "Notebooks and jeans, notebooks and jeans, notebooks and jeans . . . yeah! Notebooks and jeans!"

So goes my day, working the best that I can while navigating a myriad of distractions, hybrid chores/games, hugs, and threats.

Thankfully, Tony gets home from work early enough for me to visit Dad during dinnertime. His on-time arrival is almost enough to erase the memory of the vein-bulging argument we had this morning about who gets to go to work. I lost this one, but the consolation is that I'll get the free pass the next time around. It doesn't strike me as odd yet that arguments of this nature aren't the dynamic that I want our daughter to grow up hearing.

After goodbye hugs for him and Summer, I'm headed to Panera to buy Dad's baked-potato soup and then to McDonald's for a drive-thru shake. He's not been eating as much, and even his favorite soups aren't coaxing his appetite. But we've seen this before, and he usually bounces back. He doesn't look good, though. He has a sallow pallor, and it seems to me that the bluish tinge of the veins in his arms and the dark brown age spots have never been more pronounced. His once-strong hand, now with paper-thin skin, supports his head, resting just above his brow, shielding ever-shut eyes. His clothes are baggy because of weight loss, and with his slumped posture he looks so frail. It doesn't help that he insists on being able to sleep in his chair, saying, "I'm just resting my eyes," or "I'm just taking a catnap." Always refuses the offer to be helped to bed. I pass much of the time holding his hand and rubbing his arms to warm him up. He feels so cold, and I leave concerned. But then, that's nothing new.

Triumphantly, the first day of school finally arrives and it's giddy excitement with a touch of nerves all around. Summer is up and dressed (several times over) before anyone. "Yup, I'll finish the last sausage in a minute, but no more apple slices, okay?" she says, sliding off the kitchen stool on her way upstairs to change back into the original shorts that were planned before she'd decided, "Stupid."

"At least she has an appetite," Tony says, stealing a bite of her sausage dibs.

"Really, Tone? Can you try and spare me the headache and not eat the stinkin' sausage today of all days? Can you help me distract her from the outfit, please?"

"I'm on it." At the foot of the stairs, he calls up in his best concerned tone of voice, "Hey, Summer, can you come down now? The bus will be here any minute and I need to tell you one last thing."

This should be good. I put dishes in the sink and wrap part of the sausage link in a paper towel just like she likes it, with the nibble end concealed. As I begin to overenthusiastically wipe the counters, releasing nervous energy, I know I have my resting face on. It's well-known in my family that I don't have a pleasant resting expression. During a visit to see the *Oprah* show back in the day, I was one of three members of the "unsuspecting studio audience" to have their resting faces interpreted by the panel expert. Subsequently, before a national viewing audience, the Queen concurred with the expert: "Oh, yeah, that's unpleasant." As a result, I'm pretty sure I'm more conscious about my mug than the average person. Sometimes I'll remember to plaster a false Joker-style grin on my face at, say, a traffic light, where it's well-known one's resting face is most likely to appear. Try as I might to be forever diligent, however, I suppose it's made several appearances in the office as well.

With the beginning of a structured school schedule and the end of makeshift childcare arrangements, there's something about the back-to-school prospect that really feels like a new beginning, even more so than New Year's Eve. But rather than being steeped in melancholy and too many martinis, I've just had a little too much coffee. Tony notices.

"Smiles, smiles, everyone," he says in his best *Fantasy Island* Ricardo Montalbán imitation, making a grand, sweeping gesture with his arm, as if we're waiting to greet our guests or putting on a show. I giggle, and he takes it a step further. "Little does she know her fantasy will soon turn to danger. . . ."

He takes away the dish sponge and hugs me. It feels good and I snuggle in immediately. It's such a simple thing but exactly what I need. "I don't know why I'm this uptight, Tone," I say into his shoulder. "It's been a slog, you know?"

"I know, Sa, and it's going to get better."

I'm glad he lets me be the one to break the embrace. "Do you think it's crazy to try and attend this conference in Florida? Will I really be able to leave everything? You, Sum, my father?"

"No, not crazy, but it's weeks away. Let's cross that bridge when we get to it. Today we're getting on the bus and getting to work on time. Right?"

"Right."

Summer comes down in her originally planned outfit, which is obviously no longer stupid. "Oh good, honey, I think you look wonderful and you'll be comfy, not too hot." I try to hand her the sausage in its paper-towel blanket, but she dismisses it with a quick shake of her head. Instead I hand off her new messenger-style backpack with the black-and-white polka dots and pinned on bling. More so than clothes or shoes, the challenge this year was to find the right backpack. At last, after visits to stores galore, she found the perfect shoulder bag amid the visual explosion of colorful accessories at Claire's.

"I don't know, you might be hot. It's supposed to be hot out today," Tony adds, and I shoot him a look. "But of course you look nice. Why wouldn't you?"

We're in shameless helicopter mode as we try to keep things light, and I'm hoping she doesn't notice.

"What did you want to tell me, Dad?" she asks, sighing, half annoyed, half worried.

"I just wanted to remind you that bees will be riding to school with you," he says in his best straight-man delivery as we all walk down the stairs toward the side door.

"Bees?"

"That's right, probably quite a few."

Now I'm curious. Was there some ordinance for pest spraying that I didn't read?

"They will? Why?" She's clearly worried.

"Because they always take the *school buzz!*" he says, and gives us each a fist pump.

Summer laughs and it's infectious.

As we walk down the driveway, our laughter trickles away, and we stand on the sidewalk as a family, comfortable together and with our thoughts in the warmth of the morning sun.

Summer breaks the silence. "Um, are you *both* planning to get me on the bus?" she asks politely, just as transparent as our helicopter fly pattern probably was.

Tony takes his cue. "No way, man, I'm outta here. I wouldn't be caught dead standing with you two. He bends to kiss the top of her head, kisses my cheek, and reaches for the sausage that I've forgotten I'm walking around with. We watch him drive away and wave.

With Summer about to pull away in a school bus, I suddenly feel the need to recap some of the highlights of the past few months. "Remember the last day of school, Summer, and—"

"You mean the party at Derek's house with the invitation that said 'pool party, bring your bathing suit'?" she says with a smirk.

We laugh about it, as we have several times before, because in my hurried mind-set, I did *not* pack a bathing suit. What's more, I didn't even notice it was a pool party. At pickup time, I was one of the last to arrive and found Summer with a couple of the remaining kids joyfully bobbing around in the water in her summer dress and underwear, happy as a clam. At the time, I was embarrassed for my oversight, but more proud of her childish abandon.

Unfettered, joyful, and confident—that's my wish for my beautiful girl, I realize. And remember my own summer highlight: the patio visit with Dad and learning his life wish for all of us.

Before I can mention any more good times, the bus rounds the corner and noisily labors up the street. I grab her in tight and we give each other a heartfelt hug and a hard squeeze. "This is it. What a great summer! It flew by so fast, didn't it?" We both laugh hard because she gets my sarcasm. I must have yelled to the heavens a dozen times during the swelter of the past week, in increasingly melodramatic fashion: "When will it end?! When will this summer *end*?!" Right up to yesterday, when she was bouncing off the walls while I tried in vain to work.

She hops up the stairs onto the bus at the promised eight-thirty arrival time. There are no forced smiles today. I'm grinning ear to ear and wave as she settles into her seat. And as the bus pulls away, she smiles back, just as glad. I walk back up the driveway, grab my laptop case from the entryway and lock up the house. Backing out of the driveway, I roll the windows down. *Such a day this is shaping up to be.* I had my hair done over the weekend, during the same errand to have Summer's hair cut for school, so it's all colored and as styled as I can muster, and I'm feeling pretty good about the little things in life. *Thank you, God, for the blessings of this day.*

The morning commute is a breeze and I'm at work in record time. It's 8:50 when I press the power button on my laptop. And my phone isn't blinking with messages, which is a relief and an indication that my time yesterday wasn't entirely a wash. *Oy, I should water my plants.* I grab my watering pail to fill in the kitchen, but when I turn to the door, Twenty-Eight is standing there, apparently having appeared from out of the blue.

"Hi, S. B. Do you have a few minutes to talk?"

"Sure. Want to stay here or your—"

She's already headed down the hall.

I put down the pail, grab my trusty, well-worn day planner in case I need to take notes, and hurry to catch up.

This impromptu request comes as a surprise, as Twenty-Eight would typically schedule a meeting. As we walk, I try to figure out what this could be about. *Maybe she's annoyed that I didn't say much during the team-meeting conference call yesterday.* Truth be told, I kept my phone muted as much as possible to buffer the noise factor. Granted, they were happy sounds of child's play, but not appropriate in any professional capacity.

We sit at her table, and with no pleasantries, she lays it on me.

"We're putting you on a performance improvement plan," she says, direct and to the point in demeanor and tone.

Silence.

I feel as if I've been punched in the stomach.

No explanation. Just more silence.

I'm in shock and disbelief and say the only thing that comes to mind. "Ahh, no I'm not."

It goes without saying that this is the ultimate blow to my ego. *Me?* The master of organization and preparedness, always forward-thinking and having contributed so much to the department over the years? *Haven't I? Isn't it obvious how much I've done? How much I'm doing? Can't they see how much I'm juggling?*

Then I remember. Twenty-Eight's drive-by on Friday. Her concerns about my pipeline. My certainty that they couldn't be anything urgent. Urgent is finding trusted people to watch my daughter for a one-off summer vacation day when summer camp is no longer an option (and subsequently using a personal vacation day—to work). Urgent is when your child is sick and all your plans for the day (or days, depending on the illness) collapse like a house of cards. Urgent is trying desperately to sell your father's treasured collections in the hope that they might be worth something so he can live out his final days in his home. Urgent is answering the phone to various shift nurses at all hours of the day and night with perpetual news of his decline.

Work, and how I view my business development process, is the opposite of crisis mode. It's a deliberate, systematic strategy of moving the ball down the field. The goal, the end game, is my revenue target, and it's always back of mind. It's a method of well-planned outreach to meticulously drawn-up distribution lists of prospect contacts via calls and conversations to uncover and address their needs. I've worked hard to develop a natural conversational approach and demeanor so as never to sound urgent, which can come off as desperate. For anyone in sales, it's a surefire way to limit your career. I know that I'm perceived much better by clients than colleagues. Perhaps the confident calm I bring to account dealings comes across to them as smug? Maybe my cut-to-the-chase style, seen by clients as a way of valuing their time, seems dismissive?

It's a lesson I'm smack-dab in the middle of learning. I may have inadvertently fueled flames when I eagerly pressed for an answer about the conference-panel invitation. It's stating the obvious to say I should have taken that casual chat much more seriously. Sitting across from Twenty-Eight now, my mind races and I wonder if this is my chance to share everything that's going on. *How do I begin? Now it will look like an excuse and defensive. She won't understand. What if I break down? Just say it—he's not eating.* But I don't say it. I know that if I do, I'll crack wide open. *I can't show how vulnerable I am right now. I can't!* Instead, as if on autopilot, I steel and toughen, calling on my now deeply ingrained mantra of *just get through.* To use a sales term, I mirror and match the tone that's been set and hear myself speaking in an authoritative, almost patronizing way, something along the lines of "Just you hold your horses, little lady."

As if trying to demonstrate my value and my understanding of how she should be thinking in a manager's capacity, I wax eloquent on the importance of knowing what motivates members of your team. I go so far as to name people and what drives them. "Say, Thurston Howell, the consummate salesperson who cares about dollars. Bonus bumps and incentives mean everything to him. Wide-eyed Mary Anne? She just wants to be liked. Take every opportunity to shower her with public praise and acknowledgment and she'll be happy as a wrangler in a greasy-pig contest. How about sly Ginger? Having been here the longest, she just wants to feel like she's in the know, on the inside, you know, in the club? Wink-wink."

True to form in my encounters with her, I'm unnerved and rambling while she sits, well, gaping. I'm hoping she'll ask about me, take the prompt so we can have that discussion. What motivates me? What do I need? When she doesn't, I go there anyway.

"What I could really use right now is the ultimate currency: time. I need flexibility and time." What I don't add is "and understanding." Compassion.

Her expression is now controlled staring. Composed, silent staring.

Clearly, we're not of the same mind. Couldn't be further apart.

Feeling discouraged, I think about when I used to report to the dean. That was before the department ballooned and grew from all our success and hard work. Older and wiser, "the Skipper" was the reason for my accepting this job. During the interview, he had made it clear that there were no roadmaps for how to do the job, no defined sales territories or methodologies, just an open playing field for someone self-motivated and self-directed. *Perfect, heaven, my dream job!* Plus, I'd worked with plenty of young managers climbing corporate ladders, and here was my chance to work with someone who'd proved himself. Someone who'd climbed to see the view as opposed to having climbed to *be* viewed, as they say. While the key value sought in a business development manager at the time of my hiring was self-reliance, the current focus is all about alliances and interdependence. In a sense, I'm caught between the generational styles of the idealistic, hard-working values of my initial baby-boomer manager and the all-things-team-and-interactivity millennial. Through my own Gen Xer, autonomy-loving lens, such collaboration seems more about oversharing and handhold-ing. There are constant team meetings and daily disputes over role definition that I shy away from in my quest to be productive, focused, invisible.

"I know the dean is on vacation this week, but I would like to talk to him." I say, remembering when he used to make the rounds to each of our offices, checking in and asking if we were having fun. "Oh, he knows about this." She leaves it at that and continues to stare.

I'm stunned all over again. I can't imagine that he would let this play out in this way. The Skip used to start every conversation with three simple words: "How are you?" And much of the Yogi Berra wisdom he imparted was along the lines of my favorite: "If you need help, ask for it!" That easily, he created an environment of openness and transparency, which, in crystal-clear hindsight, I should have taken advantage of. But I didn't, opting for the proud, self-assured approach, and now I have to believe this edict delivered by Twenty-Eight is less about recent performance than about not fitting in. The irony being just that: the timing. Having been brought to my knees by months of being overextended, I'm no longer harried and proud. I'm worn down. Long gone is the overconfident persona. If anything, I'm overly deferential to just about everyone. The pendulum has swung in the other direction, and it's now more common for me to apologize my way through the day. *Avoid conflict and petty office drama at all costs.*

I try my best to share this, but it falls short. "I'm not how I used to be. I feel like I've been chipped at for so long that I've lost a piece of who I am. No job is worth that." She offers no reply. In fact, I'm not sure it's even possible for her to comprehend what I'm talking about. At her age, I would never have understood. In comparison, I had as much depth as a Dixie cup, enjoying the pre-9/11 innocence of the nineties, romping around dog-friendly parks and, for that matter, the globe, with people and places—life itself—viewed at arm's length, as I might view a beautiful Renaissance painting in the Uffizi Gallery.

The reality is that Twenty-Eight, while driven and laser-focused, is also fair and straightforward in her dealings with the team. I've witnessed the savvy of this young woman in diffusing hypersensitive issues of role definition and toe-stepping. And a dedicated loyalty to rival that of anyone seated at the round table. She has one of the longest commutes of anyone but still always manages to be the first one in the office. As for business acumen, she knows the pulse of faculty developments and has introduced formalized sales training, thereby creating a common language, tool set, and best practices as a foundation on which to build. Based on past office squabbles and various interpersonal disputes, I know she's capable of understanding and advising, but not here, not now.

Now that I can admit to finally needing help, it seems no longer an option. I realize that I've been operating all along as if Skip were still at the helm.

"Things sure have changed a lot around here," I say, aware that I sound a lot like the Beav.

"Yes, they have," she says, "and they'll continue to."

I can no longer meet her direct stare and look down. Deflated. I'm quiet, letting it sink in that this is no longer the place where I belong. I finally get that this conversation is not going to soften. I sigh and get up to leave. *No one here is going to ask, "How are you?"* This feels like a situation where someone has been waiting since Friday to check this task—me—off the list.

After the meeting, I bolt back to my office and with shaking hands fumble to shut down my system and get my laptop out of the docking bay. Feeling physically ill, I can't breathe. My mind races. *I can't work today. How can I stay here?* The fight-or-flight instinct has kicked in.

I look up and Twenty-Eight is in the doorway again. "I forgot to mention, don't make any plans to attend the conference."

"I need to go home," I manage to say. "I'm not feeling well." But it's barely a whisper, and I'm not sure if she heard me before she turned to walk away. Feeling foolish for possibly talking to myself in my empty office, I debate whether to leave a voice-mail saying that I need to leave for the day. But I know I've lost my voice. I don't trust how I'll come across. Defiant? Distraught? Instead, I flee.

I'm blinded with tears and anger on the ride home, tears and anger stemming from years of hard work and recent heartache. Angry at myself for not speaking up more, I recall good practices I've had a hand in and defend my work style to myself. *Family first, make the rounds, check the list, steer away from younger colleagues calling me out in the name of not feeling appreciated, and learn from the subtle, sometimes biting inferences from women with grownup children, to the effect of,* "deal with it, like I did." It's a study in self-preservation.

I chew over instances of feedback ignored, meetings where others were recognized and I was forgotten, meetings where I should have been present but wasn't invited. In the name of efficiency and not rocking the boat, I would always push aside the slight, real or imagined, and focus on the job at hand. *Don't make it about you,* I'd tell myself, *and do the right thing.* And now these microinequities that I've allowed to accumulate over time represent a mountain of injustices to me. At the core, I'm embarrassed and grappling to understand what has happened, confused by the difference between how I've been perceived, who I've been, and who I've become. *Is this who I want to be?*

By the time I'm home, the digital clock on the now-cold pot of coffee blinks "10:00." Less than two hours ago we were basking together in the sun while waiting for Summer's bus, and I was looking forward to what the day would bring. Now I know, and begin my internet search for a lawyer.

Watch, stand fast in the faith, be brave, be strong.
1 Corinthians 16:13

Heaven Sent

21

September 2012

Here, back in the quiet of the house, picking up toys, folding clothes, and tending to everyday household duties, I'm content. Lighter. *It's been a process for sure.* With the break from the university and from working full-time, I have time to figure out what I want to do next. A luxury and a blessing. Sitting in our back screened-in porch with a cup of hot apple cinnamon tea, I take in the falling leaves and crisp September air. Soon it will be too cold to sit out here for long stretches. It was just a couple of weeks ago when I had the "sprinkler moment" and find myself looking for it again, in the middle of the backyard. That's where I saw the most beautiful surreal rainbow through the mist of the sprinkler.

But it was more than that. It was late afternoon of the same day I'd left work early and contacted a lawyer. Still tense from the high emotions of the day, I had put a pot of water on the stove to prep for dinner. While waiting for it to boil, I had turned on the sprinkler to water the browning grass and wilted plantings. As I sat down on the love seat on the porch, that fresh earth smell came up and, breathing it in, I finally relaxed, for the first time all day. Drained and bone-tired, I watched the steady motion of the sprinkler, swaying back and forth, the water arcing high into the air.

In an almost meditative state, I experienced something amazing and surrendered to something greater than myself. It was more than witnessing the usual rainbow effect that we learn about (and forget) in junior high science, where, from just the right angle, you can see light bend and refract in the spray. I've seen countless minirainbows and plays of light, but this was different, breathtaking and comforting at the same time. It was a glimpse into something not of this world, where colors are golden, effervescent, and richer in clarity, almost musical. The vibrancy is impossible to describe, soothing beyond anything I'd ever experienced. I don't remember the thoughts I had, just awe and a deep sense of serenity as time seemed to stand still.

When Summer came running out, panicked, to tell me the water was boiling, the sprinkler moment dissipated. It was an unexpected occurrence that I didn't want to end. It left a yearning pain in its wake. As I made dinner, though, the yearning disappeared and I felt refreshed, at peace.

I'm not sure what it was, but it was something. Something special had happened and I knew everything was going to change and it would be all right.

A few days later, my father died.

After zipping my plum fleece sweater all the way up to my chin, I tear myself away from reliving that memory and flip to an empty page in my purple notebook. I'm in a pattern of listening to my favorite radio pastors out here on the porch, taking notes, and jotting random remembrances. I feel better listening to Scripture and the word of God. It beats back the self-doubt, anger, and humiliation that sometimes creep in for not handling it all differently. For not knowing better. Today, though, I don't have my radio companions, preferring the solitude of my wandering thoughts and the rustle of leaves.

I stare down at the blank page, and again the stirrings of a book come to mind. *Is my story something I should share? Can I even write a book—who do I think I am?* I think about the journey I've taken during these past few years, being closer to family, carrying the weight of responsibility, and I feel secure in what I've learned. I smile to know, to finally know, that difficult times that disrupt our busy lives are quite often divine moments and lessons from God. From this experience, I can better understand, relate to, support, and encourage others who have gone through this, too, and give a heads-up to those who will. Hopefully, I can show that even in mistakes, strife, and unpreparedness, we are connected, that God's grace is sufficient.

A recurring message from almost all the radio pastors is that we need to welcome challenges and even give thanks for them *because trials grow us up.* I think about it and chuckle to myself, trying to imagine talking about it without seeming pious, never mind figuring out how to write it. I suppose the simplest explanation is a process of spiritual maturing—sanctification, in biblical terms. Of becoming in practice what we are in position, of ordering our lives around understanding of the will of God.

I laugh out loud as I imagine possible book titles and cover art. I picture a bird's-eye view of myself in this moment, sitting catatonic in the screened porch and staring at the grass. The way I'm sitting, both feet on the ground, reminds me of Louanne, prehospice, when she would sit and stare for long spans. *Hmm, maybe she was on to something. Maybe she was a budding writer.*

I laugh harder. I'm not laughing at my sister—it's more of a silliness that comes from sitting still with your thoughts, a joy that sort of bubbles up from self-acceptance and knowing that God is in control.

Now I sigh. *I need to put down my heavy baggage or at least try to. But if I write about this, how will I even begin?* The memory of my father's last day comes to mind. I'm not surprised. I think about it often. Like the sprinkler moment, it's something I'll always treasure. He passed less than a week after my decision to move on, inspired by the meeting with Twenty-Eight. Unfortunately, during those last precious days, I was full-on preoccupied with my work situation and it seeped into everything. The shock of a performance improvement mandate for my prideful, hardworking self, rattled me to the core. My perception of my capabilities was all wrapped up with ego and embarrassment about what others would think. There were ad nauseam conversations with my husband and siblings regarding concerns about my reputation, calls with the lawyer, documenting of this or that, and other minutiae. There were never any plans to sue the university, although Tony certainly pondered the idea. Rather, I was obsessed with moving forward, with extricating myself from the situation as a means of self-preservation. Having a lawyer meant getting noticed and being heard. I assumed it meant I finally had a voice, a hired mouthpiece to represent everything I was feeling. Except, even on my best day, I myself couldn't actually articulate what that was. When I tried, I would inevitably dissolve, sobbing, emotionally raw and bereft, and become incoherent, stringing together example upon example of real or imagined injustices by colleagues, friends and, most painfully, siblings.

And at the time, amazingly enough, Dad seemed to have bounced back and was having a good spell. I was there for his last exam with the doctor, and he was in good spirits, very alert and conversational. He seemed fine, so it was easy to be preoccupied. Why worry when everything is okay?

Except it wasn't.

The call comes early Thursday morning, the kind you dread the most—when you're still in bed. "Your dad is not doing well, Sarahbeth," the overnight shift nurse says. "You need to come right away."

That's all it takes to be pulled out of self-concern and back to real time, to what really matters. Instant wake-up call. Any thoughts of reputation, lawyers, and pipeline forecasts abruptly take a backseat.

When I rush in, he's in bed, wheezing heavily and in pain from the necrotic tissue on his shins. He winces when the nurse leans on the bed to take his temperature or adjust the sheet, no matter how gently. As she sets him up on the vitals machine, I lean in to hug him and see fear in his eyes.

"Hi, Dad. They told me you're having a bad day."

With the slightest nod, he strains to answer, breathing heavily. "I'm glad you're here." He pauses, more breathless. "I don't feel good."

"I know, Dad, I know. I am here and I'm going to hang around all day if you want, to see if we can get you more comfortable. Just try and relax if you can."

"His pulse ox is 85 percent and his blood pressure is falling," the nurse tells me in a quiet voice.

I nod and pull up the side chair. Taking his hand in mine, I feel how cold he is, and a subtle shock wave goes through me.

"Can we get some extra blankets?" I ask the aide in the room. "Oh, and would you mind putting that navy blue bead bag"—I motion to the bottom bureau drawer—"with the moose pattern on it in the microwave for five minutes to heat up?" A colleague from work made me the microwavable heating wrap with dried corn inside, and I left it in his room weeks ago. He hasn't used it, but to me, it was another tangible, comforting thing I could leave with him, and we're both glad for it when the aide returns. As Dad lies on his side, I tuck the wrap lengthwise against his chest and stomach, and he folds his hands into the covering and closes his eyes. Even though his breathing is still labored, it appears that he's starting to relax, or trying to.

"See, these moose are glad to finally snuggle up," I say, rubbing his arm, feeling a strong need to keep a physical touch. Suddenly, I'm self-conscious about whether it had been okay to say that. *That's something I would say to Summer.* Although I'm trying to act calm and be myself, I'm questioning little details I normally wouldn't. And I'm scared.

"I'm just going to make a few calls in the hallway while you rest, Dad. I'll be right back."

As soon as I step out of his room, I see the lineup along the hall. The word is out on the street, and all the familiar faces we've known on this floor for the past six months, and some we don't, have wheeled their chairs around the nurses' station. I see his roommate, Jeb, his eyes sad but full of understanding. He nods to me, and for the first time that day I cry.

"Thank you, Jeb," I say softly even though he hasn't said a word, and I wipe the tears away.

The nurse comes over with a box of tissues and pats my arm. "Sarahbeth, his blood pressure has been falling. It was 92/56 overnight and now it's 84/48. Just before you arrived, we put in a catheter so he won't have to get up. It's obvious that he's in distress trying to breathe easily. We have doctor's orders to give him morphine to make him more comfortable."

I'm in agreement and give my consent.

"I'll prep and be in right away." As she disappears behind the nurses station, I make a call to Tony to let him know that I'm staying and ask him to call my sisters.

"Okay, I'll let them know, Sa. Don't worry about Summer. I'll stay home from work and get her on the bus. Then I'll be right up. What do you want me to bring?"

"Just a coffee and maybe a box of doughnuts for everyone."

"For who?"

"I don't know, for everyone. For my sisters or patients on the floor or just to have something in his room for people who might stop in and help us get through today. You know how it goes. Oh, and can you bring me a sweater?"

"Okay, Sa, relax, I'm on doughnut duty. Don't bite my head off for this next one. Here it comes—which sweater?"

It makes me smile and shifts my mood. I'm sure he can tell from my tone. "Any one. It doesn't matter. I'm suddenly so cold. Thanks, honey."

Next, I leave a quick message for the Skip at work, informing him of the situation and letting him know I won't be in. It's funny how I always turn to him when the chips are down. Technically, the correct person to inform is Twenty-Eight, but even when I'd reported to kindhearted Penny, my instinct was to call the Skip directly when my sister died. Work-related reporting structures and office political correctness take a backseat in matters close to the heart.

Back in Dad's room, I hold his hand and rub his arm as the nurse administers the morphine. "Dad, I'm right here and you're okay. Colette and Pat are coming up to be with you too." He doesn't say anything, but I know he's not a fan of these drugs or anything that will take away his self-control. I'm unsure, sensing his wishes but needing to trust the medical expertise and experience of the nursing staff. The rigidness of his grasp releases and he begins to breathe in a steadier rhythm.

By late morning, the vigil of sitting bedside begins. This is a familiar scene for all of us. So much so that when Colette arrives, after embracing and checking on Dad—who's comfortable now, lying with his eyes closed but not necessarily asleep—she comments that there's no comfort cart available for the family. "Remember how thoughtful it was when we sat with Mommy and Louanne and they brought in the cart with the coffee, teas, and pastries?" I notice Pat roll her eyes. *Not today, no bickering today.* Instead, she says, "I could use a comfort cart of a different kind," and we laugh together.

All of us know the waiting and tension of what's to come and remain polite. We talk to pass the time, mindful that he can probably hear us. I'm guilty of the occasional shush and finger wag in the name of keeping the conversation appropriate. Actually, it's more of a pointing motion with exaggerated pursed lips and a raised-eyebrow stare. I get very annoyed when anyone brings up details of the funeral service. We made that mistake at our mother's bedside, and I feel strongly that it's crass and disrespectful to make plans in the presence of your loved one. It's kind of like saying, "Hey, that's a wrap. Cue the sunset, plan the lunch."

"Stop being so directive," Colette tells me.

"Yah, and bossy!" Pat chimes in.

Touché. I note her clever way of dissing both Colette's "high-falutin'" word choice and me at the same time. When I leave the room a few minutes later, I hear them laugh like kids.

"We'll say whatever the hell we want, right, Dad?" Pat says.

The truth is, I bet he'd think it's funny too.

The nurse comes in regularly to check vitals, and we notice that the urine in his catheter is very dark and lessening in volume throughout the day. And the pauses between his breaths are lengthening. Taking turns, we're mindful to periodically swipe his mouth and lips with cool water—another rite we know well.

There are solemn moments of quiet and shared memories of how it was when we said goodbye to Mom and Louanne. There are also childhood memories. "Hey, Dad," Colette says playfully, "remember when we drove to the Cape and you missed the exit to take in the rotary? You drove around the second time and when Mommy said, 'Don't miss it again, Ben,' you drove right on by! Then on the third time, all of us kids were hysterically laughing. Mommy was clutching the door handle screaming, 'Cut it out Benny, cut it out!'" Smiling to herself, she launches into another. "Or how about when we used to go to Zayre or Caldor's and us kids would be walking behind you"—her voice breaks—"and you would zigzag in and out of the clothes racks just to see if we would follow"—crying now—"and we always did."

During the course of the day, several aides who have cared for him stop in to talk with us and say what a good person he is. Some take a doughnut, some don't but tell a little story, like the agreeable younger woman from the admissions office who comes in cautiously. "I heard that your dad isn't feeling well today," she says, "so I wanted to come in and check on him and all of you." She turns to him and, louder than we've been talking, says, "Hi,

Benny." Then she stops short, appearing unsure, as if she wants to say more, but instead she turns back to us. "I'll always remember a day during his first few weeks of staying with us when I walked by him sitting in his chair in the hallway. I didn't say anything because his head was down and I thought he was asleep. Honestly, I wasn't having a good day. You know, not feeling that good about myself, or anything really. Maybe I woke him up, because after I passed by, I heard, 'Nice boots.' When I turned around, he winked at me and smiled. It caught me so off guard and made me laugh, you know?"

We all laugh, too.

She turns to him again. "You made me feel better that day," she says, softer now, "and I want to tell you how glad I am to know you. You're a sweet and funny man."

The kindness of people uplifts us and makes the time pass quickly. During lunch, the middle-aged daughter of a patient we've gotten to know stops by and politely gives her regards. On the run, she's squeezing in a quick visit with her mom, and her hair and business clothes are a little askew. More than surface reflection, I see myself in her tired expression. I can relate to the cadence of her days and have genuine compassion.

I remember how wary I was of this environment in the early days after Dad was first admitted, but I've found instant connections here that I never expected. I've met elderly people with personality plus, with stories to share and more zest for life than many you meet in the day-to-day grind. People show their authentic selves inside these walls, where it's not so much about status and title in life as about being a good son or daughter. When I could, I was glad to bring an extra Coney Island hot dog for my dad's hallway companions, and other families returned small kindnesses for us as well. Blessings.

Later in the afternoon, Emily-Anne, our special nurse from Pinnacle, comes in like a burst of sunshine. Seeming right at home in these situations, she says a familiar hello close to Dad's ear and affectionately smooths the hair around his temple. It's reassuring to see that she also uses constant touch. There's something grounding about this practice that some people do almost instinctively. Not only as a means of comfort, I think, but also to press in body heat and life force, to keep the dying reminded of their earthly body and this physical plane.

"Well, Benny," Emily-Anne says, "I'm sure you're right at home with all of us ladies fawning all over you. Such attention you're getting and keeping us on our toes. You're the buzz at the nurses' station, you know." Standing bedside, physically near, during her entire stay, she rubs his arm and reminds him of his charming ways with little comments and quips. Before she leaves, she helps the nurse on shift to freshen him up and reposition him so that he's lying on his back, with his head and chest propped up with pillows, the thin nasal oxygen device on. When we hug goodbye, I know I'll miss Emily-Anne. She's made a difference by helping us through this period. I'm grateful for having met someone immersed in her life's purpose and so full of light.

As the day progresses, the mood in the room becomes calm and quiet, growing more reverent in step with Dad's decline. Tony has been stopping in to check on us during the vigil and, once school was out, returned with Summer in hand. She joined Colette's girls, also just arrived from school, who were down the hall in the TV room having their snack before coming in to say goodbye. Colette senses their unease when they enter.

"Why don't you each share a favorite memory or special thing that you love about Grampa?"

They do, and the shyest, Summer, goes last. "Grampa, I liked that you got me Eddy" she says quietly, referencing the toy bouncy horse on springs. She leans in further to add in a whisper, "and please check on Buddy for me. I think he'll be glad to see you." Afterward, they all know without being told to kiss his cheek. The scene is as beautiful as it is heartbreaking.

When Pat's boys, who are older, arrive, we step out to give them each their time alone. As they say their goodbyes, I reflect on all of the visitors Dad has had, not just today but since coming here. He's had weekly scheduled reading time with the kind woman assigned from the Pinnacle program since he became unable to focus on the page. When I was working and couldn't be here, I'd take consolation in the fact that she was. More blessings. There were also regular visits from church members and our pastor and the occasional lunch with his brothers, who from the start seem to have had a hard time seeing Dad in this condition. Not to mention all his children and their spouses. He's been visited almost daily since he arrived here in April, and I try and take comfort in this. *Here he had more companionship and help than the Walmart days, when he was living at home, alone on the red couch.* I already know that in the days ahead, I'll recall this accounting to try to stave off pangs of guilt and remorse. We all know he would have preferred being at home with his pets.

Just after the dinner hour, everyone begins to slowly clear out, spilling into the hallway, consoling each other, and saying goodnight with red-rimmed eyes. We agree that I'll stay overnight, and just before Colette leaves, she and I call Will, who ultimately had moved back to Florida. It's his turn now to say goodbye, and I hold the phone to Dad's ear. I don't know what Will says to him, but he has a knack for knowing what to say in the toughest times.

When we hang up, Colette and I sit together in the still of the room, hearing only the slowed rhythm of his breathing. Our chairs are on either side of the bed, each of us holding one of his hands.

"Sa, you know I can come back if you want, once I take the girls home," Colette says, as if reading my thoughts.

Part of me wants her to stay, to be here to spare me from enduring the hardest part alone. "Nope, that's okay. It's been an emotional day for you, too, and with everyone gone, I'm glad for the quiet time." Being sure to include him, I add, "Right, Dad? It's been Grand Central Station." He doesn't respond.

When Colette hugs me at the foot of the bed, I surprise myself by not crying. I feel like I'm all cried out.

Hallway conversation drifts in as she leaves, and amid it I hear her voice. "Oh, for heaven's sake, of course Jeb can go in!" It dawns on me that poor Jeb has been estranged from his room all day. Kofi, my favorite male aide, wheels Jeb in, and Jeb puts his good hand out to signal that he wants to stop at the end of Dad's bed. There are tears on his cheeks.

I get up to hug him. "Are you going to be all right being in here with us now?"

He nods emphatically and forces a slurred reply. "Weee're aaall okay." He motions to indicate that he means Dad and me as well.

"She's okay, you're okay—no one ever asks if I'm okay, eh?" Kofi jokes in his Ghanaian accent, lightening the solemn moment, before wheeling Jeb to his side of the room. He hums a soothing melody, and through the drawn curtain, I hear him ready Jeb for the night, kind and thorough as always.

"Heh, would you mind if Jeb watches his programs?" Kofi asks politely, drawing back the privacy curtain just a little.

I nod, and he stands a few minutes at the foot of Dad's bed before he leaves, not saying anything but, I suspect, paying his respects.

After Kofi is gone, the sounds of *Wheel of Fortune* play softly in the background. Sitting with Dad's hand in mine, I take in the details of the room. The picture of him in service, topside on the USS *Joseph P. Kennedy Jr.* A young man, unknowingly part of the greatest generation. Handmade cards from his grandchildren and church-sermon transcripts pinned to the corkboard. In the quiet of the dimly lighted room, I notice that his breathing is very shallow and that the deafening pauses between each breath are becoming longer.

I stand and gently put one hand on his heart and the other on the top of his head. I don't know why, but it seems a natural thing to do. I stand that way for a few minutes before sitting on the edge of his bed. I know it won't be long, and I'm no longer self-conscious about what to say, how I sound, or if Jeb hears me.

"Well, we got through today, Dad. It's nice that everyone was here." Leaning in and straining to hear each breath, I lower my voice and put my arms around him. "We all love you so much, you know. Thank you, Dad, for being such a wonderful father." My voice catches as I begin to cry. "Such a life you've had. You should be proud. I'm proud to be your daughter and couldn't have asked for more." The hymn *Angels We Have Heard on High* comes to mind, and I sing it softly in a shaky voice. Crying and holding him tight, I don't know why I sing. It just came to mind. And while I do, he takes his last breath.

Then I recognize the same feeling of utter peace I had while making dinner after the sprinkler moment. Cleansing. Like ozone before a heavy rain and the freshness that comes afterward.

I sit up and wipe away my tears, knowing he's gone. It's a different room now, absent of pain. Now there's only peace.

> *Be still, and know that I am God.*
> Psalm 46:10

Growing Up

22

A gust of wind in the trees pulls my attention back to the porch. There's a definite chill, and the blank page still waits in front of me. Sum, with her clamor of energy, will be home from school soon, which is truly the best part of my day, but it's not so easy to write then.

My focus with her lately is to help her become more self-sufficient. The reality is that she should be taking on a little more. At her age, I was sliding a chair over to the kitchen sink to stand on to wash dishes. It's been said that moms who do too much usually have husbands and children who do too little. Jus' sayin'. But in fairness, I'm grateful for how these years have strengthened my relationship with Tony. The daycare drop-offs, the silent tears, the morning workouts, the distracted chats over the blare of TV—all of it is the stuff of our shared life, our happily ever after. Now that life has slowed down, we have time to talk again, to have actual meaningful conversations about growing old and the inescapable truth of how fleeting our time is. No doubt, most of Dad's elderly companions in the nursing home had once run around crazy busy and raising families just like us. And just like him.

We've also talked about the world of caregivers to which our eyes have been opened. We've been witness to kindness, compassion, and hands-on help as the norm. It's so vastly different from the formalities and the competitive landscape we've grown accustomed to in the corporate world.

Pen in hand, I look down, wondering how to summarize this ordeal—the uncertain ground of eldercare, the equally uncertain ground of childcare, work-related pressure, the navigating of office dynamics, sibling tensions, the insecurities associated with growing up in a hoarding home. It's a clutter of memories for me to take and leave what I choose.

Ever present is how I handled things at work, and not just this last position but previous roles as well. Not seeing things the way they are or seeing people for who they are. Lacking discernment and moving through life with either rose-colored glasses, timidly forgiving overbearing personalities by looking at their circumstances, or having impatient, unrealistic expectations for others and myself. Especially myself. Taking bullish behavior that I experienced in one corporate culture to the next and then swinging from overconfidence to meekness. I never knew how to stand up for myself in a mature, articulate way. I didn't take full advantage of the FMLA time I was allowed, not having begun soon enough or recognized when a four-day workweek still wasn't enough. And as a result, I burned out.

At least I can laugh about it now with a little help from Tony. He's perfected his imitation of the meek, mumbling Milton from the movie *Office Space*, with whom I felt a kinship: "Um, um, have you seen my stapler? I believe you have my stapler." That wasn't who I wanted to be, so I rejected it with everything in my power, and in doing so, I stepped closer to God and into *his* power. And with God everything is possible.

With so many thoughts swirling, it's overwhelming to try to write. My foot is jiggling under the table, and I've been tapping my notebook with my pen all this time. So I say a prayer to settle my mind and ask how to begin.

It comes to light effortlessly. In fact, it's been back of mind all along. *When I am weak, then I am strong.* It gives me goose pimples, and I'm thrilled at the prospect of a start! I don't even know if I have the Bible quote correct or if I understand the full meaning, but I know I want to find out. Though a little nervous about how this will work, I'm fully committed.

In the distance, I hear the familiar low, grinding sound of the school bus's engine and the squeal of the brakes as it makes stops down the street. At the top of the driveway, I wave to Summer as she sprints off the bus, beaming. Talking nonstop all the way into the house, she barely takes a breath.

Inside, she transitions seamlessly to the subject of her after-school snack. "I want to make my own snack and drink today, Mom, just like we practiced. Oh, and don't worry—I'm going to make *good choices*, something healthy."

"Oh? That's great! Let me sug—"

"And if it's okay, I don't want you to watch, so you can keep doing what you were doing, 'kay? Maybe I can make cheese on toast?"

"Sure, there's also peanut butter on crackers. Just be sure to use a paper plate."

Out on the back porch, I gather up my notes and smile as themes to explore in my story come to mind: the best-laid plans; saying goodbye, not only to loved ones but to lifestyles and philosophies that we mature beyond; flaws and forgiveness; serving; and, ultimately, the necessity of compassion, for each other and ourselves. I'm excited about the prospect of beginning something new even though I'm not quite sure what that will be. *I just pray I can prove worthy of the gifts I've been given.*

That's when I hear the crash, the sound of snack-making gone wrong. Summer runs out to the porch, out of breath and fighting tears.

"Don't be mad."

"Uh-oh, mad about what?"

"I was going along just fine, did the peanut butter and got my own drink, but the pitcher slipped." No longer able to hold back the torrent, she breaks into sobs. "It's *bro-ho-ken.* I broke it and made a mess!"

Inside, the cracked plastic mixing jug lies in a large pool of traveling lemonade. "Sheesh, I guess you did. It's a pretty good one, too."

When she sees that I'm not really mad, her tears slow, but I know it's her pride that's been hurt. She was determined to do it on her own. My heart swells as I pull her close to me for a hug.

"Look, Mom, it's spilled on the new clean rug. I don't think it will stain if we catch it, will it? I think it's okay."

"It *is* okay, honey. Let me help you clean up. It seems to me that stains and messes are part of life. And it's okay to ask for help. We all need a little help sometimes, that's why we have each other."

I know there are more days ahead where I'll find myself in either a race, a steady state, or a crawl, but for now, I'm on my knees, alongside my daughter, which is just fine.

> *Trust in the Lord with all of your heart and lean not on your own understanding. In all your ways acknowledge Him and He shall direct your paths.*
> Proverbs 3:5–6

Topics for Discussion

1. The title, *Run, Walk, Crawl: Caught Between Generations,* has a dual meaning with regard to Sarahbeth feeling pulled between generations at home and in the workplace. Have you had similar experiences personally or professionally?

2. Rather than joining the numerous books available offering tips and best practices, Sarahbeth chose to share her story without prescriptive advice and overt lessons learned. How does this help or hinder the story?

3. Sarahbeth makes note of hearing her father's voice offering maxims and advice. For example, "Walk with a purpose." "Eat what you like, just not a lot of it!" Do you replay family sayings or rules to live by in your mind?

4. Early in the story, Sarahbeth references a string of deaths among her immediate family and friends, and mentions reliving memories about them as akin to posttraumatic stress disorder (PTSD). How did family illness and prolonged grieving impact her decision to resign?

5. Did you find yourself interpreting anything from *Run, Walk, Crawl* through the lens of personal experience? Specifically, topics and themes relating to:
    — Childcare, eldercare, and self-care
    — Sibling viewpoints
    — Sleep deprivation
    — Conflict avoidance
    — Women and stoicism
    — Persistence

6. Faith plays a large role in Sarahbeth's journey and becomes her source of strength. What moments resonate and why? What strengthens you?

Afterword

This is not an Afterword in the typical sense, where I simply provide an update on what I've been doing in the five years since the main events of this book ended. I'll include such an update, but I also feel compelled to address in more detail the workplace aspects of my story. In large part, I was motivated by everything I experienced to write this book for proverbial corporate America.

Out of respect for former colleagues, I did not add many details about office life. Sharing my story was *never* about finger-wagging or harming reputations. I harbor no ill will against my former manager, coworkers, or place of employment. Or any previous employers for that matter! In nearly every position I've ever held, I've thanked my lucky stars—first, for the challenging work, and second, for the opportunity to learn from so many gifted and professional colleagues.

Nor do I think anyone at my former job had any personal vendetta against me. But I do believe there's unconscious bias in the workplace with regard to understanding the challenges that family caregivers face. What might be perceived as lack of commitment, could be just the opposite—a necessary drawing back to simultaneously conserve time and energy while juggling personal issues and the requirements of a demanding job. I would like companies that espouse the "we're all one big family" work ethic to examine carefully how they view and respond to employees struggling during such all-too-common life situations—and make sure they really mean what they say.

At a recent women-in-business networking event, a highly regarded female senior executive did a masterful job of explaining how she handled a situation similar to mine when she needed extra flexibility for caregiving purposes. With a little finesse and by flipping the question, she was able to illuminate (to a stereotypically stodgy, older, male manager) an even better precedent—of a progressive environment where employees would feel supported and respond, in turn, by being all the more dedicated. The manager gave her a chance to prove that her commitment to her job would continue in spite of an unconventional schedule. She made it work.

And that's what this, my story, my current focus, is all about. Well, sort of. Flexible schedules are just one part of the equation. The message I now champion is: Retention, loyalty, and morale increase when employees feel supported. That may seem like stating the obvious. But the reality is that, in most companies, those in leadership roles don't always know who within their organization is a family caregiver, or understand the extent of the strain they are under. I'm living proof.

In all fairness, I should share that the university from which I fled *did* ask me to stay. (They even offered to send me to the dang Florida conference!) Their request was for a pipeline discussion to review my sales-related activity from a legitimate business perspective. That conversation *should* have happened, but it never did. The truth is I fell completely apart every time I considered the thought. I was so emotionally raw, bereft, and angry that I know, with absolute certainty, that had I attended such a meeting, I would have railed and sobbed. So I declined.

I'm pretty sure time moved forward for everyone else who would have been in that meeting, while for years I remained emotionally stuck in September 2012. Full writer-weirdo disclosure: I've had both sleeping and wide-awake dream versions of that discussion, rehashing and defending my less-than-perfect way of handling everything that led up to it.

I toyed with the notion of beginning this book with the day-dream version of that meeting—the hook, as they say in writing terms, to provide shocking insight into my hysterical self. Let's just say my draft copy rant was best left on the cutting-room floor. Had the pipeline review request come before the damning performance review or, even better, a few weeks after my father had died and I had had time to rest, things might have transpired much differently. Instead, it came while I was in the throes of the Five Stages of Grief. Specifically, the Anger Stage—so I resigned and hired an attorney as a mouthpiece to represent what I was feeling. Somehow, I thought she would be better able to succinctly explain what ultimately has taken me years to understand and articulate! Caregiving can do that. You can lose yourself in the process and in grief (both during and after) and make impetuous decisions out of character.

This from someone who dated for ten years before marrying, deliberated another ten on whether to have children, opened a college fund for a fetus, worked full-time while taking on a full-course load toward a master's degree, and held just about every on-staff position for a minimum of five years. For that matter, it's taken over five years to publish my story, even though the meat and bones, if you will, were written very soon after my father's passing. Steady as she goes—reflecting, planning, and preparing—is kind of my thing.

So is work. I'm all about the identity, purpose, and dignity that working provides. I know now that much of my anger was misplaced. I sincerely hope that the underlying message and reason for sharing my story—as a caution to other working family caregivers and their colleagues, to managers, and to Human Resource professionals—have come across as intended.

In the language of corporate culture, or HR-speak, I believe my story is one of diversity and inclusion (emphasis on *inclusion*), or "D&I." Typically D&I conversations deliberate gender equality/pay equity issues, and encompass the concerns of minority and LGBTQ groups—not so much middle-aged caregiving women. Again, I'm living proof that family caregivers are overlooked and excluded, inadvertently or not. It's been the norm to use a blanket categorization for that subset of employees seen as "uncommitted," "absentminded," or "wound a little too tight," as they bolt a little too quickly from the office at the sound of the lunch bell or the five o'clock whistle. Never mind that their workdays might be bookended by racing to work and flying home again—to a slew of tasks in aid of children, aging parents, or spouses or other family members with chronic illnesses, leaning in to provide emotional support, tie shoelaces, change Depends.

In addition to the physical, emotional, and psychological toll, caregivers are often struggling to rebuild their lives around the prospect of substantial financial loss. Here are just a few statistics, gathered from multiple sources: (namely, caregiving-related support websites)

- An estimated 43.5 million adults (20 percent of the nation's population) are unpaid family caregivers.

- Most have children ages seven through seventeen living at home.

- The average income lost by caregivers each year is a whopping 33 percent.

- Caregivers pay for many caregiving expenses out of their own pockets, at an average $10,000 per year.

- Overall, 11 percent of caregivers end up having to quit their jobs to care for someone at home around the clock.

- If a woman has to leave her job due to caregiving needs, the loss in wages, pension, and Social Security benefits over her lifetime totals more than $300,000.

- By 2030 there will be a national shortage of paid direct-care workers and an estimated 70 million unpaid family caregivers.

These are sobering figures and I find myself squarely in the mix. There's sadness to it, and not just for me. For the thousands of women whose lives were and will be changed from their caregiving experiences, it's one thing to read the statistics, another to live them intimately; understanding the impact that it means to your livelihood and life path. I'm one of the lucky ones. Initially for having had the means to help my family, but more importantly, for understanding how God helped me use the experience to switch course to a career that's far more fulfilling and meaningful.

As with all things, this change came about gradually. Occasionally there are days where I lament the financial contribution I could have been making to my family. But the good news is that my pity parties are now fleeting and less frequent. For a while after my father died and I left my job, in the quiet of the house, I was the epitome of all-dressed-up-and-nowhere-to-go. Ironically, in the aftermath of family caregiving, with my daughter a little older and off to school on an earlier bus, it would have been easier to be that in-the-office, in-your-seat employee and more-engaged teammate. Going above and beyond on tasks, being an undistracted lunchroom chit-chatter, taking water cooler and coffee breaks, maybe even going out for drinks after work as well.

But at the risk of beating my drum to a bloody pulp, my main intent was to expose sad glimpses of my experience as a caution, a white flag, if you will. A real-life story behind the data points, and only one of thousands.

At human resources events and conferences, I'm privy to in-depth presentations and discussions about administering policies. Time and again, I hear skepticism that errs on the side of reducing FMLA abuse and protecting against FMLA litigation. Understandable, as there will always be those who try and cheat the system. But let's not miss the mark. There are far fewer conversations—in most cases, none—about the stress, the burdens, the genuine toll felt by working family caregivers. There's a hands-wiped mentality that thinks ticking a coverage box for the Employee Assistance Program (EAP) option, or telecommuting, or eldercare referral service, is enough. Unfortunately, it's not.

A lens of unconscious bias about those "train wreck" working caregivers (my words and my younger-self perspective, you'll recall) may be coloring what's right in front of you. Look again and realize those FMLA "swindlers" you're so concerned about are leaving the workforce in droves not because they want to, but because they don't feel fully supported. It will be extraordinarily difficult for them to rejoin the workforce once their caregiving obligations have ceased. Jus' sayin'.

As for me? It's no longer a daily litany of self-reproach and woulda, coulda, shoulda regrets! In the years since my father passed and I left my job, I've regained so much of my joy and cheerfulness. Beginning with good health (thanks to regular "reverse aging" tips from Dr. Oz) and more good hair days (due to faithful trips to the hair salon for coloring), few would guess that I'm a card-carrying member of AARP! Honestly, I have a feeling of well-being and contentment for the first time in my life. Sleep has a lot to do with it. I eat much better, more healthily, now too. Not that I frequent the farmer's market or buy strictly organic (no disrespect and hats off to those who do) but I am proud that my drive-thru to home-cooked meal ratio has flipped.

The endless list of daily to-dos that once wore me down, no longer does. Being there (at home, present in body and mind) for my husband and daughter means everything. Don't get me wrong, it still tires me out, but not to the point of being comatose, empty, or exhausted. It's more like the satisfied feeling of taking off your bra at the end of the day, putting on the softest pajamas you own, and knowing that you were there for the mash-up of mundane, blessed daily tasks—finding the lost iPhone charging cord, washing out sports water bottles, filling the bird feeders, and keeping the junk mail pile at bay.

Tony, Pat, and Collette are there for my worried rants about raising a now-teenager. I've bemoaned Summer's insecurities while sharing my own—how-do-you-survive-slammed-doors-and-hypersensitivity? Admittedly, I do often remind her to be careful (a.k.a., make good decisions!) when she leaves the house.

And where would I be without my lifelong best friend and husband? I can't even imagine and don't want to. Unapologetically, Tony and I have become the kind of parents who hold back that sleepover or phone time to keep some semblance of 1950s-style manners and polite discourse. According to Summer, we are the strictest, most overly cautious and protective parents in our town. From what I'm told, nobody else has parents who care how often their child goes to the "*Maaaallll.*"

From a career perspective, I didn't realize at the time that my decision to resign was also an inadvertent decision to leave the ranks of the full-time employed. Oh, I tried. I applied for many positions over the years, dozens in fact, and in some instances came down to being a final candidate. But nothing panned out. From necessity, I said goodbye to the corporate world in that butt-in-seat, commuter nine-to-five capacity, and turned to accepting freelance assignments. The previous guilt pendulum now swings mostly on the fashion front, from dressy days when I have a corporate engagement to facilitate, to sweatpants and a medley of faded, well-worn Life Is Good T-shirts.

I like the person I am now and think others do as well. Just think how improved workplace productivity and team dynamics could be if everyone put aside the false narrative of being in perfect control and showed up in their humanity.

In my walk, learning Bible verse and wisdom, I've come to appreciate so many blessings, not the least of which is free will. We have the gift to choose whether our experiences make or break us. As a card-carrying, lifelong learner, I can ask, "What role did I play in this?" not "Why was this was done to me?" I have also asked, "What can I learn and share from this?" The stoic depends on himself. But I would much rather depend on God's grace.

Toward that end, my focus as a consultant is on helping companies retain and develop talent by offering seminars that address work-life balance issues. I still enjoy being a working mom, and now I am able to walk through various companies' doors, with peace in my heart and something to offer—family caregiving seminars and support for the working professional.

There's much to be done to recognize and retain hard-working, valuable employees—good work and good business for everyone involved. To stay in touch and continue the conversation about family caregiving and the workplace, please visit my website: www.wearesharingthesun.com.

Acknowledgments

I would like to gratefully thank:

My husband and daughter—my heart and soul. There are no words. Although, if I had to, I probably could muster up a few more stories about your quirky ways and goodness. (Sounds like more fun, right?) I'm amazed at your capacity to love and, when necessary, steer clear away from the distracted, doubting, moody, needy, manic writer that I may have been on occasion. Your carefully delivered "feedback," support and encouragement meant everything. You are my greatest blessings.

Toni and Doug at Winword Literary services, for coaching and developmental editing. Toni somehow magically showed up in my life at just the right time and offered lightness and a *c'est la vie* vibe that nurtured the process of healing through writing. Together we took initial steps to get started and, for the first time, I felt permission to consider myself a writer. Doug's steady support and quiet patience were the right counterbalance to a very emotional process for me.

Mary Ann Faughnan, Editorial Director at Bauhan Publishing, for copy edits and thoughtful insights. It meant a lot that you took the time. Your professional validation that a hodge-podge of chapters and memories could really become a book was fuel to keep plugging away.

Cheryl Cory, author of *Must've Done Something Good* and co-Founder of the Worcester Writer's Collaborative, for much needed, much appreciated writer-support coffeehouse dates. We had the best laughs! You have a unique ability to turn a meh day into one of inspiration and encouragement.

To extended family, and friends who are duly noted as angels and princesses within these pages. Everyone should be so lucky! I thank you for your endless support. I suspect you wondered, after years of casual mention, if there really was a book in development. It's good you kept a straight face. I needed that.

I like to think we're connected to our deceased loved ones, even though they're doing far more interesting things in heaven than surveying us running around, fretting on some days and skipping on others. During any given moment of excessive wallow or morose, the perfect echo of my Mother saying, "That's enough of that" pulled me through and cracked me up. I'm immensely grateful for the parents I was blessed with and for my, (at times provoking, overbearing, boundary ignoring,) mostly kind, good-hearted siblings. ;-)

And to Meadow's successor, Bo. Also a black-and-white tuxedo cat, who supplied endless head bump interruptions and is a lovey, love love.

About the Author

Sarahbeth Persiani is the founder of *We Are Sharing the Sun,* a consultancy supporting the over 40 million Americans currently providing informal care to a family member. *We Are Sharing the Sun* helps companies address the demands of the modern caregiver-cum-employee, who has both children and aging parents to attend to.

Sarahbeth has held senior managerial roles in the field of corporate learning, development and professional education in both traditional and corporate universities. A board member of the Elder Services of Worcester and the Millbury Council on Aging, Sarahbeth is active at a number of other community organizations including the Human Resources of Central Massachusetts Diversity Council, Dementia Friends and her church, Emanuel Lutheran in Worcester, MA.

She holds a Masters of Business Administration from Northeastern University, and a Bachelor of Arts in Humanities & Social Sciences from the University of Massachusetts, Dartmouth. She lives with her family in the Worcester county area of central Massachusetts and they spend as much time as possible at their cottage on Cape Cod.

Made in the USA
Middletown, DE
08 June 2020